MEMORIES OF SOCRATES

XENOPHON (*c.*430–*c.*354 BCE) lived through one of the most dramatic periods of Greek history, from the start of the Peloponnesian War between Athens and Sparta to the rise of Macedonian dominance in the mid-fourth century BCE. Like others brought up in upper-class Athenian society, and like other young associates of Socrates, Xenophon was broadly unsympathetic to radical democracy, and was ultimately exiled from Athens for pro-Spartan activity. For some seven years from 401 BCE he served as a mercenary in Persia and Thrace, and then under Spartan command: his *Anabasis* recounts his own role in leading 10,000 marooned Greek mercenaries on a perilous retreat in 400 BCE through central Asia to safety at the Black Sea—'The sea! The sea!' He then spent nearly thirty years in comfortable exile in the Peloponnese, and returned to Athens for the remaining ten or so years of his life after his sentence of exile was repealed in about 367 BCE. In mid- and later life he was a prolific and remarkably versatile writer. His works include history (the *Anabasis*, and the larger-scale *Hellenica*, which starts where Thucydides left off in 411 BCE and is our main source for the next fifty years of Greek history); biography; political, military, and economic theory; practical treatises reflecting his own interests and expertise (cavalry command, horsemanship, hunting); and philosophy, an interest kindled by his youthful association with Socrates. His four Socratic works, *Memorabilia*, *Apology*, *Oeconomicus*, and *Symposium*, are his tributes to an admired teacher and role model.

MARTIN HAMMOND was born in 1944 and educated at Winchester College and Balliol College, Oxford. He has taught at St Paul's School, Harrow School, and Eton College, where he was Head of Classics from 1974 to 1980, and Master in College from 1980 to 1984. He was Headmaster of the City of London School from 1984 to 1990, and of Tonbridge School from 1990 to his retirement in 2005. He has translated the *Iliad* (Penguin, 1987), the *Odyssey* (Duckworth, 2000; Bloomsbury, 2014), the *Meditations* of Marcus Aurelius (Penguin, 2006), and for Oxford World's Classics Thucydides: *The Peloponnesian War* (2009), Arrian: *Anabasis* and *Indica* (2013), Josephus: *The Jewish War* (2017), and Artemidorus: *The Interpretation of Dreams* (2020).

CAROL ATACK studied Government at the London School of Economics, and Classics at Lucy Cavendish College, Cambridge. She is currently a Fellow and Director of Studies in Classics at Newnham College, Cambridge. Her books include *The Discourse of Kingship in Classical Greece* (Routledge, 2020), and *Anachronism and Antiquity* (Bloomsbury, 2020, with Tim Rood and Tom Phillips); she has published many articles on topics in classical Greek political thought, and is currently working on a book on the temporality of Platonic dialogue.

T0019907

OXFORD WORLD'S CLASSICS

*For over 100 years Oxford World's Classics have brought
readers closer to the world's great literature. Now with over 700
titles—from the 4,000-year-old myths of Mesopotamia to the
twentieth century's greatest novels—the series makes available
lesser-known as well as celebrated writing.*

*The pocket-sized hardbacks of the early years contained
introductions by Virginia Woolf, T. S. Eliot, Graham Greene,
and other literary figures which enriched the experience of reading.
Today the series is recognized for its fine scholarship and
reliability in texts that span world literature, drama and poetry,
religion, philosophy, and politics. Each edition includes perceptive
commentary and essential background information to meet the
changing needs of readers.*

OXFORD WORLD'S CLASSICS

XENOPHON

Memories of Socrates
Memorabilia and *Apology*

Translated by
MARTIN HAMMOND

With an Introduction and Notes by
CAROL ATACK

OXFORD
UNIVERSITY PRESS

OXFORD
UNIVERSITY PRESS

Great Clarendon Street, Oxford, OX2 6DP,
United Kingdom

Oxford University Press is a department of the University of Oxford.
It furthers the University's objective of excellence in research, scholarship,
and education by publishing worldwide. Oxford is a registered trade mark of
Oxford University Press in the UK and in certain other countries

First published as an Oxford World's Classics paperback 2023

Impression: 1

Published in the United States of America by Oxford University Press
198 Madison Avenue, New York, NY 10016, United States of America

British Library Cataloguing in Publication Data

Data available

Library of Congress Control Number: 2022939678

ISBN 978-0-19-885609-2

Printed and bound in the UK by
Clays Ltd, Elcograf S.p.A.

PREFACE

XENOPHON was an almost exact contemporary of Plato, and both were part of the circle of mainly upper-class young Athenians who were associates and admirers of Socrates, forty years their senior, in the late fifth century BCE. After Socrates' execution in 399 BCE both Xenophon and Plato, and others of the Socratic circle, wrote works in justification of Socrates, and dialogues exemplifying the Socratic method. For all the various adventures and fortunes of his later life, Xenophon never lost his admiration of Socrates, and his four Socratic works, *Memorabilia*, *Apology*, *Oeconomicus*, and *Symposium*, are second only to Plato's in the light they shed on the historical Socrates, the man, his teaching, his methods, and his philosophy.

There are differences between the Xenophontic Socrates (practical, genial, down-to-earth) and the Platonic Socrates (cerebral, ironic, intent on higher things): Xenophon sees Socrates more as a benign educator, Plato as a strikingly and uncomfortably original thinker. These two pictures of a clearly complex figure, reflecting the viewpoints of two very different men of different interests and abilities, are best seen as complementary rather than incompatible. Plato's is the stronger voice, and his increasingly Platonized Socrates has been the dominant influence on much of subsequent philosophy, but for a balanced assessment of the historical Socrates in his lifetime, Xenophon also must be given credit and taken into account as a 'second opinion'.

Xenophon's is the more intimate portrait, and his Socrates the more human and attractive figure: he writes with a clear affection, as well as admiration, for his subject. In a series of representative mini-dialogues and shorter vignettes Xenophon presents a wide range of types and individuals exposed to Socratic inquisition or given avuncular advice—from arrogant members of the *jeunesse dorée* and self-confident cynics to artists and artisans, a sparky courtesan, and his own rebellious son—and by this means puts flesh on the main themes of Socrates' teaching and the main tenets of his philosophy. Xenophon, as he tells us, was present at several of these reported conversations, and even gives himself a small and not very glorious part in one of them (*Mem.* 1.3.8–13). Some of the vignettes, for example at *Memorabilia* 2.13–14, are delightfully Boswell and Johnson. As Xenophon left Athens in 401 BCE, he was reliant on the testimony of others for his account of Socrates' trial and execution in 399 BCE.

The dialogues in *Memorabilia*, interspersed with Xenophon's own commentary, present a picture of Socrates at his characteristic and lifelong work. That work was education, in which Socrates claimed to be an expert, and more specifically moral education, which he thought must begin with self-knowledge. Socrates wished success for his associates, but he redefined 'a successful life' as the virtuous life, shaped by the cultivation of a rational self-control: and virtue is knowledge. Redefinition extends to the traditional upper-class term of approbation, *kalos kagathos* (literally 'beautiful and good'), frequently used in *Memorabilia*. It is hard to translate, but in its traditional Athenian use there were mainly aesthetic and social connotations, something like 'a fine figure of a gentleman'. Socrates urged his associates to work, by study and practice, towards becoming *kaloi kagathoi* themselves, but in his teaching to that end he crucially added both moral and intellectual dimensions to the concept. For the term in Socrates' use we have adopted the translation 'a man of quality'.

Xenophon's portrait of Socrates offers insights into the intellectual and political debates at a critical time in the Greek world, and so has its place in the history of ideas. It also has considerable interest for the social historian, as the conversations reported by Xenophon incidentally reveal much about the social and cultural mores in Athens in the late fifth century BCE, and the effects on morale and living conditions in the later stages of the long war with Sparta. Some examples are the attitudes to and treatment of slaves, the boundaries of what was socially acceptable in Athenian pederasty, the procedure and 'entertainment' at men-only club dinners, the prevalence of trumped-up prosecutions to blackmail the wealthy, the plight of once-prosperous Athenians dispossessed by the Spartan invasions of Attica.

This book is a collaboration. It has been a constant pleasure, and an education, to work in tandem with Carol Atack, who has improved my first drafts on almost every page of the translation, and given expert advice on all matters philosophical.

   I am responsible for the translation, the Notes on the Greek Texts, and the Index: Carol for all the rest of the book. We gladly share responsibility for the book as a whole.

MARTIN HAMMOND

Just as Socrates learned from watching artists produce their works, I have learned a great deal from watching Martin Hammond craft a translation which does justice to Xenophon's witty and stylish Greek. In writing the Explanatory Notes I have benefited from the collective wisdom of a global community of Xenophon scholars; particular thanks are due to Tim Rood and Emily Baragwanath, and to Newnham College, Cambridge, and the Center for Hellenic Studies, Washington DC, for their support.

CAROL ATACK

Note

In the text of the translation an asterisk indicates an entry in the Explanatory Notes.

CONTENTS

ABBREVIATIONS

Aristotle (Ar.)	*NE*	*Nicomachean Ethics*
	Pol.	*Politics*
[Aristotle] [Ar.]	*Ath. Pol.*	*Athenaiōn Politeia* (Constitution of the Athenians)
DL		Diogenes Laertius, *Lives of the Philosophers*
Hdt.		Herodotus, *The Histories*
Plato (Pl.)	*Ap.*	*Apology of Socrates*
	Phd.	*Phaedo*
	Rep.	*Republic*
	Smp.	*Symposium*
Thuc.		Thucydides, *The History of the Peloponnesian War*
Xenophon (Xen.)	*Ages.*	*Agesilaus*
	Anab.	*Anabasis*
	Ap.	*Apology*
	Cyn.	*Cynegeticus* (The Expert Hunter)
	Cyr.	*Cyropaedia* (Education of Cyrus)
	Hell.	*Hellenica* (History of Greece)
	Lac. Pol.	*Lacedaimoniōn Politeia* (Constitution of the Spartans)
	Mem.	*Memorabilia* (Memories of Socrates)
	Oec.	*Oeconomicus* (The Estate Manager)
	Smp.	*Symposium* (The Banquet)

References to ancient texts follow the established divisions into books and chapters, and the standard numbering system of Stephanus pages (Plato) and Bekker pages (Aristotle).

INTRODUCTION

IN the conversations gathered in the *Memorabilia* Xenophon memorializes Socrates, the Athenian thinker, who did not himself write any philosophical works, but who inspired a new generation of thinkers as well as providing an example of how to live. In the decades subsequent to Socrates' trial (on charges of introducing new gods and 'corrupting the young') and execution in Athens in 399 BCE, Xenophon and others sought to demonstrate their connection to Socrates through written examples of his conversational style, even as they revised and developed his teachings in line with their own views. Together, these writers produced an interconnected body of work that would be foundational for the project of philosophy in the western European tradition.

Xenophon, who had experienced Socrates' teaching but was probably writing some decades later, combined the project of commemorating Socrates with some sharp political analysis and critique of the ideas of his own contemporaries, including Socrates' most famous associate, the philosopher Plato. '[S]hall we wait to make our proposals until we have moved on from guesswork to knowledge?': Socrates' question to the ambitious young Athenian Glaucon encapsulates Xenophon's view of the importance of preparation and a firm grasp on detail for the would-be leader (*Mem.* 3.6). This sharp dialogue is rendered even more ironic by the fact that Glaucon is Plato's older brother. Socrates takes Glaucon to task for hoping to take on a key political role in the city without having done his homework first, pointing out the kinds of details which a good leader should know in order to devise good policies, persuade others to adopt and follow them, and deliver a successful outcome for household, army, or city. Xenophon's Socrates would have been a formidable opponent across the dispatch box in the House of Commons for any government minister not on top of his or her brief; Xenophon was familiar with the rough ride given to leading politicians and generals in the Athenian democracy of his time, frequently put on trial for failures of policy or military loss, and fined, exiled, and in some notorious cases executed.

Xenophon, like Plato, represents Socrates as placing immense value on knowledge, as part of a highly practical set of leadership skills together known as the 'royal art'. While there had been much philosophical debate on whether there was a master craft or form of knowledge, Xenophon's characters treat it as the body of skills and knowledge taught by Socrates to his followers, of which the most significant part is self-knowledge. Although the command to 'Know yourself' inscribed on the temple of Apollo at Delphi was familiar to all ancient Greeks, it played a specific role for Socrates, who emphasized the importance of self-knowledge and exemplified its consequences.

For Xenophon, the knowledge which underpinned the 'royal art' remained practical and specific; his Socrates thinks that a leader can know too much advanced theoretical science, and although he is aware of Plato's philosophical ideas he does not ascribe any of them to the Socrates he depicts. For Xenophon, self-knowledge primarily consists of a keen practical ability to match up one's own capabilities and the resources at one's disposal against the demands of the present situation. This is the knowledge offered by Socrates to a potential pupil, Euthydemus, after he is disabused of any confidence in his existing knowledge (*Mem.* 4.2).[1]

Xenophon's Socratic dialogues offer a vivid glimpse into the intellectual and social world of Socrates, and the political culture of Athens during two key points in its intellectual history, the late fifth century BCE and the early decades of the fourth century, in which Socrates' successors competed over his legacy. They are delivered by Xenophon with characteristic wit and humour, leavening the occasionally heavy-handed repetition of exhortations to moral virtue and practical competence.

Xenophon's contributions, contained in his *Apology* (account of Socrates at his trial, including a defence speech), *Memorabilia* (a series of interconnected dialogues containing Socratic advice for life), *Oeconomicus* (specific advice on running a wealthy aristocratic estate and household), and *Symposium* (an account of a dinner party at which Socrates explores the topic of love), portray Socrates as a witty and occasionally spiky character who encourages his fellow citizens to take their obligations to their families and communities seriously, and to use their talents and energies for the collective good. The biographer Diogenes Laertius, writing in the third century CE, claims

---

[1] C. Moore, *Socrates and Self-knowledge* (Cambridge: Cambridge University Press, 2015), 216–35; D. M. Johnson, 'Xenophon at His Most Socratic (*Memorabilia* 4.2)', *Oxford Studies in Ancient History*, 29 (2005), 39–73.

that Xenophon was the first to take notes of Socrates' conversations and to publish written versions (DL 2.48); and while this view is chronologically implausible, the priority of Xenophon's account as a true account of Socrates and his thought has had many supporters, through the long period in which these works have been enjoyed.

At other times, Xenophon's contribution, and his version of Socrates, have been undervalued, although renewed interest has shown both the depth and the importance of Xenophon's account. The readability and human interest of Xenophon's stories and character vignettes, and the use of his stylish prose in the schoolroom for the teaching of classical Greek, may have contributed to a reluctance to treat his work as seriously as it might be (see the 'Responses to Xenophon' section, below).

Xenophon and Athens

Although Xenophon includes some autobiographical detail in his work, our understanding of his life is far from complete. He was born into a wealthy family in Erchia, a deme (administrative subdivision) of Athens in an agricultural area to the east of the city, around 430 BCE, so in the first years of the Peloponnesian War. As a young adult, finishing his education with the aim of reaching political and military office, he encountered Socrates as a teacher. However, Xenophon's progress towards the career typical of a wealthy Athenian citizen was cut short by events at the end of the Peloponnesian War, as he reached adulthood and began to participate in civic life. He appears to have remained in the city at the end of the war under the oligarchy of the Thirty Tyrants which was put in place by the victorious Spartans (404/3 BCE). He may even have fought as a cavalryman against the pro-democracy faction who, after leaving the city or being exiled, regrouped at the city's port, the Piraeus, and attacked and defeated the oligarchs. One of the most remarkable episodes in the turbulent history of Athenian democracy was the amnesty put in place by the restored democracy, intended to enable those who had fought on each side to reintegrate into political life together.

Xenophon, however, appears at this point to have chosen a different path away from his home city. In his autobiographical *Anabasis*, he tells how he accepted an invitation to travel with a mercenary force supporting Cyrus the Younger, younger brother of the reigning Persian

king Artaxerxes I, in his campaign to overthrow his brother. This plan
came to an end when Cyrus was killed in battle at Cunaxa (401 BCE),
and the Persians captured and killed the expedition's leaders.
Xenophon famously narrates the journey of the Greeks back home
through hostile territory, in which he himself comes to display the
kind of leadership skills which would have been valued in public service for his city, had he stayed there. While Xenophon's Socratic writings are focused on questions of how to live in the context of democratic
Athens and the challenges faced by its elites, he spent much of his life
living outside his own polis as a client of the Spartans, and did not
exercise leadership in any official role or capacity. This paradox may
leave traces in his ambiguous treatment of some characters in the
Memorabilia, such as the young Aristippus, whose desire to live independently from the framework and constraints of the polis leads
Socrates to tell him the story of the Choice of Heracles (*Mem.* 2.1).

Xenophon continued in service as a mercenary for Sparta under
the Spartan king Agesilaus, who was fighting the Persians in Asia
Minor up to 394 BCE when he was recalled home (*Hell.* 4.2.1). By this
point Xenophon had been exiled from Athens (DL 2.51), either
because he fought among Spartan ranks against the city's troops at
the Battle of Coronea (394 BCE, *Hell.* 4.3.15–18), or as a consequence
of previous political machinations between Athens and Persia, in
which his engagement with Cyrus was seen as disruptive to Athenian
overtures to Artaxerxes.

Xenophon's adventures abroad had, therefore, kept him away from
Athens at the point at which Socrates was put on trial (399 BCE); his
accounts of the trial and charges in the *Apology* and *Memorabilia* cannot be those of an eyewitness, although he emphasizes that they draw
on the testimony of others who were present, such as Hermogenes
son of Hipponicus, a member of the Socratic circle whom Xenophon
reports as a source (*Mem.* 1.2.48, 2.10.3, 4.8.4; *Ap.* 2).

Instead, Xenophon for many years lived a quiet life in territory
controlled by Sparta, at Scillus close to the Panhellenic sanctuary of
Zeus at Olympia; he is also said to have had his sons Gryllus and
Diodorus educated in the Spartan system of military education, the
notoriously brutal *agōgē* (DL 2.54). However, Xenophon's idyll proved
temporary; the Spartan defeat by Thebes at Leuctra in 371 BCE lost
them control of the region, and Xenophon moved on, most likely to
Corinth; he may have returned to Athens, or at least resolved his

relationship with the city. That his son Gryllus was killed while serving in the Athenian cavalry in an encounter just before the Battle of Mantinea (362 BCE) suggests that the family had strengthened its Athenian connection. Xenophon himself died a few years later, probably after 354 BCE, based on the likely composition date of the *Poroi*, a pamphlet on Athenian state finance thought to be his final work (see below).

One challenge of Xenophon's biography is understanding when he wrote the works that we have. Whether Xenophon wrote throughout his adult life, or only in his later years after his reconciliation with Athens, remains a topic of scholarly controversy. Adherents to the former view are 'developmentalists', and to the other 'unitarians'; the latter group have also made stronger claims about a unity of purpose and theme across Xenophon's many works.[2] Allusions to the work of Plato across Xenophon's work suggest composition dates later in his life, lending some weight to the unitarian view; but the vivid detail of Xenophon's reportage of events, especially his travels outside the Greek world, suggests to some that those works, or at least early drafts of them, could have been composed soon after the events they depict.

The variety of Xenophon's work—which, unusually, has survived to the present day more or less complete—has confused some interpreters into failing to observe the underlying organizing principles and concepts which run throughout his writing. One can read Xenophon's historical and narrative works as illustrating the political and ethical qualities which he sought and valued: this applies in particular to portraits of leaders in the *Hellenica*, his account of the history of Athens and other Greek cities between 411/10 BCE (the end point of Thucydides' account of the Peloponnesian War) and 362 BCE, and the *Anabasis*, his lively narrative account of his time as a mercenary stranded deep in enemy territory. Such preoccupations also find their way into more practical works of instruction, such as the manuals for hunting (*Cynegeticus*), horsemanship (*De Re Equestri*), and for leading cavalry (*Hipparchicus*). There is some suspicion that some or all parts of these shorter works are, like the *Constitution of the Athenians* transmitted along with them in the manuscript tradition, not Xenophon's own work. The *Cyropaedia*, a philosophical narrative analysing the rise to power of Cyrus the Great of Persia, depicted as an exemplary

---

[2] The question of the composition dates of Xenophon's work has been deemed unanswerable by Michael Flower: see his introduction to M. A. Flower (ed.), *The Cambridge Companion to Xenophon* (Cambridge: Cambridge University Press, 2017), 8–9.

leader, defies categorization by genre, but echoes many of the topics discussed in the *Memorabilia*.

But there is as little certainty over the dating of Plato's dialogues across the forty or so years in which they might have been written. The concept of 'publication' is less meaningful in a culture in which works circulated in manuscript copies; Xenophon may well have kept up to date with Athenian affairs and intellectual life while he was away from the city, or plunged himself back into its culture if he returned. He had clearly read the major Platonic dialogues in which Socrates features before composing the *Memorabilia*; Book 4 in particular connects directly to discussions in dialogues such as the *Republic*, *Gorgias*, and *Protagoras*. Characters from Plato's dialogues—such as Charmides and Critias, from the *Charmides*, and Glaucon from the *Republic*—reappear in the *Memorabilia*, often in a pointed contrast with Plato's depiction. Xenophon's *Apology* shows a familiarity with Plato's *Apology*.[3] Such allusions and shared details led to suspicions that Xenophon's dialogues were at times second-hand rehashes of Platonic originals (a view expressed most strongly by the classicist John Burnet in the early twentieth century).

Plato in turn appears to respond to Xenophon's work in his later writings, notably the *Statesman* and the *Laws* with their discussion of the shepherd-king figure and of Cyrus the Great.[4] There is agreement that a short pamphlet on improving Athens' finances, the *Poroi*, is one of Xenophon's later works, and the close focus on the city's economy and its specific problems suggests that its author might have returned to the city. The encomium of the Spartan king Agesilaus must have been written after the death of its subject, in 360/59 BCE.

Although Xenophon lived much of his adult life away from Athens, its practices remained central to his thinking; the *Poroi* is full of ideas for boosting Athenian state revenues, as the city adjusted to lower revenues in the second quarter of the fourth century BCE. In several works, Xenophon depicts characters performing the roles and activities that

---

[3] Xenophon responds to other works by Plato, notably the *Phaedo* and the *Charmides*, in the *Memorabilia*; Plato scholar John Burnet criticized him for this dependence on Plato: see the introduction to J. Burnet, *Plato's* Phaedo (Oxford: Clarendon Press, 1911).

[4] G. Danzig, 'Did Plato read Xenophon's *Cyropaedia*?', in S. Scolnicov and L. Brisson (eds), *Plato's* Laws: *From Theory into Practice* (Sankt Augustin: Academia, 2003), 286–97; C. Atack, 'Plato's Statesman and Xenophon's Cyrus', in G. Danzig, D. M. Johnson, and D. Morrison (eds), *Plato and Xenophon: Comparative Studies* (Leiden: Brill, 2018), 510–43.

citizens undertook as they participated in Athenian democracy: Socrates himself, for example, was once randomly selected to chair the assembly, on a critical day, that of the Arginusae trial in 406 BCE, a point which Xenophon repeats from work to work (*Hell.* 1.6-7; *Mem.* 1.1.18, 4.4.2; see below). Male Athenian citizens were allocated to ten 'tribes', depending on their deme, a local administrative area, in a system established by the reforming politician Cleisthenes in 508/7 BCE. Fifty members of each tribe were selected by lot to serve as councillors each year, and each tribe took a turn 'in prytany', staying in residence continuously for thirty-six or thirty-seven days in the council office in the agora; one of this group would be selected at random to chair each meeting of the council and assembly, and so Socrates came to hold the role on a particularly fateful occasion.

Other characters, like Plato's brother Glaucon, aspire to leading roles, formal and informal, particularly the most significant elected position as one of the city's ten generals (*Mem.* 3.2–6). As the generalship was, unusually for Athens, an elected role, candidates needed to win support from the citizen electorate, a process which Xenophon depicts as not always straightforward (*Mem.* 3.4). Other roles requiring expertise, such as some treasury posts, were also elected positions, again reflecting the view that citizens should evaluate the skill and expertise of potential office-holders, a theme emphasized by Xenophon in the *Memorabilia*.

The *Memorabilia* can also be read as a source for details of Athenian political culture. While it is dangerous to assume that Socratic dialogues as a genre contain accurate evidence for social practices—neither settings nor conversations can be taken as historical representations—Xenophon's characters and their situations represent aspects of the city's life, often keyed to the difficulties of the 400s BCE. At that time war closed the routes by which food was imported, any crops on the city's surrounding agricultural land were likely to be harvested by invading forces, and the citizens endured considerable hardship. Xenophon's insights extend to the lives of Athenian women; archaeological evidence in the form of innumerable loom weights confirms the centrality to women's lives of wool-working and clothing production, which Socrates recommends that Eutherus monetize in order to feed his extended family (*Mem.* 2.7). While Xenophon presents Socrates' wife Xanthippe as a bad-tempered harridan (*Smp.* 2.10), he also depicts her as a caring mother who deserves more respect from her ungrateful son Lamprocles (*Mem.* 2.2).

Finally, Xenophon draws on his own experience of growing up as an elite Athenian to touch on the social practices of education and the construction of citizen friendships, by which such Athenians could support each other's citizen careers. An Athenian had many social connections to his fellow citizens. Some would be members of his own family, others members of his local deme—Athenians were known by the name of their deme, although Xenophon often prefers to use their patronymic (father's name). Other connections derived from affiliation to cults, shared experience of military service (as with Socrates and Alcibiades), or membership of more shadowy dining clubs with political and social goals (*hetaireiai*). Unlike Sparta, Athens did not require its youth to participate in a set form of education organized by the city. Young men like Xenophon would be educated at home until late boyhood, when they might attend classes with a sophist as well as physical training at a gymnasium, all focused on the skills needed to participate in political and legal debate and to succeed in military campaigning.

One form of social connection between elite Athenian citizens was the intense relationship between an older and younger male sometimes known as *paiderastia* ('boy-love', Plato, *Smp.* 181c). Such relationships were attested in many older Greek societies and some testimony presents them as a rite of passage for boys reaching adulthood and taking up the activities of citizenship. At least as depicted in Socratic dialogues, an older citizen (*erastēs*, 'lover') pursued a younger boy (*erōmenos*, 'beloved') with poetry and other gifts. Such relationships are a theme of the painted drinking cups and vessels used in the elite symposium or dinner party, with many drinking cups from the early fifth century BCE showing older bearded men offering gifts to younger beardless youths. By the time Xenophon and Plato were writing such depictions were much less common, and the intricacies of the historical practice of pederasty among the elite of fourth-century Athens, the exact age of participants, and what was involved in such relationships, remain disputed.[5] While the older vases depict physical sexual contact within these relationships, other literary evidence from the

---

[5] Two competing interpretations of Athenian pederasty are offered by K. J. Dover, *Greek Homosexuality* (London: Duckworth, 1978; new edn 2016) and J. N. Davidson, *The Greeks and Greek Love: A Radical Reappraisal of Homosexuality in Ancient Greece* (London: Weidenfeld & Nicolson, 2007); for a recent summary of the debate, see A. Lear, 'Was Pederasty Problematized?', in M. Masterson, N. S. Rabinowitz, and J. Robson (eds), *Sex in Antiquity: Exploring Gender and Sexuality in the Ancient World* (New York: Routledge, 2015), 115–36.

mid-fourth century, such as Aeschines' speech *Against Timarchus*, suggests that the behaviour of the *erastēs* might be policed by boys' families, and any relationships which did not follow the socially sanctioned form were subject to social and even legal censure.

Both Plato and Xenophon use pederasty as an analogy and metaphor for education, with Socrates taking on the role of the *erastēs* (and occasionally, as in Plato's *Symposium*, that of the *erōmenos*). Xenophon represents Socrates' pursuit of the potential student Euthydemus as an intellectual version of pederastic courtship (*Mem.* 4.2–3, 5–6); hints of pederasty and the symposium permeate Socrates' earlier conversation with Crito's young son Critobulus on friendship (*Mem.* 2.6). Unlike Plato, Xenophon is markedly ambivalent about the practice. In his only direct participation in conversation with Socrates in the *Memorabilia*, he presents Socrates advising him against engaging in erotic pursuit (*Mem.* 1.3.8–13), perhaps reflecting a biographical tradition that Xenophon pursued Cleinias, another elite youth of the Socratic circle, in this way (DL 2.49). Elsewhere, he treats it as potentially damaging and corrupting for both parties (*Mem.* 4.2.35). In the *Constitution of the Spartans* he presents an idealized and entirely chaste version of the practice, in which young Spartans benefit from an innocuous form of mentorship (*Lac. Pol.* 2.12–14). Nonetheless, the transmission of values and status through a range of erotic relationships serves as an important analogy for Socratic education. In one of the *Memorabilia*'s liveliest chapters, Socrates treats the relationship between the *hetaira* Theodote and her clients as an analogy for his relationship with students (3.11), describing his followers as his 'girlfriends'.

Socrates on Trial

For Plato the trial and execution of Socrates in 399 BCE was a life-changing event, to which he returned constantly throughout his writing, setting many dialogues in the last few weeks of Socrates' life (*Theaetetus, Euthyphro, Sophist, Statesman*) and on the occasion of his death (*Phaedo*). For Xenophon, Socrates' trial and death parallel other injustices in democratic Athens, such as the trial of the Arginusae generals (*Hell.* 1.5–6). Both Xenophon and Plato provide accounts of Socrates' speech in his own defence (*Apology*), although each emphasizes different aspects of Socrates' arguments. They also include the charges laid by the prosecutors, led by Meletus and Anytus, that Socrates 'commits a crime in not recognizing the gods recognized by the city, but introducing new divinities, and commits a crime for corrupting the young' (DL 2.40). They may also be responding to other written accounts of the charges and trial circulating in Athens, such as a pamphlet by Polycrates (DL 2.39). Both Plato and Xenophon clearly feel that Socrates was unjustly prosecuted, convicted, and punished, but more recently some have argued that in the febrile political circumstances of the newly restored democracy it was understandable that an eccentric figure associated with some of the leading figures of the oligarchy would become a focus for discontent.[6]

In the Athenian legal system, there was no public prosecutor; individual citizens prosecuted each other for breaking the city's laws, and cases were often politically or financially motivated. Hearings were held in front of juries of various sizes, and accuser and defendant spoke for themselves, perhaps engaging a speech-writer to compose a compelling case for them to present to the jury. Socrates' case was heard before a large jury of 501, in the court of the King Archon in the agora, so the uproar in court reported by both Plato and Xenophon may well reflect the size of the crowd watching the case, as well as a negative view on democracy and social order. The jury was selected at random from a standing pool by a complex multilevel process; both contemporary description ([Ar.] *Ath. Pol.* 63–6) and surviving machinery for allocating jurors to courts show how the Athenians were concerned to avoid the possibility of jury-rigging or court-packing.

The charges against Socrates were not typical; most cases heard in the Athenian courts revolved around property and personal injury, or failure to perform the various duties of a citizen. The charges against Socrates appear to have been brought under an impiety regulation, the Decree of Diopeithes, introduced in the mid-fifth century and possibly also used against the philosopher Anaxagoras.[7] Unfortunately, all stories about prosecutions of philosophers in surviving written sources are heavily patterned after the literary accounts of Socrates'

[6] P. Cartledge, *Ancient Greek Political Thought in Practice* (Cambridge: Cambridge University Press, 2009), 76–90; see also I. F. Stone, *The Trial of Socrates* (London: Jonathan Cape, 1988).

[7] Xenophon takes particular care to distinguish Socrates' thought from that of Anaxagoras and others; see *Mem.* 1.4, 4.7.

trial; the theme of the persecuted philosopher was a common one in ancient biographical sources, and there is no independent evidence for prosecutions other than those of Socrates and the Athenians caught up in the scandal of the revelation of the secrets of the Eleusinian Mysteries in 415 BCE (Thuc. 6.28–9). The cult, based at Eleusis in Attica, offered initiates details of the afterlife revealed in secret ceremonies; a group of Athenians, including Socrates' associate Alcibiades, was said to have staged a mock performance of the rituals at a dinner party in front of non-initiates.[8] On each of these occasions the religious crisis appears symptomatic of a broader political malaise within Athenian democracy.

Xenophon, highlighting the secondary charge of corrupting the youth, robustly assesses that the charges against Socrates had a political component, based on his association with Alcibiades and Critias, politically controversial figures who played important roles in the city's defeat and, in the case of the latter, led the extreme and brutal oligarchy of the Thirty in 404/3 BCE.[9] The Thirty were prominent and wealthy Athenians established as oligarchs ruling their fellow citizens by Sparta, after Athens' defeat in the Peloponnesian War, and their brief period in power was marked by the brutal suppression of opposition. Their opponents then led a civil war which led to restoration of the democracy. There was then an official amnesty, in which citizens' actions during the period of the oligarchy could not become the basis for legal action.[10] This aimed to reconcile citizens and keep disputes from the period of civil war out of the courts, but as is shown by the speeches of Lysias, the pre-eminent speech-writer of the period and himself a victim of the Thirty's persecution, litigants did not shy from emphasizing whatever good or bad actions from this period supported their cases.

Athenian comedy provides the earliest evidence for the activities of Socrates and the responses of his fellow citizens. Aristophanes' *Clouds*

---

[8] While Alcibiades was pursued in the courts and exiled in absentia, cases related to this incident were still being prosecuted at the time of Socrates' trial; the defence speech of Andocides, *On the Mysteries*, is from a trial also held in 399 BCE.

[9] Xenophon's narrative of the rise and fall of the regime of the Thirty, in his *Hellenica*, is particularly concerned with the characters of leading oligarchs such as Critias.

[10] On the political climate of the restored democracy, see A. Wolpert, *Remembering Defeat: Civil War and Civic Memory in Ancient Athens* (Baltimore: Johns Hopkins University Press, 2002), and J. L. Shear, *Polis and Revolution: Responding to Oligarchy in Classical Athens* (Cambridge: Cambridge University Press, 2011).

was first performed at Athens in 423 BCE, shortly after Socrates had fought with courage for his city at Delium in Boeotia, an early and significant defeat for Athens in the Peloponnesian War. The *Clouds* is set in a philosophical school run by Socrates and his friend Chaerephon, in which the students study both natural phenomena and sophistic debating techniques. Such study is explicitly linked with new religious thinking; the Socrates of the play worships the Vortex, a power which appears to be based on the philosopher Anaxagoras' model of movement in the cosmos being driven by reason (*nous*), rather than by the traditional supreme god Zeus. The *Clouds* depicts a Socrates engaged in natural philosophy; he enters aloft on the stage crane so as to appear suspended above the stage as he studies the heavens. Plato, writing some decades later, suggests that these comic depictions of Socrates were responsible for some of the hostility to him in Athens; in his *Apology*, Socrates refers to the 'old accusations' (Pl. *Ap.* 19bc).

Both Plato and Xenophon show Socrates moving away from this kind of philosophy. Plato depicts Socrates turning to the study of ethical questions, which he identifies as a 'second (*deuteron*) voyage', using an alternative method as with switching from sails to rowing (*Phd.* 99d). Xenophon emphasizes Socrates' interest in applied philosophy, assisting with the education of leaders and the resolution of practical social problems, rather than indulging in cosmological speculation or more abstract forms of categorization and analysis. Yet education was also a controversial area; Aristophanes' *Clouds* also links Socrates' teaching to a new form of rhetorical training, in which students were trained to be able to argue either for or against the same proposition. Plato took great care to depict Socrates as rejecting such forms of argumentation, which he associated with educators such as Gorgias of Leontini and Protagoras of Abdera, influential visitors to Athens during Socrates' time whom Plato labelled 'sophists', transforming the term from a general description of an educator to a critical and negatively loaded term. Xenophon does not depict Socrates engaging directly with this debate, but his inclusion of a conversation between the young Alcibiades and his guardian Pericles, in which Alcibiades uses sophistic forms of argument (*Mem.* 1.2.40–6), distances Socrates from such methods.

In emphasizing Socrates' piety, Xenophon nonetheless depicts a figure who has novel thoughts about religious matters, as is shown in two key chapters of the *Memorabilia*, 1.4 and 4.3, in which he out-lines the case for intelligent design in the cosmos and in the special place of humans within the cosmos. Some scholars have argued that the creationist views in these chapter are so unconventional for their time that they might be an interpolation from a later source (sugges-tions for authorship have included the radical early Stoic Zeno of Citium); more recently others have argued that they offer a genuine insight into Socrates' own thought, or possibly contain Xenophon's own contribution to a developing creationist view of the cosmos. John Dillery has noted how Xenophon combines established conservative ideas with a new sense of the gods as 'an awesome, invisible force working for good throughout the universe', while David Sedley points to their anthropocentric view of the purpose of the cosmos.[11] Sedley concludes that the arguments presented are authentically Socratic, preserved by Xenophon in works which predate the later dialogues (*Phaedrus*, *Laws*) in which Plato attends to these issues. Xenophon emerges as an important witness to a key development in ancient religion and cosmology.

Philosophy in Fourth-Century Athens

After Socrates' death, a new generation of thinkers and educators emerged in Athens, taking his thought in new directions and engag-ing with philosophical ideas from other Greek traditions. Xenophon's depiction of many leading figures of this time in the *Memorabilia* offers important insights into the earliest stages of the development of ideas that would be taken up by Cynics, Cyrenaics, and later Stoics and the other Hellenistic schools of philosophy which began to emerge in the century or so after Xenophon's death. Followers of Socrates such as Antisthenes (*Mem.* 2.5, 3.11.17; DL 6.2) and Aristippus of Cyrene (*Mem.* 2.1, 3.8; DL 2.65) would later be seen as important founding figures for these traditions; Diogenes Laertius tells the stories of twelve first-generation Socratic authors (DL 2.47).

---

[11] J. Dillery, *Xenophon and the History of His Times* (London: Routledge, 1995), 187: D. N. Sedley, *Creationism and Its Critics in Antiquity* (Berkeley and Los Angeles: University of California Press, 2007), 80–1. Thomas Pangle strikes a different note, argu-ing that Xenophon fails to provide a sufficient account of Socrates' connection to the divine (T. L. Pangle, *The Socratic Way of Life: Xenophon's* Memorabilia (Chicago: University of Chicago Press, 2018), 53–4).

These figures and their views are less evident in Plato's accounts of Socrates; Plato rarely names the opponents at whom the critiques he gives to Socrates are aimed. Xenophon, in depicting Socrates in conversation with figures representing key rival Socratic traditions, suggests the rivalries between those who followed Socrates and the contest over his legacy (DL 2.65).

Writing became an important way of doing and communicating philosophy in the fourth century, in parallel with developments in other genres of prose literatures including historiography and rhetoric, both of which can themselves be seen as rival tools for elite education. The 'Socratic *logos*' emerged shortly after Socrates' death as a way of recording the ideas of Socrates—who, as mentioned, did not produce any written works—but also as a way of laying claim to his legacy and developing those ideas. Neither Plato nor Xenophon was the originator of this genre; while Diogenes Laertius lists many authors of Socratic dialogues, only fragments survive from authors such as Antisthenes and Aeschines the Socratic (not the same writer as the orator cited above). Socratic dialogues typically focus on a specific topic; both Plato and Xenophon tend to structure dialogues around a problem introduced by one of the characters, which turns out to revolve around the understanding of some aspect of virtue. In Plato's *Laches*, for example, the discussion about the teachability of virtue, and the failure of families to transmit virtue to their sons, develops into a more philosophical conversation about the definition of courage, and whether that confirms its position as a key form of virtue. The dialogues feature Socrates in conversation with other Athenians and characters from the Socratic circle; Xenophon and his wife are themselves characters in Aeschines' *Aspasia*, preserved in a quotation by Cicero (*On Invention* 1.31.51–2).

This new literary tradition enables us to see the connections and debates between those who came after Socrates. Xenophon's interactions with Plato's dialogues are significant. At several points in the *Memorabilia*, the discussion appears to track or summarize passages from them. This is especially apparent in Book 4, which sets out a syllabus for Socratic education through an account of Socrates' conversations with a student, Euthydemus. Interactions with works by other Socratics whose works do not survive are more difficult to spot, but Xenophon does show Socrates' ideas being challenged by the more hedonistic thought of Aristippus (*Mem.* 2.1, 3.8) and Antisthenes (*Mem.* 2.5).

Xenophon does not, however, depict Socrates using the same argumentative technique as that which dominates Plato's Socratic dialogues, the question-and-answer structure of the 'elenchus', as Socrates' dialogic approach is known. As a criticism of Xenophon, this difference can be overplayed; Xenophon marks key forms of Socratic practice in his text, such as the hunt for definitions beginning with the key question 'What is x?', as seen in chapters 3.9 and 4.6. One could just as easily argue that Plato's Socrates makes too little use of the 'protreptic' approach, using encouragement and persuasion through positive examples, that Xenophon's Socrates favours. Plato's *Euthydemus* offers an interesting comparison, as Socrates there does engage in protreptic, in contrast with the extreme and destructive 'eristic' version of the elenchus deployed by the sophist brothers Euthydemus and Dionysodorus. Plato does not have an answer to Xenophon's suggestion that Socrates used the elenchus to attract students and to dismantle their preconceived ideas, turning to other methods once he had an established teaching relationship in place (*Mem.* 4.2.40). The 'Socratic method' is held up as an educational ideal, yet the fictive examples of it in ancient dialogues are hardly a sufficient basis on which to proceed, and Xenophon's testimony suggests that caution is required.

The question of whether education of any sort could improve students was itself a topic of frequent discussion, especially in the fourth-century context in which Plato and his slightly older contemporary, the rhetorician and educator Isocrates (*c*.436–338 BCE), offered rival approaches to the final stages of the education of elite young men. Were the attributes of students fixed? It was a commonplace idea that some kinds of personal excellence were innate, and attributable to family background; the idea that some men enjoyed good birth (*eugeneia*) which endowed them with superior qualities was familiar, and developed further in the more monarchical contexts of the Hellenistic world. Yet the possibility of improvement—and deterioration—of any individual remained; innate attributes needed to be drawn out by educators, and developed through practice. Even those from the best families might fail to realize innate potential skills without the correct guidance and education; famous fathers might neglect their sons as they pursued their own political careers, the scenario in which Socrates is called in for educational advice in Plato's *Laches*. The competition to provide education to such young men is

seen best in works such as Isocrates' *Against the Sophists*, which contrasts the benefits of different approaches. In placing Socrates in this
environment both Plato and Xenophon are to some extent writing
anachronistically, but competition between different approaches to
education was a feature of both the Athens of Xenophon's youth and
the fourth-century context in which Plato and Isocrates were writing
and competing.

The importance of education is also explained by ancient ideas
about psychology; that is, the make-up of the soul (*psuchē*). Xenophon
does not replicate the details of Plato's complex model of a three-part
soul, in which lower physical appetites are overseen by spirit (*thumos*)
and, above that, reason (*nous*). Plato's tripartite model is partly driven
by his further analogy, developed in the *Republic* and its account of an
ideal city, Kallipolis, between the structure of the soul and structure
of the city, in which different classes of citizen take on the role of
different parts of the soul. Xenophon is particularly interested in the
restraint and control of physical appetites, seen in many discussions
about the need to restrain appetites for food and sex, but he also connects this to practical training for military activity.

The Structure and Themes of the Memorabilia

Like most early Greek writings, the dialogues Xenophon collected
together did not originally have a title. They were referred to as
Apomnemoneumata, a term often used in ancient scholarship for notes
and unedited writings. But the arrangement of the dialogues is for the
most part careful and precise; the variety of characters with whom
Socrates converses is subordinated to an overall programme which
considers the impact of Socrates' thought in an ordered range of
social contexts.[12] As in the case of Plato's Socratic dialogues, it is difficult to treat these conversations as records of actual discussions.
Although there are few explicit anachronisms in the dialogues,
Xenophon's dialogic time is sometimes fuzzy, stretching between
Socrates' time and the time at which Xenophon was writing, and

---

[12] This arrangement has been explored by many scholars: see H. Erbse, 'Die
Architektonik im Aufbau von Xenophons Memorabilien', *Hermes*, 89/3 (1961), 257–87;
V. J. Gray, *The Framing of Socrates: The Literary Interpretation of Xenophon's* Memorabilia
(Stuttgart: F. Steiner, 1998); L. Strauss, *Xenophon's Socrates* (Ithaca, NY: Cornell
University Press, 1972).

sometimes precise, particularly in evocation of the 400s BCE, Xenophon's years in Athens as a young man and the final years of Socrates' life. On occasion, Xenophon sharpens the philosophical discussion by setting it in the context of charged personal relationships between the characters, or readers' knowledge of what had happened subsequently to either Socrates or the interlocutor.

The first book presents a detailed portrait of Socrates and an assessment of his thought and activities, in response to the charges listed in the prosecution. Its first two chapters offer defences of Socrates against the two main charges against him, of religious criminality (improperly introducing new gods, not duly acknowledging the established ones) and of 'corrupting the young'. Xenophon interprets this latter charge as an attack on the activities of Socrates' students, especially those involved in the 404/3 oligarchy and civil war. Are teachers responsible for the political actions of their former students? Xenophon carefully shows how Critias and Alcibiades, two of Athens' most notorious politicians of the late fifth century, failed to learn the self-control that Socrates had tried to teach them (1.2), and how other influences—such as the teachings of the sophists, as well as their own excessive ambition—also informed their behaviour. After this explicit defence, Book 1 continues with more detailed exploration of Socrates' personal qualities and ideas, seen through conversations he held with friends and associates, such as Aristodemus, an obsessive fan who imitates Socrates' practices but has dangerous and unconventional atheistic views (1.4), and Antiphon the sophist, who criticizes Socrates' asceticism as a poor example for his students (1.6). These conversations set out Socrates' intellectual context, and while they are not as detailed as some other ancient accounts of early philosophy, such as the opening book of Aristotle's *Metaphysics*, they show that Xenophon had a good grasp of the ideas in circulation in Socrates' time.

Book 2 is focused on the family, and wider household, and the personal connections which structure citizens' lives; it presents Socratic ideas on friendship and close relationships, along with practical advice on navigating economic and social problems. Xenophon adds a twist with his preoccupation with the practical benefits of personal friendship, as an instance of the benefits of reciprocal support between individuals. The book begins with perhaps the most famous chapter in the work, Socrates' discussion with the young Aristippus of the importance of active participation in one's own political community (2.1). The fraught discussion in which Aristippus rejects any political obligation leads Socrates to recount a fable of the 'Choice of Heracles'. Xenophon's Socrates attributes this story to another of his contemporaries, the sophist Prodicus of Ceos, well known in Athens as an educator. However, the fable's emphasis on typical Xenophontic themes such as the importance of personal action governed by reason suggests that Xenophon is not simply reporting the work of others. The story offers an assertion of the values which Xenophon in turn attributes to Socrates. This frames the subsequent shorter discussions throughout the book, which start within Socrates' own household as he persuades his son Lamprocles to show more respect to his mother (2.2). Familial obligations extend to brothers; Chaerecrates must learn to get on with his brother Chaerephon (2.3). Yet maintaining a household is costly and difficult, especially amid the disruption caused by war—a citizen might need to support a large number of women, might not have access to his agricultural estate, or have been deprived of holdings overseas (2.7–8).

The lives of citizens in the polis are also connected through other forms of relationship, notably *philia* or friendship. The discussion of friendship between citizens (2.6) echoes explorations of the same theme by Plato (notably the *Lysis*), and both can be seen as precursors to Aristotle's detailed account of the role of friendship in communal life, books 8 and 9 of the *Nicomachean Ethics*. Xenophon's dialogue, with Critobulus the son of Crito, echoes the erotic and pederastic context of the *Lysis* and other Platonic dialogues, in which Socrates engages with young members of the elite.

Book 3 considers the political and communal life of the individual, taking up the societal obligations introduced in earlier discussions (1.2, 2.1) and considering how individuals should respond to the demands of public life. Again, the Xenophontic emphasis on education and personal development, and on commitment to participation and public service, is stressed from the opening words. The first chapter contrasts Socrates with a visiting educator, Dionysodorus, whose teaching on generalship is shown to be deficient because of its focus on a single aspect of the task, the formation of troops on the battlefield. Xenophon moves on to give a positive account of how conversations with Socrates were of practical and educational value to young men seeking to win high office in the city, such as Pericles

Junior (3.5) and Plato's brother Glaucon (3.6); the outcome of Socrates' conversation with Plato's uncle Charmides (3.7), notorious as one of the Piraeus Ten who managed Athens' port for the 404/3 oligarchy, is perhaps more ambiguous. In these dialogues, Xenophon makes many witty and ironic allusions to the work of Plato as well as to Athenian politics and political debates. Socrates' conversation with Pericles Junior foreshadows the premature end to that young man's career: his execution as one of the generals put on trial after the battle of Arginusae in 406 BCE. Xenophon uses this dialogue to engage with Athenian patriotic myths, noting the 'great deeds' familiar from the rhetoric of the Athenian funeral speech, but pointedly omitted in the funeral oration which Thucydides gives to Pericles Senior (Thuc. 2.36); the example of Erechtheus, a mythical Athenian king who protected the city from war with neighbouring Eleusis, stands alongside the more recent defence by the Marathon generation (3.5.9–11). Yet the elegiac tone has a political point; in his historical writing, Xenophon is keen to point out how Athens failed to support its military leaders while holding them responsible for defeat and loss.

In contrast to Plato, Xenophon shows Socrates in conversation with Athenians from outside the narrow elite circles represented in Platonic dialogue. After the discussion with Charmides (3.7) the book changes direction; Straussians wonder about the possibility of a missing dialogue with Plato himself, although arguably the discussion with Aristippus in 3.8 fulfils any need for a politically disengaged philosopher as interlocutor. Chapter 3.10 shows Socrates engaging in philosophical conversation with artists and artisans, and 3.11 is a literary tour de force in which Socrates engages in a playful debate with the courtesan Theodote. The subsequent conversation with the slothful Epigenes (3.12) is a lively evocation of Xenophon's interest in physical fitness, placed in the mouth of Socrates.

Book 4 turns to education; several chapters feature the young Euthydemus, who is eager to learn but despite his enthusiasm lacks the sense and experience to direct his own studies. Throughout this book, Xenophon engages with topics explored in the Platonic corpus, often using the same examples as key Platonic texts such as the *Republic*, the *Gorgias*, and the *Apology*, and making close reference to them. The book opens with a survey of Socrates' method of engaging with students (4.1), and the benefits he aimed to provide for them; it closes with a reiteration of the apologetic framing of the opening chapters of Book 1. This final book illustrates Socrates' skill with a case study of Socrates' engagement with one student, Euthydemus. Several chapters (4.2–3, 5–7) provide a Socratic curriculum for the personal development of an elite youth who seeks to deploy skills in speech and action to the benefit of his city. These dialogues restate Socratic ideas on important virtues and qualities: self-control, justice (for this particular discussion, chapter 4.4, Xenophon matches Socrates with the feisty sophist Hippias of Elis rather than the feeble student Euthydemus), restraint of physical appetites, and skill in philosophical argument and analysis. These discussions of justice are a key starting point for the natural law tradition. With the Socratic programme sketched out, Xenophon returns for the closing sections to the explicit defence of Socrates, overlapping with some of the contents of the *Apology*, and echoing the opening chapters to offer a formal closure to the work.

Key Themes and Concepts in Xenophon's Thought

The discussions of the *Memorabilia* explore and define a series of concepts and definitions which Xenophon attributes to Socrates. While many of the concepts intersect with those explored in Plato's dialogues, Xenophon builds an independent and distinctive model of what it means to be a good man and citizen and to use one's developed personal capacities for the public good. Recent scholarship on Xenophon has focused on the model of good leadership and active citizenship which Xenophon develops.[13] However, incorporating Xenophon's thought into any modern prescriptions for good leadership is challenging because of the hierarchical structure he sets out and the way in which the virtuous man is opposed to the enslaved.[14] The figure of the virtuous self-sufficient and self-mastered man depends by antithesis on the figure of the enslaved person, deprived of all opportunity to display or develop any form of agency, moral or otherwise. Xenophon draws repeatedly on this opposition, starting in the opening chapter, which lists the virtues and skills that the 'man of

[13] N. B. Sandridge, *Loving Humanity, Learning, and Being Honored: The Foundations of Leadership in Xenophon's* Education of Cyrus (Cambridge, MA: Harvard University Press, 2012).

[14] For a different assessment of Xenophon's thought on virtue, see Pangle, *Socratic Way of Life*, 6–7.

quality' (as we translate Xenophon's phrase *kalos kagathos*) should possess:

His own discourse was always on human subjects, investigating how we should define piety and impiety, beauty and ugliness, justice and injustice, good sense and madness, courage and cowardice, the state and the statesman, the government of men and the qualities of a governor—and all the other areas of which understanding, he thought, was a requisite for men of quality, and of which the ignorant could properly be described as no better than slaves. (*Mem.* 1.1.16)

As a list, this does summarize topics covered in these dialogues, but it does not offer any organizing principle. Yet Xenophon does suggest various structures; the unity of the virtues, the importance of reciprocal acts of giving (*charis*) as an organizing principle for human interaction, and the special status of a 'master art' which describes both the special skill of the ruler and the skill set imparted by Socrates as an educator.

THE KALOS KAGATHOS *OR MAN OF QUALITY*

The central concept in Xenophon's model is the 'fine and good man', the *kalos kagathos* (the Greek word elides two adjectives for 'beautiful' and 'good'); the aim of Socratic education is to produce such a man. This phrase has traditionally been translated 'gentleman', but that translation presupposes a system of social and cultural structures of hierarchy and deference which may be less apparent to twenty-first-century readers, even if the resonances of 'gentleman' may be equally conservative in ancient and modern times. Xenophon's primary example of the *kalos kagathos* is Ischomachus, the wealthy Athenian estate owner whose discussion with Socrates is reported in the *Oeconomicus*, and whom Socrates identifies as his teacher in practical matters.

Although Socrates encourages his interlocutors in the *Memorabilia* to develop their capabilities and become 'gentlemen', none of them, even the established adult Charmides, is treated as being so in the way that Ischomachus is. (We have translated *kalos kagathos* as 'man of quality' rather than relying on the analogical translation 'gentleman' or falling back on a literal translation such as 'fine and good man' (for example at 1.1.16), but when the adjectives as a pair are applied to other objects and practices we have retained the pairing 'fine and good' or 'beautiful and good' (for example at 1.2.23). However, one should not lose sight of the aesthetic evaluation implicit in the phrase.)

What makes a *kalos kagathos* good in the sense of admirable and imitable is his attainment of a set of skills operated under a specific set of values. While these were described in summary by the Greek term *aretē*, representing a general form of excellence, this does not have quite the same connotations as the English term 'virtue'. Sophists and Socratics alike were concerned with identifying the characteristics which made up this excellence, and the extent to which they might simply be the same excellence applied in different ways, or if they were a constellation of separate characteristics, whether one was predominant and whether there was an organizing principle. Some argued for the unity of virtue, others generated lists showing how a virtue might be instantiated differently in a list of different types of people, a method which Plato's Socrates criticizes (*Meno* 72ae). The questions of whether virtue could be taught, and whether education was more a process of drawing out innate natural qualities, were the focus of the *Meno* and other Platonic dialogues. Xenophon, in *Memorabilia* Book 4, provides a list of virtues that equates to a syllabus for Socratic education, although there is no evidence that the historical Socrates offered a structured education with a syllabus. Xenophon's model might represent an idealized form of education or at least a set of goals to aspire towards.

Several virtues vie for the position of key value in this system: justice and wisdom are important along with courage, but for Xenophon the most important of the four traditional 'cardinal virtues' is *sōphrosunē*. The complex connotations of this word are hard to capture in a single word in English; the translation favoured by many is 'moderation', but Xenophon uses the concept to cover a series of personal qualities, a mode of behaviour, and a manner of responding to difficulties. Closely linked to *sōphrosunē* is a series of values related to personal conduct: *enkrateia*, internal rule or self-mastery; *karteria*, physical endurance; and *autarkeia*, self-sufficiency. On some readings, gaining physical self-control must precede the development of the mental quality of *sōphrosunē*; on others, moderation is a core virtue which necessarily underlies and enables all other virtuous activity including control of physical appetites. The latter reading gains support from the pre-eminent position granted to *sōphrosunē* in the Socratic system of education sketched in Book 4.

Enkrateia has a particularly important role as a form of self-mastery critical to many activities of the *kalos kagathos*. By controlling his desires and managing the way in which he fulfils them, an individual gains access to more satisfying forms of pleasure and more resilience against misfortune and deprivation. Socrates himself exemplifies the enkratic life by demonstrating through his own austere lifestyle that fulfilment can be achieved with limited resources; just as Plato's Glaucon mocks Socrates for sketching a 'city of pigs' devoid of any luxuries (*Rep.* 2.372cd), Xenophon's Antiphon criticizes his thread-bare clothing and meagre diet (*Mem.* 1.6).

A key manifestation of virtue in political frameworks was justice. For Plato, justice operated both at the level of the city, in a harmonious ordering of the different constituent groups within it, and at the level of the individual, in the harmonious ordering of the *psyche* under the control of reason; his *Republic* explores these two systems as analogies for each other. Xenophon takes a different approach to justice, exploring its relationship to law (*Mem.* 4.4).[15]

Xenophon sees similarity in managerial functions which maintain order in both collective enterprises and the individual. He is concerned with *epimeleia*, the activity undertaken by rulers, generals, and managers of households in overseeing and managing those over whom they exercise authority, and also used by analogy to indicate the self-management of individuals ruling their own passions and desires. This sense of *epimeleia* as care of the self develops in later Greek philosophy into a framework for conscious practices of philosophical self-management, another way in which Xenophon's presentation of Socratic thought prefigures ideas developed by the Hellenistic schools of philosophy, which traced their heritage back to the Socratics.

Another social framework in which individual qualities become apparent is that of *charis*, the network of reciprocal obligations between individuals.[16] In the *Memorabilia*, *charis* is an important system underpinning citizen and familial friendship, comprising a range of acts which individuals must learn to perform effectively

---

[15] L.-A. Dorion, 'L'Exégèse straussienne de Xénophon: Le Cas paradigmatique de *Mémorables* IV 4', *Philosophie antique*, 1 (2001), 87–118; also (translated) in V. J. Gray (ed.), *Xenophon* (Oxford: Oxford University Press, 2010), 283–323.

[16] Vincent Azoulay has mapped the centrality of these relationships to Xenophon's thought: V. Azoulay, *Xenophon and the Graces of Power: A Greek Guide to Political Manipulation*, trans. A. Krieger (2004; Swansea: Classical Press of Wales, 2018).

and appropriately in order to cement relationships and demonstrate their commitment to the shared life of the city.

ELEUTHERIA — *FREEDOM AND UNFREEDOM*

Xenophon's theory of psychology, like Plato's, echoes hierarchical social structures. The normative presupposition contained within this hierarchy introduces a difficult aspect of Xenophon's thought, his use of the long-standing Greek analogy between the personal statuses of freedom and enslavement and political relationships and situations. This analogy ran alongside the connection between freedom and citizen status established when the Athenian politician Solon's political reforms abolished debt bondage for citizens and both sharpened and politicized the distinction between the status of the free and the enslaved, events which were thought to have taken place in the early sixth century BCE.[17]

In this Athenian view of freedom, monarchical rule was identified as analogous to or even as a form of enslavement: this form of the analogy runs through Aeschylus' *Persians*, and Herodotus' histories, seen in the famous claim made by Herodotus that the Athenians became more successful in battle once the city became a democracy, and its citizens were empowered by their freedom (Hdt. 5.78). The Athenian citizen who participates in the city's democratic self-governance stands to the disempowered subjects of monarchical regimes such as the Persian Empire in the same way as a free person (whose status includes the capacity to own and control enslaved persons) does to an enslaved person.

Xenophon incorporates this analogy into his aesthetic ethical model. The qualities of the *kalos kagathos* are aligned with the possession of the political status of freedom; Xenophon makes frequent use of a new adjective, *eleutherios*, which had come into use to describe the (possession of) characteristics ideally attributed to free persons, rather than simply ascribing the status of being free, for which an older term, *eleutheros*, was used. This nuance was a key development of Greek political thinking in the fourth century.[18] Its effect was to turn a political status into what was effectively a character virtue. An

---

[17] [Ar.] *Ath. Pol.* 5–12 gives an account which includes fragments of Solon's own poetic summary of his actions; Plutarch's *Life of Solon* 14–15 contains further details.

[18] K. A. Raaflaub, *The Discovery of Freedom in Ancient Greece*, trans. R. Franciscono (Chicago: Chicago University Pres, 2004) (1st published in German, 1985).

individual's status as a free person was demonstrated through behaving in certain ways, which were opposed to the behaviour of the 'unfree' (*aneleutheros*) or 'slavish' (*douleios, andrapodōdēs*). The personal virtues valorized by Xenophon remain out of the reach of the enslaved, often through the deliberate actions of whose who control them; in the *Cyropaedia*, for example, Cyrus uses hunting expeditions to train his elite companions in *enkrateia*. They restrain their appetites and do not eat or drink while in the field, but the enslaved support team, along with the dogs and horses, is fed and watered (*Cyr.* 8.1.43–4). Unlike Aristotle (*Pol.* 1.5.1254a17–1255a3), Xenophon does not give an explicit account of so-called 'natural slavery', in which the enslaved are identified as suited in physiology and character for that status, through lacking the capacity for reason. His account of self-mastery is defined against a group of people whose situation in life deprived them of agency and of the opportunity to exercise their intellectual capacities. This theme is introduced in the first chapter of the *Memorabilia*, and plays a significant role in the account of Socratic education in Book 4, notably in the discussion on self-mastery (4.5).

TECHNĒ — *THE CRAFT ANALOGY*

Both Plato and Xenophon show Socrates using analogies with productive crafts and professional skills to describe the work and skills required of political and military leaders. But the craft analogy has some inherent problems: some skills have obvious outputs, the material objects produced by the skilled, such as the furniture produced by the skilled carpenter, or other material goods, while others do not. The products of some crafts may be intangible, though still identifiable: the helmsman delivers the ship and its passengers safely to its destination, the doctor restores patients to full health. Such crafts involve the mastery of a distinct body of knowledge as well as practical skills.

For other activities, their status as a craft and whether there is an associated body of knowledge might be disputed. Is rhetoric a *technē*, or simply a knack that is used by the practitioners of other crafts? Socrates discusses this with the rhetorician and educator Gorgias, in Plato's dialogue of that name. For Xenophon, skill in public speaking is a skill that potential leaders should possess in order to carry out their role.

Xenophon has a particular interest in skills which involve managing and allocating resources, and overseeing the activities of the practitioners of other crafts; this has some parallels in Plato's investigation into the possibility of an architectonic master craft (*Charmides*) but in Xenophon has a more pragmatic and tactical focus. He regards these managerial and leadership skills, concerned with the management of households, armies, and cities, as placing similar requirements on the leader/manager, even if exercised at different scales and over different organizations. At the highest level this craft is identified as the 'royal craft' or 'art of kingship' (*basilikē technē*); it is unclear whether it is called so because it is the craft exercised by kings, or because it is concerned with ruling over the practitioners of other crafts and their products, or both these reasons. But it also provides a label for the skills Xenophon shows Socrates teaching to his elite pupils in the *Memorabilia*; both Aristippus, who declines to be taught (2.1), and Euthydemus, who eagerly takes up Socrates' teaching (4.2), identify it as such (2.1.17, 4.2.11). With this label, Xenophon acknowledges that there are some uneasy aspects in the relationship between Socratic thought and Athenian democracy, and also affirms his belief in the critical importance of good leadership for that democracy.

Responses to Xenophon

What makes Xenophon's account important and useful? Xenophon was a sophisticated interpreter of the diverging strands of applied philosophy that followed in the decades after Socrates' death. He was a keen theorist of leadership ethics, a significant issue in the turbulent world of a fourth-century Greece racked by continuing conflicts both between cities and between factions and individuals within them. He was also a valuable reporter of Athenian daily life, particularly within the household, enabling later readers to understand how the Socratic tradition was rooted in that specific social and political context. Xenophon takes us not just into the houses of the elite, but also into the workshops of ordinary craftsmen, the homes of citizens struggling to support their families in the midst of grave social and economic crises, and even into the elegant home of a glamorous courtesan. While Xenophon's Socrates talks to a wide range of Athenians, his work is also in dialogue with the writings of Plato and others, sometimes literally so through the use of common characters and themes.

Responses to the *Memorabilia* across the centuries have followed changing trends in education and culture. Xenophon's works were widely admired in antiquity, providing models for later writers in various genres. One episode from the *Memorabilia*, the story of the young hero Heracles (Hercules in Latin versions) at a crossroads faced with the choice between the lives of virtue and vice, was particularly popular. The Roman orator and philosopher Cicero, for example, summarized the Choice of Heracles story (*Mem.* 2.1) in his philosophical work *On Duties*, citing both Xenophon and Xenophon's claimed source Prodicus as authorities for the story (*On Duties* 1.118). Cicero observes that most ordinary mortals do not get the assistance that Heracles receives in choosing the kind of life to follow, although they perhaps receive more direct assistance from their parents. Xenophon's military-themed works have always had their admirers. The second-century CE historian Arrian, for example, wrote an *Anabasis* which covered the expeditions and conquests of Alexander the Great, imitating the structure of Xenophon's work, as well as a hunting manual updating Xenophon's *Cynegeticus*. The fourth-century historian and educator Eunapius used Xenophon's interest in the lives of eminent men (such as Socrates, the Spartan king Agesilaus, and Cyrus the Great) to frame his own *Lives of the Philosophers and Sophists*, pointing to the unusual combination of writing and action evident in Xenophon's own life.

Xenophon's use of exemplary lives as a framework for analysis and argument animated much interest in him in early modern Europe. They proved particularly amenable to incorporation into new forms of political thinking, such as the 'mirror for princes' advice manuals for princes and politicians which proliferated at this time of political change and state formation. Xenophon's work was read and translated by courtiers in Tudor England.[19] The Florentine political adviser and writer Niccolò Machiavelli (1469–1527), for example, saw Xenophon's Cyrus the Great as an exemplary figure to rank alongside Moses, Theseus, and Romulus as an agent of political transformation and the successful establishment of new imperial powers (*The Prince*, chapter 6). The Choice of Heracles story (*Mem.* 2.1) was taken up during this period, at a point when the depiction of a personified supreme Virtue became more culturally acceptable than it had been to earlier generations of Christian

[19] J. Grogan, *William Barker: Xenophon's* Cyropaedia (Cambridge: Modern Humanities Research Association, 2020), 6–13; N. Humble, 'Xenophon and the Instruction of Princes', in Flower (ed.), *Cambridge Companion to Xenophon*, 416–34.

thinkers.[20] The Italian poet Petrarch (1304–74) alludes to it twice (*De Vita Solitaria*), and many artists, including Albrecht Dürer (1471–1528) and Paolo Veronese (1528–88), found that the story offered a compelling scene to depict, with its muscular hero and contrasting female figures of Virtue and Vice. Later, the Earl of Shaftesbury (1671–1713) thought the Choice of Heracles such an inspiring and educational scene that he commissioned the artist Paolo de Matteis to create a new version, in which the choice is presented as a tough one for the young hero.[21]

Throughout the early modern period, Xenophon's writings served to educate the elite in Greek language and to instil the knowledge needed to participate in politics. Xenophon was treated as the authentic source for Socrates as an exemplary figure, in works such as Johann Jakob Brucker's *Historia Critica Philosophiae*; the widely read English translation states that Xenophon offers a 'much more accurate' picture of Socrates than Plato does, demonstrating that his 'distinguishing character' was 'that of a moral philosopher'.[22] Such sentiments were echoed by other readers; Thomas Jefferson, one of several founding fathers of the United States who read and praised Xenophon's work, noted in a letter of 1819 that 'of Socrates we have nothing genuine but in the *Memorabilia* of Xenophon'.[23]

This view was upturned by developments in philosophy as an academic discipline, which saw Plato's work promoted as prefiguring the modern discipline, and his version of Socrates given more weight. Again, German scholars led the way, with Friedrich Schleiermacher's presentation of Plato and his work exemplifying a trend in scholarship that downplayed Xenophon's understanding of the philosophical

[20] T. E. Mommsen, 'Petrarch and the Story of the Choice of Hercules', *Journal of the Warburg and Courtauld Institutes*, 16 (1954), 178.

[21] T. Rood, 'Xenophon's Changing Fortunes in the Modern World', in Flower (ed.), *Cambridge Companion to Xenophon*, 435–48.

[22] J. J. Brucker, *The History of Philosophy: From the Earliest Times to the Beginning of the Present Century*, trans. W. Enfield (London: J. Johnson, 1791), 183.

[23] T. Jefferson, 'Thomas Jefferson to William Short, 31 October 1819' (Founders Online, 1819); https://founders.archives.gov/documents/Jefferson/98-01-02-0850. On the Founding Fathers as readers of classical texts, including Xenophon, see the essays in P. S. Onuf and N. Cole (eds), *Thomas Jefferson, the Classical World, and Early America* (Charlottesville: University of Virginia Press, 2011), and also C. J. Richard, *The Founders and the Classics: Greece, Rome, and the American Enlightenment* (Cambridge, MA: Harvard University Press, 1994), and T. E. Ricks, *First Principles: What America's Founders Learned from the Greeks and Romans and How that Shaped Our Country* (New York: HarperCollins, 2020).

developments he reported.[24] A succession of Plato scholars found
Xenophon's moral philosophy lacking compared with Plato's explorations of epistemology and metaphysics. Xenophon's temporal and
spatial distance from Socrates' Athens brought his recollections under
suspicion; his historical writings were under similar attack from the
new discipline of scientific historiography, and it is for inconsistencies
and chronological errors that Plato scholars such as John Burnet found
his account of Socrates lacking; political philosopher Leo Strauss
(1899–1973), who treated Xenophon as a significant political thinker,
characterizes Burnet as identifying Xenophon as 'not very intelligent'
with 'the mind of a retired colonel rather than a philosopher'.[25] Other
philosophers, such as the great Plato scholar Gregory Vlastos, followed
suit; he found Xenophon's Socrates 'tirelessly didactic' and 'mono-
tonously earnest', and even in lighter episodes 'arch and strained'.[26]

However, Xenophon remained of more interest to political philosophers seeking to strengthen that subdiscipline's connection to the
past by tracing the heritage of political and ethical ideas. Machiavelli's
citation of Xenophon was one reason that led Strauss and his followers to pay particular interest to his work, as part of a conservative
project that sought to reject modern philosophies and methodologies
in favour of what they saw as the pure philosophy of the ancients.[27]
Strauss developed a methodology, drawing heavily on that used to
explore Jewish religious writings and philosophy, which sought to
excavate hidden meanings from texts, arguing that writers under
threat of political and religious persecution conceal their deepest
thoughts, which might run contrary to the surface meanings perceived
by non-expert and uninitiated readers. The skilled reader, Strauss
advised, should be alert to gaps and absences in the text. For example,
Strauss noted of Socrates' conversation with his son Lamprocles
(*Mem.* 2.2): 'one must pay attention not only to what Xenophon says,

[24] F. Schleiermacher, 'Über den Werth des Sokrates als Philosophen', in A. Patzer
(ed.), *Der historische Sokrates* (Darmstadt: Wissenschaftliche Buchgesellschaft, 1987),
41–58; L.-A. Dorion, *L'Autre Socrate: Études sur les écrits socratiques de Xénophon* (Paris:
Les Belles Lettres, 2013).
[25] Burnet, *Plato's* Phaedo; L. Strauss, *The Rebirth of Classical Political Rationalism:
An Introduction to the Thought of Leo Strauss; Essays and Lectures*, ed. T. L. Pangle
(Chicago: University of Chicago Press, 1989), 127.
[26] G. Vlastos, *Socrates, Ironist And Moral Philosopher* (Ithaca, NY: Cornell University
Press, 1991), 30.
[27] Strauss, *Rebirth*; Strauss, *Xenophon's Socrates*, 41.

but also to what he does not say. His Socrates does not for a moment consider it wise to talk over his son's complaint with his wife.'

While Strauss and his followers often excavate interesting and subtle points about Xenophon's works, the Straussian method can focus on minor details, on which a great deal of weight is placed and which are granted specific significance, without due consideration of the context in which those details are included. For example, Strauss and his followers meticulously count the number of oaths sworn in each dialogue. Yet considering which god is named, or other ways in which the historical context of classical Athens is reflected in characters' words and actions, is essential if any weight is to be given to these details. Xenophon himself expects readers to place the characters with whom Socrates converses in their historical context. Charmides (*Mem.* 3.7), Plato's uncle and one of the board of Ten oligarchs placed in charge of Athens' port during the oligarchic regime of the Thirty in 404/3 BCE, is one example. Socrates encourages him to involve himself in public life, yet his turn to the political life was disastrous for Athens, and ultimately for him personally. Aristippus (*Mem.* 2.1, 3.8), who has already been identified as rejecting the political life, is an appropriate character to follow (*Mem.* 3.8), as Xenophon devotes a couple of chapters to a consideration of philosophical and political education.

However, attention from Strauss and his followers played a significant part in returning Xenophon to consideration as a serious analyst of Athenian thought and society, inspiring new evaluations by classical scholars, such as W. E. Higgins's *Xenophon the Athenian*.[28] More recently, there has been a resurgence of interest both in the *Memorabilia* in its own right, in the counterbalance it offers to Plato's depiction of Socrates, and in Xenophon's thought more broadly in the context of the social and intellectual history of classical Greece, and in the operation of Athenian democracy.[29] A particularly significant contribution was the major multi-volume edition of the *Memorabilia* in the French Budé series of classical texts, including an

---

[28] W. E. Higgins, *Xenophon the Athenian: The Problem of the Individual and the Society of the Polis* (Albany, NY: State University of New York Press, 1977).
[29] See M. R. Christ, *Xenophon and the Athenian Democracy: The Education of an Elite Citizenry* (Cambridge: Cambridge University Press, 2020) for a detailed exploration of Xenophon's political thought in the context of Athenian democracy.

immense and detailed commentary by Louis-André Dorion, perhaps the foremost present-day scholar of Xenophon's Socrates.[30]

While critical of many aspects of the operation of Athenian democracy, Xenophon still depicts a Socrates who urges his followers to make useful contributions to society and the common good. At a time when the role of expertise and truthfulness in political leadership has become a central topic of debate, Xenophon's insistence that leaders must work hard and get to grips with important details has a renewed resonance.

[30] L.-A. Dorion and M. Bandini, *Xénophon: Mémorables*, 3 vols (Paris: Les Belles Lettres, 2000–11).

SELECT BIBLIOGRAPHY

Editions

Denyer, N., *Plato, The Apology of Socrates and Xenophon, The Apology of Socrates* (Cambridge: Cambridge University Press, 2019).

Dorion, L.-A., and Bandini, M., *Xénophon: Mémorables*, 3 vols (Paris: Les Belles Lettres, 2000–11).

Gigon, O., *Kommentar zum ersten Buch von Xenophons Memorabilien* (Basel: Reinhardt, 1953).

Gigon, O., *Kommentar zum zweiten Buch von Xenophons Memorabilien* (Basel: Reinhardt, 1956).

Macleod, M. D., *Xenophon: Apology and Memorabilia I* (Oxford: Oxbow, 2008).

Marchant, E. C., *Xenophontis: Opera Omnia*, 5 vols (Oxford: Clarendon Press, 1900–20).

Marchant, E. C., and Todd, O. J., *Xenophon: Memorabilia, Oeconomicus, Symposium, Apology* (Loeb Classical Library, Cambridge, MA: Harvard University Press, 1923).

Ollier, F., *Xénophon: Banquet, Apologie de Socrate* (Paris: Les Belles Lettres, 1961).

On Xenophon

Anderson, J. K., *Xenophon* (London: Duckworth, 1974).

Atack, C., 'Plato's Statesman and Xenophon's Cyrus', in G. Danzig, D. M. Johnson, and D. Morrison (eds), *Plato and Xenophon: Comparative Studies* (Mnemosyne Supplements; Leiden: Brill, 2018), 510–43.

Azoulay, V., *Xénophon et les grâces du pouvoir: De la charis au charisme* (Paris: Publications de la Sorbonne, 2004) = Azoulay, V., *Xenophon and the Graces of Power: A Greek Guide to Political Manipulation*, trans. A. Krieger (Swansea: Classical Press of Wales, 2018).

Chernyakhovskaya, O., *Sokrates bei Xenophon: Moral—Politik—Religion* (Tübingen: Narr, 2014).

Christ, M. R., *Xenophon and the Athenian Democracy: The Education of an Elite Citizenry* (Cambridge: Cambridge University Press, 2020).

Dillery, J., *Xenophon and the History of His Times* (London: Routledge, 1995).

Dorion, L.-A., *L'Autre Socrate: Études sur les écrits socratiques de Xénophon* (Paris: Les Belles Lettres, 2013).

Flower, M. A. (ed.), *The Cambridge Companion to Xenophon* (Cambridge: Cambridge University Press, 2017).

Higgins, W. E., *Xenophon the Athenian: The Problem of the Individual and the Society of the Polis* (Albany, NY: State University of New York Press, 1977).

Hobden, F., *Xenophon* (London: Bloomsbury, 2020).

Hobden, F., and Tuplin, C. J. (eds), *Xenophon: Ethical Principles and Historical Enquiry* (Leiden: Brill, 2012).

Johnson, D. M., *Xenophon's Socratic Works* (Abingdon: Routledge, 2021).

Moore, C., *Socrates and Self-Knowledge* (Cambridge: Cambridge University Press, 2015).

Narcy, M., and Tordesillas, A. (eds), *Xénophon et Socrate: Actes du colloque d'Aix-en-Provence (6–9 novembre 2003)* (Paris: J. Vrin, 2008).

Rood, T., 'Xenophon's Changing Fortunes in the Modern World', in Flower, M. (ed.), *The Cambridge Companion to Xenophon*, 435–48.

Sandridge, N. B., *Loving Humanity, Learning, and Being Honored: The Foundations of Leadership in Xenophon's Education of Cyrus* (Cambridge, MA: Harvard University Press, 2012).

Strauss, L., *The Rebirth of Classical Political Rationalism: An Introduction to the Thought of Leo Strauss; Essays and Lectures*, ed. T. L. Pangle (Chicago: University of Chicago Press, 1989).

Tuplin, C. J., and Azoulay, V. (eds), *Xenophon and His World: Papers from a Conference Held in Liverpool in July 1999* (Stuttgart: Steiner, 2004).

Memorabilia

Erbse, H., 'Die Architektonik im Aufbau von Xenophons Memorabilien', *Hermes*, 89/3 (1961), 257–87.

Goldhill, S. D., 'The Seductions of the Gaze: Socrates and His Girlfriends', in P. Cartledge, P. Millett, and S. Von Reden (eds), *Kosmos: Essays in Order, Conflict and Community in Classical Athens* (Cambridge: Cambridge University Press, 1998), 105–24.

Gray, V. J., 'Xenophon's Image of Socrates in the *Memorabilia*', *Prudentia*, 27/2 (1995), 50–73.

Gray, V. J., *The Framing of Socrates: The Literary Interpretation of Xenophon's Memorabilia* (Stuttgart: F. Steiner, 1998).

Johnson, D. M., 'Xenophon at His Most Socratic (*Memorabilia* 4.2)', *Oxford Studies in Ancient Philosophy*, 29 (2005), 39–73.

Johnson, D. M., 'Aristippus at the Crossroads: The Politics of Pleasure in Xenophon's *Memorabilia*', *Polis*, 26/2 (2009), 204–22.

McNamara, C., 'Socratic Politics in Xenophon's *Memorabilia*', *Polis*, 26/2 (2009), 223–45.

Morrison, D. R., 'Xenophon's Socrates on the Just and the Lawful', *Ancient Philosophy*, 15/2 (1995), 329–58.

Natali, C., 'Socrates' Dialectic in Xenophon's *Memorabilia*', in Judson, L. and Karasmanēs, V. (eds), *Remembering Socrates: philosophical essays* (Oxford: Clarendon Press, 2006), 3–17.

O'Connor, D. K., 'The Erotic Self-Sufficiency of Socrates: A Reading of Xenophon's *Memorabilia*', in P. A. Vander Waerdt (ed.), *The Socratic Movement* (Ithaca, NY: Cornell University Press, 1994), 151–80.

Pangle, T. L., *The Socratic Way of Life: Xenophon's Memorabilia* (Chicago: University of Chicago Press, 2018).

Strauss, L., *Xenophon's Socrates* (Ithaca, NY: Cornell University Press, 1972).

Historical and Philosophical Background

Atack, C., *The Discourse of Kingship in Classical Greece* (London: Routledge, 2020).

Brucker, J. J., *The History of Philosophy: From the Earliest Times to the Beginning of the Present Century*, trans. W. Enfield (London: J. Johnson, 1791).

Burnet, J., *Plato's* Phaedo (Oxford: Clarendon Press, 1911).

Cartledge, P., *Ancient Greek Political Thought in Practice* (Cambridge: Cambridge University Press, 2009).

Danzig, G., 'Did Plato Read Xenophon's *Cyropaedia?*', in S. Scolnicov and L. Brisson (eds), *Plato's Laws: From Theory into Practice; Proceedings of the VI Symposium Platonicum* (Sankt Augustin: Academia, 2003), 286–97.

Davidson, J. N., *The Greeks and Greek Love: A Radical Reappraisal of Homosexuality in Ancient Greece* (London: Weidenfeld & Nicolson, 2007).

Dover, K. J., *Greek Homosexuality* (London: Duckworth, 1978; new edn. Bloomsbury Academic, 2016).

Jefferson, T., 'Thomas Jefferson to William Short, 31 October 1819' (1819). Online at: https://founders.archives.gov/documents/Jefferson/98-01-02-0850.

Kahn, C. H., *Plato and the Socratic Dialogue: The Philosophical Use of a Literary Form* (Cambridge: Cambridge University Press, 1996).

Mommsen, T. E., 'Petrarch and the Story of the Choice of Hercules', *Journal of the Warburg and Courtauld Institutes*, 16 (1954), 178.

Nails, D., *The People of Plato: A Prosopography of Plato and Other Socratics* (Indianapolis: Hackett, 2002).

Osborne, R., and Rhodes, P. J., *Greek Historical Inscriptions: 478–404 BC* (Oxford: Oxford University Press, 2017).

Raaflaub, K. A., *The Discovery of Freedom in Ancient Greece*, trans. R. Franciscono (Chicago: University of Chicago Press, 2004) (1st published in German, 1985).

Rhodes, P. J., *Aristotle: The Athenian Constitution* (Harmondsworth: Penguin, 1984).

Rhodes, P. J., and Osborne, R., *Greek Historical Inscriptions: 404–323 BC* (Oxford: Oxford University Press, 2003).

Schleiermacher, F., 'Über den Werth des Sokrates als Philosophen', in A. Patzer (ed.), *Der historische Sokrates* (Darmstadt: Wissenschaftliche Buchgesellschaft, 1987), 41–58.

Sedley, D. N., *Creationism and Its Critics in Antiquity* (Berkeley and Los Angeles: University of California Press, 2007).

Shear, J. L., *Polis and Revolution: Responding to Oligarchy in Classical Athens* (Cambridge: Cambridge University Press, 2011).

Vlastos, G., *Socrates, Ironist and Moral Philosopher* (Ithaca, NY: Cornell University Press, 1991).

Wolpert, A., *Remembering Defeat: Civil War and Civic Memory in Ancient Athens* (Baltimore: Johns Hopkins University Press, 2002).

CHRONOLOGY

(All dates BCE)

490   Persians under Darius launch invasion of mainland Greece and are defeated by the Athenians at Marathon.

483   Funded by silver from the mines at Laurium, Athens builds its naval capacity under military leadership of Themistocles.

480–79   Persians under Xerxes invade Greece, sacking Athens. They are defeated at sea by the Athenian navy at Salamis, then by combined land forces at Plataea.

472   Pericles begins his political career by funding a production for a civic festival, Aeschylus' *Persians*.

c.469   Birth of Socrates.

451   New law restricts Athenian citizenship to legitimate children of two Athenian citizens.

447   Athens defeated by Thebes at Coronea.

431   Start of Peloponnesian War between Athens and Sparta.

c.430   Birth of Xenophon.

c.428/7   Birth of Plato.

429   Plague in Athens; death of Pericles and his older sons.

424   Battle of Delium, in which Socrates serves with distinction: Athens defeated.

421   Peace of Callias brings Athens–Sparta war to a temporary close.

415   Athenians vote to send an expeditionary force to support Sicilian cities against Syracuse, beginning a new phase of the Peloponnesian War.

413   Sicilian Expedition ends in defeat, with a catastrophic loss of men and resources for Athens.

411/10   Regimes of the Four Hundred, and then the Five Thousand, at Athens. After a brief interlude, democracy is restored.

406   Battle of Arginusae; and subsequent trial and execution of the Arginusae generals.

404   End of Peloponnesian War: Athens is defeated by Sparta. Athens' walls are demolished and a pro-Spartan oligarchic regime, the Thirty, installed in place of democracy. Spartan hegemony over Greek world begins.

403 Athenian democrats regroup and after a fierce civil war democracy is restored. Critias and other leaders of the Thirty killed.

401 Xenophon joins expedition of the 10,000 Greek mercenaries to Persia (recounted in his *Anabasis*); after the attempt to overthrow Artaxerxes fails, he accompanies the surviving Greeks back to safety.

399 Trial and execution of Socrates in Athens.

396/5 Xenophon accompanies Agesilaus of Sparta on campaign in Asia Minor, and probably on his return to Sparta.

394 Battle of Coronea. Xenophon fights for Sparta, against an alliance of Thebes and Argos which also included Athenian troops. At some point during this period he was officially exiled from Athens. (The Spartans provide Xenophon with an estate at Scillus, near Elis.)

387/6 'King's Peace' or Peace of Antalcidas brokered by Artaxerxes II of Persia ends the Corinthian War and cements Spartan hegemony over the Greek world, as well as Persian influence in the Aegean.

c.385 Plato establishes the Academy in Athens.

378 Second Athenian League founded, with aim of resisting Spartan hegemony.

371 Sparta defeated by the Thebans at Leuctra; Spartan hegemony ends and Sparta loses control of Peloponnese. Xenophon leaves Scillus, probably for Corinth.

362 Battle of Mantinea ends Theban hegemony but does not restore Sparta's fortunes; Xenophon's son Gryllus is killed fighting for the Athenians.

c.360 Death of Agesilaus.

c.354 Death of Xenophon.

c.348/7 Death of Plato.

MAP I   The Eastern Mediterranean

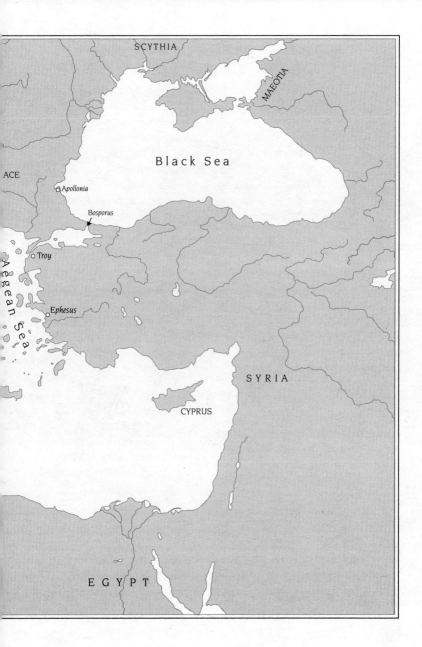

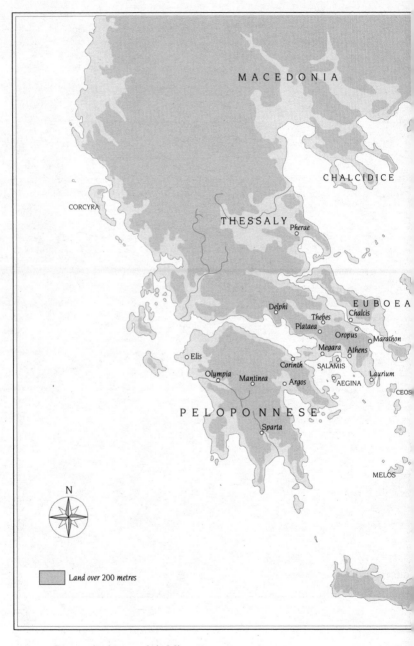

MAP 2 Greece, the Aegean, Asia Minor

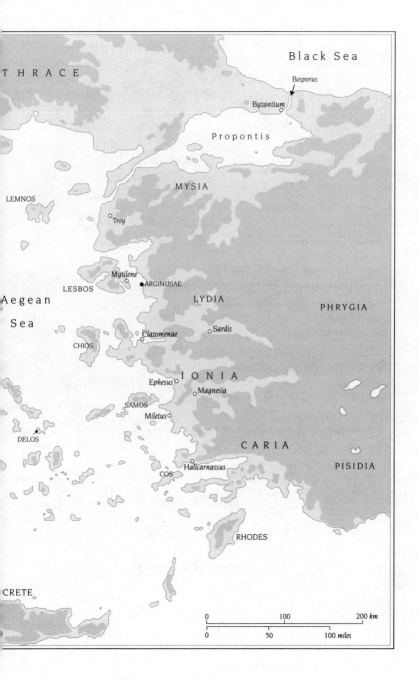

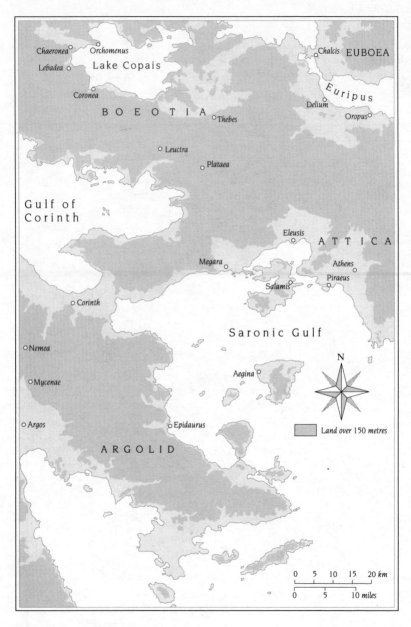

MAP 3 Boeotia, West Attica, Argolid

MEMORABILIA

BOOK 1

I HAVE often wondered* just what arguments advanced by his **1**
accusers could possibly have persuaded the Athenians that Socrates
deserved execution by the city.* The accusation against him went
something like this: 'Socrates is guilty of not recognizing the gods*
traditionally recognized by the city, and of introducing other novel
divinities: he is also guilty of corrupting the young men.'*

First, then, what possible evidence could they have used to show **2**
that he did not recognize the gods recognized by the city? On many
occasions he was quite openly seen sacrificing either at home or at the
city's communal altars, and it was hardly a secret that he made use of
divination*—it had become common knowledge that Socrates said that
his own 'divine sign'* gave him instructions: and that, I think, was in
fact the main basis of their charge that he was introducing novel divinities. But there was nothing novel in this. He was not introducing any- **3**
thing different from the divination practised by all others who make use
for that purpose of augury, significant utterances, chance encounters,
or sacrificial victims. These others do not suppose in their divination
that it is the birds or the people they meet who have knowledge of what
is to their benefit, but rather the gods communicating it by those means:
and this is what Socrates recognized too. But whereas most others say **4**
that they are either deterred or encouraged* by the birds or their chance
encounters, Socrates would say what he knew to be true: he said that it
was his divine sign which gave him instructions. And there were many
of his associates* to whom he made forecasts, telling them to do this
or not to do that, and attributing this advice to the advance notice
given by his divine sign: those who followed his advice did well out of
it, and those who did not had cause for regret. Yet who could fail to **5**
acknowledge that he would not have wanted to be shown up to his associates as a fool or a charlatan? But he would have been seen as both, if
he made forecasts supposed to be divine revelations and was then
revealed to be making them up. So clearly he would not have made his
forecasts if he was not confident that he was speaking the truth. But
who could have such confidence other than in a god? And if he was
confident in the gods, how could he not believe that there are gods?

6   Furthermore, with his close friends he also took the following approach. In straightforward matters he would advise them to go ahead with whatever action he thought would turn out for the best, but where there was real uncertainty about the outcome of any action, he would

7   send them to ask the oracle* whether that action should be taken. He said that those who were going to be good managers of a household or a city needed the additional guidance of divination. To acquire skill in carpentry* or metalwork or farming or government, or the ability to supervise such activities, exercise financial control, manage an estate, or command an army—all these and suchlike he thought were things which could be taught and learnt within the grasp of the human

8   mind. But he said that the most important elements of all these pursuits were reserved by the gods to themselves, and none of them could be clearly known by human beings. A man who has planted a field well cannot know who will reap the crop; a man who has built a house well cannot know who will live in it; a would-be general cannot know whether being in command will be to his benefit; a politician cannot know whether being head of state will be to his benefit; a man who has married a beautiful wife to give him pleasure cannot know whether she will bring him pain; and a man who has acquired through his marriage kinsmen of political power in his city cannot know whether

9   they will be the agents of his exile from the city. People who think that none of these eventualities lie with the gods, but that all lie within the range of the human mind, are themselves, he said, the victims of a god-sent delusion. Deluded too are those who turn to divination on matters which the gods have allowed humans to decide for themselves on their own understanding—for example, if someone were to ask the gods if it is better to engage a qualified or an unqualified driver for their carriage-and-pair, or to engage a qualified or an unqualified helmsman for their ship—or on matters which can be settled by calculation, measurement, or weighing. He thought that people asking such questions of the gods were committing an irreverence. The proper course, he said, was to act on our own intelligence in areas where the gods have granted us the use of that intelligence, but to try by means of divination to receive an answer from the gods on those matters which are obscured to the human view: because the gods, he said, do communicate with those on whom they look kindly.

10   Then again, Socrates was always to be seen in public.* Early in the morning he would go to the arcades and the exercise grounds; at

midday when the agora was full he was conspicuous there too; and
for the rest of the day he was always where he could expect to meet
the most people. Generally he did the talking, and it was open to
anyone who wanted to listen to him. But no one ever saw or heard *11*
Socrates doing or saying anything blasphemous or impious. Nor,
unlike most of the other philosophers, did he hold forth about the
nature of the universe* or speculate on the fabric of what the sophists call the 'cosmos'* and whatever it was that compelled the various
celestial phenomena* into being—in fact he would demonstrate the
folly of those who made such matters their study. His first question *12*
of them was whether they had somehow concluded that they already
possessed sufficient knowledge of human affairs to proceed to this
further study, or whether they thought it appropriate behaviour to
ignore the human and enquire into the divine. And then he would *13*
express his astonishment if it was not obvious to them that these
things are impossible to discover. Even those who prided themselves
on being the expert lecturers on this subject could not agree with
one another, but differed among themselves as widely as the various
types of madmen. Some madmen have no fear even in clear danger, *14*
and others are afraid when there is no cause for fear; some cannot see
any disgrace in saying or doing anything, even in the middle of
a crowd,* and others think they should not even go out in public;
some have no respect for any temple or altar, or anything else to do
with the gods, and others worship stones, odd bits of wood, or wild
animals.* So it was with those who theorize about the nature of the
universe. Some thought that all that exists was a single indivisible
entity,* others that there was an infinity of separate components;*
some held that all things are in perpetual motion,* others that nothing could ever be moved; some thought that all things were subject
to generation and extinction,* others that nothing could ever be generated or extinguished.

He had further questions of them too. Students of human affairs, *15*
he would say, think that there is practical effect which they can apply
from whatever knowledge they gain to their own benefit and that of
anyone else they choose. Do these investigators of divine phenomena
make a similar assumption of practical effect? Do they think that
when they have understood the causes which compel each of these
phenomena into being they can then create at will winds, waters, seasons,* or anything else of that sort which may be required? Or is it

that they do not even hope for anything like that, but are simply content to understand how such things come to be?

16   This, then, was the sort of thing he used to say about those who busy themselves with such speculations. His own discourse was always on human subjects,* investigating how we should define piety and impiety, beauty and ugliness, justice and injustice, good sense and madness, courage and cowardice, the state and the statesman, the government of men and the qualities of a governor—and all the other areas of which understanding, he thought, was a requisite for men of quality,* and of which the ignorant could properly be described as no better than slaves.*

17   Now it is no surprise that the jurors came to a wrong judgement of him on those matters where his opinions were not open and obvious. What is surprising—is it not?—is that they took no account of what
18 was common knowledge. There was one occasion when he was a member of the Council,* and had taken the Councillors' oath, which included the duty to exercise their office in accordance with the laws. He happened to be president of the Council at a meeting of the assembly when the people were fired up to demand a single resolution at one go for the execution of nine generals,* Thrasyllus and Erasinides* and all their colleagues, and that was against the law. Socrates refused to put the motion to the vote, even though the people were angry at him and many powerful men added their threats. But he thought it more important to abide by his oath than to give in to an illegal popular demand or protect himself against intimidation.

19   The truth is that Socrates did believe that the gods care for human beings, but not in the way that is commonly thought. Most people think that the gods know some things about us, but not others. Socrates on the other hand thought that the gods know everything, what we say, what we do, what we secretly intend; that they are present everywhere; and that they use signs to communicate with human beings on the
20 whole range of human affairs. So I do wonder how on earth the Athenians were persuaded that Socrates was not serious about the gods. This was a man who never said or did anything irreverent in his relation to the gods, but whose words and actions in matters of religion would be in anyone else the very model of piety, and recognized as such.

2   I AM also amazed that some people were persuaded that Socrates was a corrupter of the young. Firstly, apart from what I have already said, of all men he had the strongest control over his appetites* as regards both sex and belly; secondly, he showed exceptional endurance* in cold, heat, and all other physical hardships;* and then he was so disciplined to modest requirements that, though he possessed very little, he was very easily content with that as a sufficiency. How then, if that 2 was the sort of man he was, could he have caused others to be irreligious, criminal, greedy, sexually incontinent, or physically soft? In fact there were many whom he stopped from going that way by inspiring in them a love of virtue, and giving them hope that, if they took care of themselves, they would become men of quality. And yet he 3 never professed to teach how to achieve that end: rather, by manifestly displaying that character himself, he made those who spent time in his company hope that, if they followed his example,* they would develop the same character as his.

A further point is that he himself did not neglect his bodily health, 4 and had no time for those who did. He disapproved of excessive eating* followed by excessive working off, but approved of just enough exercise to digest an intake with which one's rational mind was happy: such a regime, he said, was healthy enough and no impediment to the care of the soul.* And there was nothing at all foppish or pretentious 5 about his clothing, footwear, or general style of life. Nor, most certainly, did he instil any love of money* in his associates. He put an end to their other desires, and charged no fee to those whose desire was to be with him. His view was that by making no charge* he was ensuring 6 his independence: he used to call those who did take a fee for their tutorials 'self-enslavers', because they were obliged to converse with anyone who had paid their fee. He found it astonishing that someone 7 who professed to teach virtue* should demand money for it, and rather than considering that his greatest reward would be gained by the acquisition of a good friend,* was evidently afraid that the resulting man of quality would not show the greatest gratitude to his greatest benefactor. Socrates never made any such profession to any- 8 one, but was confident that those of his associates who adopted his own tried and tested principles would be good friends both to himself and to one another for the whole of their lives. How then could a man like that be a corrupter of the young? Only, perhaps, if it is somehow corruption to cultivate virtue.

'But, for heaven's sake,' said his accuser,* 'he made his associates 9 contemptuous of the established order by telling them that it was

idiotic to appoint state officials by lot,* when nobody would employ anyone chosen by lot as a helmsman or a carpenter or a musician, or for any other professional role, in which mistakes cause far less damage than mistakes in affairs of state.' This sort of talk, he said, encouraged the young men to care nothing for the established constitution,*
10 and turned them to violence.* But in my opinion those who are in the habit of rational thought,* and consider that they will be able to show their fellow citizens where their best interests lie, are the least likely to resort to violence. They know that violence is accompanied by enmities and dangers, whereas persuasion achieves the same results without danger and in a spirit of friendship: people who have been subjected to violence* resent what they see as a deprivation, but people who have been won over by persuasion welcome what they see as a benefit conferred. So violence is not the way of those who exercise reason, but rather the characteristic behaviour of those who combine
11 power with lack of judgement. Moreover, anyone attempting violent change would need a good number of supporters, whereas a man capable of persuasion would need nobody else: he would be confident of his ability to persuade on his own. And such men are the least likely to commit bloodshed: who would rather kill a man than win him over and have his living support?
12   'But', said the accuser, 'Critias* and Alcibiades* had been associates of Socrates, and these two did more harm to Athens than anyone else. Critias was the most grasping, violent, and murderous of all in the oligarchy, and Alcibiades likewise the most dissolute, overween-
13 ing, and violent of all in the democracy.' For my part I shall not make any defence of those two for any harm they did to Athens, but I shall
14 explain how they came to be associated with Socrates. These two men were innately the most ambitious in all Athens: they wanted to have everything under their own control and to achieve greater fame than anyone else. They knew that Socrates lived a completely self-sufficient* life on very little money and had complete discipline over all pleasures of the flesh, but when it came to argument could do as he
15 liked with any interlocutor. Given that they could see this, and were the sort of men I have described, I wonder whether anyone would say that their desire for Socrates' company was out of enthusiasm for his way of life and self-discipline, or rather a calculation that keeping company with him would make them supremely capable in both
16 speech and action. My own thought is that if god gave them the

choice of living their whole life in the way they saw Socrates living his
or of dying, they would both have preferred death. This became clear
from their conduct. As soon as they thought they had reached the top
of the class, they immediately bolted from Socrates and turned to
political activity, the purpose which had drawn them to him in the
first place.

Perhaps someone might retort that Socrates should not have *17*
taught politics to his circle before teaching them self-discipline. I do
not dispute that, but I observe that all teachers give a personal example to their pupils by the way they themselves practise what they
preach, as well as adding persuasive arguments. And I know that this
was true of Socrates also—he gave his associates an example in his
own person* of the man of quality, and his discourse on virtue and all
other human concerns was quite brilliant. I know too that both these *18*
men did exercise self-discipline for as long as they associated with
Socrates: and this was not through any fear of being punished or
beaten by him, but because they believed at the time that this was the
best way to behave.

Now perhaps many of those who claim to be philosophers might *19*
say that the just man could never become unjust or the self-disciplined
man a lecher, nor could anyone who has once learnt any other teachable
subject ever unlearn that knowledge. Here I disagree. My perception
is that, just as those who do not keep their bodies in training cannot
carry out the proper functions of a body, so those who do not keep
their souls in training cannot carry out the proper functioning of
a soul: they can neither do what they should do nor refrain from what
they should not do. That is why fathers keep even sensible sons away *20*
from bad characters, on the understanding that good company is
a training* in virtue, and bad company is its ruin. The poets* bear
witness to this too. One says:

> 'You will learn what is good from men who are good: but if ever
>   you consort with the bad, any good sense will be gone.'

And another says:

> 'But a good man can sometimes be bad, and at other times noble.'

And I can add my testimony to theirs. Just as those who do not make *21*
a constant study of the epic poets forget the verses they have read, so
too I observe that people who do not keep in mind what their teachers

have told them tend to forget it. Whenever anyone forgets his course of instruction he has also forgotten the state of mind which made his soul eager for self-discipline: and when he has forgotten that, it is not

22 surprising that he has also forgotten the self-discipline. I also observe that those who have been led to drink or embroiled in love affairs are less capable of taking thought for what they should do and refraining from what they should not do. Many who could keep control over their spending before they fell in love can no longer do so once love has struck: and then, when they have spent all their money, they do not hold back from the sort of profiteering which they had previously

23 shunned as shameful. How then can it be impossible for those who were once self-disciplined to lose that discipline later, or those who were once capable of right action to be incapable later? In fact it seems to me that all which is fine and good needs practice for its cultivation, and especially self-discipline. The appetites for pleasure which inhere in the same body as the soul are urging the soul to abandon self-discipline and give both them and the body immediate gratification.

24   And so it was with Critias and Alcibiades too. As long as they were associated with Socrates, they were able with him as their ally to win control over their baser desires. But once they were parted from his company, Critias went into exile in Thessaly,* and began to associate there with men given more to lawlessness than to just behaviour. As for Alcibiades, he was pursued for his good looks by many grand ladies,* cosseted by many powerful flatterers for his influence in Athens and among the allies, and looked up to by the common people. His supremacy was easily won, and just as athletes who win an easy supremacy in the games neglect their training, so he too neglected himself.

25   So under those circumstances, with both of them conceited by their birth, elated by their wealth, puffed up by their power, and cosseted by so many—with all these corrupting influences, and so long away from Socrates, is it any surprise that they became high-handed?

26 And then does his accuser blame Socrates for whatever faults were shown by these two? Does the accuser think that Socrates deserves no credit for giving them self-discipline when they were young and at the age when the greatest irresponsibility and lack of control were to be expected? That is certainly far from the judgement we make in other

27 cases. For example, what professional teacher of pipe- or lyre-playing, or of any other art, is held accountable if he has made his pupils

proficient, and they then deteriorate after moving on* to other teachers? And what father, with a son kept sensible under one mentor, but who later goes to the bad under another, will hold that earlier mentor responsible, rather than giving the first all the greater credit the more his son was clearly getting worse under the second? And fathers themselves who live with their sons are not blamed when their sons go wrong, if they themselves live a disciplined life. This would 28 have been the proper way to make a judgement on Socrates also. If there were anything discreditable in his own behaviour, he could reasonably have been thought a bad influence: but if he himself showed consistent self-control, how could it be right to hold him responsible for a vice which was no part of his own nature?

Nevertheless, even though he never did anything bad himself, he 29 could rightly have been censured if he expressed approval when he saw those men behaving discreditably. Well, when he perceived that Critias was in love with Euthydemus* and was trying to have his way with him in the manner of those who use bodies for sexual pleasure, Socrates sought to dissuade him, declaring that it was both demeaning and improper for a man of quality to pester the object of his affection, whose high regard he desired, with the importunity of a beggar, asking for one more favour, and a dishonourable one at that. When 30 Critias paid no attention to such advice and was not dissuaded, it is reported that, in the presence of a large company which included Euthydemus, Socrates said that Critias seemed to him to have the same problem as a pig: he was as urgent to rub himself against Euthydemus as piglets are to rub against stones. The result was that 31 Critias conceived a hatred of Socrates, so that when he was one of the Thirty and became a legislator along with Charicles,* he took out his grudge against Socrates by including among the laws which he enacted a prohibition on teaching the art of argument.* This was his way of spiting Socrates: with no other means of attack, he was exposing him to the common public complaint against philosophers in general, and so blackening his reputation with the public. I myself never heard Socrates make any such claim, and I am not aware of anyone else saying that they had heard him do so.

Socrates made his position clear enough. When the Thirty* were 32 putting many of the citizens to death (not the worst of them either), and inciting many others to criminal activity, Socrates happened to remark that he would think it strange if a man put in charge of a herd of cattle* did not admit that he was a poor herdsman if he caused a decline in both numbers and quality, but stranger still if a man appointed to lead a city and causing a decline in citizen numbers and quality feels no shame and does not consider himself a poor leader.

33   When this remark was reported to them, Critias and Charicles summoned Socrates, showed him the law, and forbade him to have conversations with the young. Socrates asked them if it was permitted to seek clarification of anything which might not be understood in this
34   prohibition. They said that it was. 'Well then,' he said, 'I am ready to obey the laws. But just in case I inadvertently break the law through not understanding it, can you please tell me clearly whether what you have in mind in your ban on "the art of argument" is to do with right argument or wrong argument? If it is to do with right argument, then obviously one would have to avoid arguing rightly: but if with wrong argument, obviously one must try to argue rightly.'

35   This infuriated Charicles. 'Since you are that clueless, Socrates,' he said, 'here is our edict in a form you will find it easier to understand: you are not to converse with the young in any way at all.'

'Well then,' said Socrates, 'to avoid any doubt, and anything I might do in contravention of your edict, tell me specifically the age up to which people should be considered young.'

Charicles replied, 'For as long as they are not allowed to sit as members of the Council, as not yet having reached maturity of judgement:* so for the same reason you must not converse with those younger than thirty.'

36   'Not even if I am shopping,' said Socrates, 'and the seller is under thirty? Can I not ask him his price?'

'Yes, of course you can ask that sort of thing,' Charicles replied, 'but the trouble is, Socrates, that your habit is to ask questions to which more often than not you already know the answer. These are the questions you must stop asking.'

'So I am not even to reply', said Socrates, 'if some young man asks me something like "Where does Charicles live?" or "Where is Critias?", if I know the answer?'

'Yes, of course you can answer that sort of question,' said Charicles.

37   And now Critias intervened, saying, 'I tell you, though, Socrates, what you will have to keep off—all that talk of cobblers, carpenters, and smiths.* I imagine that they are by now quite worn out with all the publicity you give them.'

'So,' said Socrates, 'am I also to keep off the consequent subjects—justice, piety, and other such virtues?'

'By god, yes!', said Charicles, 'and cowherds too! Otherwise you had better watch out that you too do not reduce the numbers in the herd.'

This was proof that Socrates' remark about cattle had been *38* reported to them and provoked their anger.

So much then for the nature of Critias' association with Socrates and their attitude to each other.

I myself would say that no one can take any educational benefit *39* from someone they do not like. It was not because they liked him that Critias and Alcibiades associated with Socrates for as long as they did, but because from the very start they were intent on a leading role in the state. While still in company with Socrates they were looking to hold talks with the most active politicians in preference to anyone else. It is said that before he was twenty years old *40* Alcibiades had a discussion about law with Pericles,* who was his guardian and also the leading statesman in Athens. It went something like this.

'Tell me, Pericles,' Alcibiades said, 'can you teach me what law is?'* *41*

'Certainly I can,' said Pericles.

'Well for heaven's sake please do so!' said Alcibiades, 'Because when I hear people being praised as law-abiding folk, it occurs to me that such praise could not properly be conferred on someone who does not know what law is.'

'Well, Alcibiades,' said Pericles, 'you are not asking for anything *42* very difficult, if you want to understand what law is. Laws are all that the people at large, after due assembly and approval, have enacted to declare what should and should not be done.'

'And what they have decided should be done—is that something good or something bad?'

'Good of course, my young man, not bad.'

'But if it is not the people at large, but, as happens where there is *43* an oligarchy,* just a few of them who meet together and enact what should be done—what do you call that?'

'Everything enacted by the ruling power in a state, after due consideration of what should be done, is called law.'

'And so even if that ruling power in the state is a tyrant,* and it is he who enacts what should be done by the citizens, is that also law?'

'Yes, even the enactments of a tyrant in power are also called law.'

44   'But, Pericles, what constitutes force and the antithesis of law? Is it not when the stronger* imposes whatever he wants on the weaker by means of force, not persuasion?'

'I would agree with that,' said Pericles.

'And so whatever enactments a tyrant imposes on the citizens other than by persuasion are the antithesis of law?'

'Yes, I agree,' said Pericles, 'and I take back my statement that whatever a tyrant enacts without persuasion is law.'

45   'And whatever the few enact without persuading the many, but simply because they have the power—are we or are we not to call that force?'

'In all cases,' said Pericles, 'where one party imposes a course of action on another, whether by enactment or not, without persuading him, that in my view constitutes force rather than law.'

'So when the whole people at large make enactments using their power over the propertied classes rather than persuasion, that too would be force rather than law?'

46   'Look, Alcibiades,' said Pericles, 'at your age we too were very clever at this sort of thing: we used to work up the same sort of ingenious arguments that you seem to me to be working up now.'

Then Alcibiades said, 'How I wish I had been with you, Pericles, when you were at your cleverest in these things!'

47   So then, as soon as Critias and Alcibiades fancied themselves better than the current politicians, they had no more contact with Socrates. They did not like him anyway, and if they did happen to come into contact with him, they resented being cross-questioned about the error of their ways. They began to engage in politics, which was the very reason why they had first attached themselves to Socrates.

48   But other associates of Socrates were Crito,* Chaerephon,* Chaerecrates,* Hermogenes,* Simmias and Cebes,* and Phaedondas.* These and others associated with him not to acquire the skills of public speakers or legal experts, but rather to become men of quality capable of doing their proper duty by family and household, relatives and friends, city and fellow citizens. And none of these, when either young or old, ever did anything wrong or was accused of doing wrong.

49   'But', said the accuser, 'Socrates taught sons to treat their fathers with contempt.* He persuaded them that he made those in his circle wiser than their fathers, and told them that the law allowed anyone who convicted his father of insanity* to have him actually committed

to prison: and he used that as evidence that it was legal for the ignorant
to be locked up by the wise.' In fact Socrates' opinion was that anyone 50
having someone else imprisoned for ignorance could justifiably be
locked up himself by those with greater understanding than his own.
Such questions often led him to examine the difference between
ignorance and madness. His view was that locking up madmen was in
their own and their families' best interest, but the right way for those
without the necessary understanding was to learn from those who did
possess it.

'But', said the accuser, 'it was not only disrespect for their fathers 51
that Socrates engendered in his associates, but for their other relatives also, by saying that when people are ill or involved in a lawsuit it
is not their relatives who help them, but in the one case doctors and
in the other trained advocates.'* And the accuser went on to say that 52
this applied to friends too, of whom Socrates said that their kind
intentions were of no use if they were not going to be able to give
practical help: he declared that the only people deserving respect
were those who knew what was needed and had the ability to explain
it to others. And so, by leading the young men to believe that he was
the wisest of men and the most capable of making others wise, he
induced in his associates a state of mind which had them rating everyone else absolutely nowhere compared with him.

I know that he did talk like that about fathers, other relatives, and 53
friends: and he went further still, saying that once the soul, the only
seat of intelligence, had departed, they carry out the body of their
nearest and dearest as soon as they can and put it out of sight. He 54
used to say that even in life, though his own body is dearer to him
than anything else, each of us removes, or lets someone else remove,
any part of it which is useless and serves no purpose. People remove
their own nails, hair, and calluses, and let doctors amputate or cauter-
ize, with all the suffering and pain for which they think they should be
grateful and pay a fee: and they spit the saliva out of their mouth as
far away as they can, because retaining it serves no purpose and is
much more likely to do them harm. Now this talk of his was not any 55
sort of instruction to people to bury their father alive or cut themselves to pieces, but rather a demonstration that mindless is worthless, and an encouragement to concentrate on being as mindful and
useful as possible, so that anyone wanting to be well regarded by father,
brother, or anyone else should not just rely on family connections and

leave it at that, but try to be of practical use to those whose good
regard he wanted.

56   The accuser said that Socrates used to pick out the most perverse
passages* from even the most famous poets, and use them as texts for
teaching his associates to be criminal and despotic. An example is
Hesiod's line,* 'Work is no shame: the shame is refusal to work.' The
accuser claimed that Socrates interpreted this as the poet recom-
mending that no sort of work, however wrongful or disgraceful,

57   should be shunned, as long as there was profit in doing it. Now while
Socrates would fully agree that being a worker was beneficial and
good for a man, and being idle was harmful and bad—so work good,
idleness bad—he also said that 'working' and 'being a good worker'
applied to those who were doing something good, and 'idlers' was
his term for gamblers or those doing anything else depraved or
punishable. So that would justify the saying that 'Work is no shame:
the shame is refusal to work.'

58   And the accuser said that Socrates often quoted that passage of
Homer about Odysseus:*

'Whenever he met with a king or a man of importance, he would come up
to him and turn him back with gentle words: "Friend, it would not be right
for me to threaten you like an inferior. Rather you take your seat again and
make the rest of the army return to their places." But whenever he saw
a commoner and found him shouting, he would strike him with the sceptre
and berate him, saying: "Friend, sit quiet and listen to what others tell you,
your superiors—you are a coward and a weakling, of no account either in
war or in counsel."'

The accuser alleged that Socrates interpreted this passage as the
poet's recommendation that commoners and poor men should be

59   beaten. But that was not what Socrates said—otherwise, on that view,
he would have thought that he himself should be beaten. What he did
say was that people who had nothing useful to contribute in either
word or deed, and were incapable, if need arose, of being any help to
the army, the city, or the common people, should be blocked at every
turn, especially if they were outspoken as well as useless, and no mat-

60   ter how wealthy they might be. But Socrates was the opposite of that,
and manifestly both a man of the people and a friend of humanity.*
He acquired many enthusiastic followers, both from Athens and
from abroad, but never charged any fee for his company, and was

unstinting in his gift to all of what he had to offer. Some of them took nuggets of the teaching he had given them for free and tried to sell them on to others at a price—but they were no friends of the common people as he was, and refused to talk with those who had no money. Socrates, though, enhanced the reputation of his city in the 61 wider world much more than Lichas,* who has become famous for it, did for the Spartan state. Lichas used to entertain visitors to Sparta for the Gymnopaidiai festival,* but throughout the whole of his life Socrates expended all that he had on conferring the greatest benefits on all who wished to receive them: he would always try to make his associates better men before he sent them on their way.

That was the man he was, and to my mind Socrates deserved 62 honour from his city rather than execution. Any survey of the laws would confirm this. According to the laws, death is the penalty* for anyone proved a thief, a robber, a pickpocket, a housebreaker, a kidnapper, or a temple-robber: Socrates was as far from these crimes as any man on earth. And in politics too, he was never the cause of 63 a disastrous war, guilty of sedition or treason, or responsible for any other detriment to the city. Likewise in private life also: he never deprived anyone of what was to their good, or involved anyone in what was to their harm. He was never even accused of any of the foregoing.

How then could he be guilty of the charges against him? So far 64 from failing to recognize the gods, as had been charged in the indictment, he was manifestly more observant of the gods than all other men. And so far from corrupting the young, of which he was actually accused by the prosecutor, his practice with any of his associates who had improper ambitions was manifestly to put a stop to those ambitions and urge them to be ambitious instead for moral virtue, the finest and most prestigious of all virtues, which makes for good governance in both states and households. With that record, how could he not have been deserving of great honour from his city?

I SHALL now record* all the ways I can recall in which it seemed to 3 me that he did indeed benefit his associates, whether by practical demonstration of his own character or also through his conversation.

So, in his attitude to the gods it was manifestly clear that anything he did or said was in accordance with the answer given by the Delphic priestess* to those asking what action they should take concerning sacrifice, the cult of their ancestors, or on any other such question. The response of the priestess was that those who followed the customary practice of their city were acting piously, and that was how Socrates both acted himself and advised others to do: those who acted otherwise he thought were presumptuous fools.

2   His prayers to the gods were simply that they should give good things, since the gods know best what things are for our good. To pray for gold or silver or absolute power or anything like that he thought was no different from praying for a game of dice or a battle or any-
3 thing else with an obviously unknowable outcome. In offering small sacrifices from small resources* he thought he was in no way inferior to those who made many large sacrifices from many large resources. He said firstly that it would not sit well with the gods if they took greater pleasure in the large sacrifices than in the small—that would mean that offerings from the wicked would often be more pleasing to them than those from the good—and secondly that life would not be worth living for human beings if offerings from the wicked were indeed more pleasing to the gods than those from the good. No, his view was that the gods took the greatest pleasure in the honours paid them by those with the greatest reverence. And he would quote approvingly the poet's line, 'To the best of your ability* offer sacrifices to the immortal gods'. This 'offer to the best of your ability' he said was a fine maxim for the way to treat both friends and strangers, and for the overall conduct of one's life.

4   If ever he thought that some signal* was being sent to him from the gods, he would no more have been persuaded to act contrary to that signal than if someone were trying to persuade him to take as his guide on a journey a blind man who did not know the way instead of one who could see and did know the way: and he condemned the folly of others who do something contrary to signals sent by the gods in order to preserve their reputation among men. He himself disregarded all human concerns when compared with the advice from the gods.

5   He disciplined both soul and body with a regime which would enable anyone, barring some act of god, to live a confident, secure life with no shortage of the small expense it required. He was so frugal* that I cannot imagine anyone having so little employment as not to earn what sufficed for Socrates. He took only as much food as he could eat with enjoyment, and when he came to a meal he was so

ready for it that hunger was the only sauce* he needed: and any kind of drink was a pleasure, as he did not drink unless he was thirsty. If 6 ever he accepted an invitation to dinner, it was very easy for him to avoid the overstuffing which most other people find so hard to resist. He would advise those unable to do so to avoid anything served as an inducement to eat when no longer hungry or drink when no longer thirsty: it was these, he said, which ruined stomachs, heads, and souls. He joked that he thought it was by feasting them to such excess that 7 Circe* turned many men into pigs, and that what saved Odysseus from becoming a pig was both Hermes' warning and also his own self-control in holding back from overindulgence in what was on offer. He talked like this in jest, but there was serious intent too.   8

In matters of sex* his advice was to keep resolutely clear of relations with beautiful people: one taste of such a relation, and self-control, he said, was not easily maintained. <......>.* In fact when he heard once that Critobulus* the son of Crito had kissed Alcibiades' son, who was a beauty, he put some questions to Xenophon,* with Critobulus present. 'Tell me, Xenophon,' he said, 'didn't you use to 9 think that Critobulus was a sensible sort of chap rather than a chancer—more the cautious type, and not a thoughtless daredevil?'

'Certainly,' said Xenophon.

'Well, you must now consider him a complete hothead and hell-raiser. This man would turn somersaults* into a ring of knives and jump into fire.'

'You must have seen him do something', said Xenophon, 'to make 10 you pass this verdict on him. What was it?'

'Didn't he bring himself to kiss Alcibiades' extremely handsome and attractive son?'

'Yes,' said Xenophon, 'but if that qualifies as daredevilry, I think I too would be prepared to take the risk myself!'

'You poor man,' said Socrates, 'and what do you think would hap- 11 pen to you after kissing a beauty like that? Wouldn't you at that very instant become a slave rather than a free agent, and then spend loads of money on debilitating pleasures, have no time at all to devote to anything fine and good, and find yourself forced to take an interest in things to which no one, not even a madman, would pay any attention?'

'Good heavens,' said Xenophon, 'that's some fearful power you 12 attribute to a kiss!'

'Does that surprise you?' said Socrates. 'Don't you know that widow spiders,* not even the size of a sixpence, can by simply applying their mouth cause people terrible pain and drive them out of their senses?'

'Yes, of course,' said Xenophon, 'but that is because they inject something with their bite.'

13 'You poor fool,' said Socrates, 'and don't you think that a kiss from someone beautiful injects something which you can't see? Don't you know that this creature, the thing people call "beautiful" and "attractive", is all the more dangerous than those spiders, in that the spiders must first make physical contact, but this creature does not even need contact—you only have to look at it, and no matter how far away it injects something capable of driving you mad? Perhaps that is why the gods of love are called archers, because beauty wounds from afar. No, Xenophon, whenever you see someone handsome, I advise you to run for your life. And my advice to you, Critobulus, is to go away somewhere for a year: that may only just give you enough time to recover from the bite.'

14 Similarly, he thought that people who were not reliably immune to sexual passions should limit their indulgence in sex to those activities to which the soul would only consent if the body was in urgent need, and which would not cause problems when that need arose. He himself was manifestly so disciplined in this area that it was easier for him to abstain from sexual contact with the most beautiful and attractive of the young than it is for others to abstain from the ugliest creatures well past their prime.

15 This, then, was how he had equipped himself to deal with food, drink, and sex: and he thought that he would be just as satisfied with his own measure of enjoyment in these matters as those who set great store by them—and would have much less cause for regret.

4 IF there are some who rely on a few written or oral accounts* of Socrates and think that while he was unequalled at pointing people towards moral virtue he did not have the ability to guide them along the path to it, they should consider not only the constant questioning he used by way of corrective to show up those who thought they knew everything, but also the substance of what he said in conversations with those who were daily in his company: and then let them form their judgement on whether Socrates was able to make his associates better men.

First I shall relate a conversation which I once heard him have *2*
about the divine with Aristodemus,* nicknamed 'the Titch'. On
learning that Aristodemus did not sacrifice or pray to the gods or
make any use of divination, but actually derided those who did so,
Socrates said, 'Tell me, Aristodemus, are there any men you have
admired for their artistry?'

'Certainly,' he said.

'Name them for us,' said Socrates.   *3*

'Well, my list of those I have most admired would be Homer* for
epic poetry, Melanippides for dithyramb,* Sophocles for tragedy,*
Polyclitus for sculpture,* and Zeuxis for painting.'*

'Which would you say are the more worthy of admiration—artists *4*
who create images that cannot think or move,* or those who create
living beings capable of thought and action?'

'Heaven's sake, the latter by far—as long, that is, as those living
beings are the product of conscious design and not some random
chance.'*

'Given that some things have no detectable reason for their existence, and others clearly do serve some useful purpose, which would
you judge to be products of chance and which products of design?'

'Well, it should be that those which serve a useful purpose* are the
products of design.'

'Then don't you think it was for a useful purpose that the original *5*
creator of mankind further endowed his creatures with the various
means of perception*—eyes to see what is visible, and ears to hear
what is audible? And what use would smells have been to us, if we had
not been given noses too? And what perception would we have had of
sweet and sour and all the pleasant tastes in the mouth if the
tongue had not been implanted to tell them apart? And there is more. *6*
Don't you think that all these things too look like the workings of
providence—that because the eyes are vulnerable, they have eyelids*
to protect them like shutters, opening when the eyes need to see and
closing in sleep; that lashes grow on the lids to filter out anything
harmful blown by the winds; and that eyebrows* are set like a cornice
above the eyes to prevent even the sweat of the head from being
troublesome? And then that the ears take in every sort of sound but
never get blocked full; that the front teeth in all animals act as inci-
sors, and the molars have the food passed back to them to grind it
small; that the mouth, the receptacle for what animals want to eat, is

placed close to the eyes and the nose, whereas the outlets for unpleasant excreta are diverted and removed as far as possible from the sense organs? When all these things have been arranged so providentially, are you in any doubt whether they are the products of chance or of design?'

7   'Good god, no!', he said. 'Looked at in this way they do seem very much like the workings of a clever craftsman and a friend of living creatures.'

'And what about the implanting of a natural desire to procreate children, the implanting in the mothers who have given birth a natural desire to rear their children, and in the children they have reared an intense urge to live* and an intense fear of death?'

'Undoubtedly these too look like the devices of someone who has planned the existence of living creatures.'

8   'And what about you personally? Do you think that you yourself have some intelligence?'*

'Well, ask your questions and I'll give you my answers.'

'Do you think that there is no intelligence anywhere else, even though you know that what you have in your body is only a tiny part of the vast quantity of earth in existence, and a small drop of the equally vast quantity of moisture, and that in the composition of your body you were given only a tiny helping of all the other doubtless important elements?* So is mind the only thing which exists nowhere else, and you think that by some lucky chance you have appropriated it to yourself, and in your view all these other things of massive size and infinite number preserve such good order in some sort of mindless state?'

9   'Yes, that is exactly my view—because I don't see anyone in control, unlike here on earth where I can see the craftsmen who bring things into being.'

'But you don't see your own soul either, and that is what is in control of your body. So on that argument you can say that you do nothing by design and everything by chance.'

10   At this point Aristodemus said, 'Look, Socrates, I don't disregard the divine, but I think it too exalted* to be in need of any service from me.'

'Then the more exalted the power which deigns to do you service, the greater the honour which should be paid to it.'

11   'I can assure you,' said Aristodemus, 'that if I considered that the gods had any concern for human beings,* I would not neglect them.'

'It follows, then, that you don't think they have that concern? And yet in the first place the gods made man the only creature to stand upright, a posture which allows him to see further ahead, to have a better view of what is above him, and to be less exposed to injury: and they have placed his eyes, ears, and mouth up high. Then secondly, while they have given all the other terrestrial animals feet, which simply provide locomotion, to man they have also given hands, which are used to create most of what makes our life more fortunate* than that of the other animals. Furthermore, although all creatures have a tongue, *12* it is only the human tongue which the gods have made capable of articulating speech by varying its contact with different parts of the mouth, and so enabling us to communicate whatever we want to one another. And then there is the pleasure of sexual intercourse:* to other animals they have granted it for a limited period in the year, but for us they provide it uninterruptedly right up to our old age.

'Now god wasn't simply content to take care of the human body, *13* but—and this is most important of all—he also implanted in man that rational soul* which he made our dominant faculty. What other creature has a soul which in the first place has intuited the existence of gods as creators of all the grandeur and great beauty arranged in an ordered world? And what species other than man pays worship to gods? Is there any other soul more capable than the human soul of making provision against hunger and thirst, cold and heat, or of relieving disease, training for fitness, slaving to acquire knowledge, or committing to memory everything heard, seen, or learnt? Isn't it *14* abundantly clear to you that in comparison to the other animals men live like gods,* inherently superior in both body and soul? A creature with a human mind but the body of an ox could not do what it wanted: and creatures which have hands but no rational faculty are no better off. You have been given both these inestimable gifts, and you don't think that the gods care for you? So what more are you waiting for them to do before you will believe that they are concerned for you?'

'I'll believe it when they send me advisers, as you say they do to *15* you, to tell me what to do and what not to do.'

'But', said Socrates, 'when the Athenians put a question to the gods by means of divination* and the gods give their instruction, do you not think that this instruction is meant for you too? Or when they send portents as a warning to the Greeks, or to all mankind, are they making an exception just of you, and excluding you alone from their

16 consideration? Do you think that the gods would have implanted in men a belief in the divine ability to do good and harm, if they did not have that ability, and that men would never have realized that they were all that time under an illusion? Don't you see that the most enduring* and sophisticated of human institutions—cities and nations—are where there is the greatest reverence for the gods, and that it is at the most thoughtful stages of their life that people pay most attention to the gods?

17 'Please understand, my friend,' he went on, 'that just as you yourself have a mind within you which manages your body as it wills, you should conceive in the same way of the thought which is active in the universe* disposing everything in whatever way it pleases. Your own vision may have a range of several miles, but do not think that god's eye* cannot possibly see all things at one and the same time: and your mind may be able to think about what is happening here or in Egypt or Sicily, but do not suppose that god's thought is not capable of attending to everything in the world at one and the same time. Here, *18* though, is a suggestion. In human affairs if you do people a service or a favour* you discover those who are willing to do you a service or a favour in return, and if you seek advice you come to know those who are good at thinking. So why not put the gods to a similar test by doing them service, to see whether they will be willing to advise you on matters which are obscure to the human view? If you do that, you will come to realize that the divine has the magnitude and the power to see all and hear all simultaneously, to be all-present, and to take care of all at one and the same time.'

19 So in my own opinion it was by this sort of talk that Socrates caused his associates to refrain from everything irreverent, unjust, or immoral—not only when they were in full view of their fellow humans, but also when they were alone by themselves—because they had come to think that nothing they did could ever go unnoticed by the gods.

5 Now if self-control* also is something fine and good for a man to acquire, let us consider whether Socrates promoted a path to it with this sort of homily: 'Gentlemen, if we found ourselves at war and wanted to elect a man under whose leadership we were most likely to preserve our own lives and defeat the enemy, would we elect someone who we could see was unable to resist the domination of his belly or his drinking or his sexual desires, or combat fatigue and sleep? How could we expect a man like that to save our lives or overcome the enemy? And if we were coming to the end of our life and wanted to 2 entrust* someone with the education of our male children or the protection of our unmarried daughters or the safeguarding of our property, would we consider the man with no control over himself as someone we could trust with these responsibilities? If a slave* has no self-control, would we entrust him with livestock, stores, or the supervision of work? Would we be prepared to take on a slave like that to run our household and make our purchases, even if he came as a free gift? But surely if we would not tolerate even a slave with no 3 self-control, it must be in our interest to guard against acquiring that character ourselves. Profiteers* are known to enrich themselves by depriving others of their money, but there is no parallel with the man who lacks self-control: he does not similarly harm others to his own benefit, but causes both damage to others and much greater damage to himself, if indeed the most damaging thing is to ruin not only one's own household but also one's own body and soul. Who would enjoy 4 the company of a man like that at any club dinner, knowing that he takes more pleasure in the food and drink than in his friends, and is more fond of the call-girls* than of his companions?

'Shouldn't every man consider self-discipline as the foundation of moral virtue, and establish this in his soul before anything else? Without this who could come to learn any good habit, or practise it to 5 any worthwhile extent? And what man who is a slave to his pleasures will not be compromised with both body and soul in a wretched state? By Hera,* any free man, it seems to me, should pray not to find himself with a slave like that, and anyone enslaved by such pleasures should beg the gods to let him find good masters—that is the only way that such a man could be rescued.'

That was how he used to talk, but it was in his actions yet more than 6 his words that he showed the strength of his own self-discipline. He was proof not only against the pleasures which arise from the body, but also against the lure of money: his view was that anyone who takes money from all-comers is setting up a master to dominate him, and submitting to a form of slavery as demeaning as any.

To do him justice I should not fail to record also the conversations he 6 had with Antiphon* the sophist. There was one occasion when, in an attempt to poach Socrates' circle of followers, Antiphon came up to

2 Socrates in their presence and said this: 'Socrates, I used to think that engaging in philosophy should make people happier:* but what philosophy has done for you seems to me quite the opposite. At any rate you lead the sort of life which no slave would stay to tolerate if it were the regime imposed by his master. The food you eat and what you have to drink are of the poorest quality; the coat* you wear is not only shabby, but unchanged in summer and winter; and you always go

3 about without shoes or shirt. And what's more, you don't accept money,* although its acquisition gladdens the heart and its possession makes for a freer and more enjoyable life.* So if you have the same effect on your associates as teachers of other disciplines do, turning out pupils who are replicas of themselves, then you must consider yourself a professor of misery!'

4 And this was Socrates' reply: 'You seem to have assumed, Antiphon, that the life I lead is a miserable one—so miserable, in fact, that I'm sure you would choose to die rather than live like me. So come on

5 then, let's examine what hardship you have identified in my life. Is it that, while those who do take money are obliged to see through whatever they have been paid to do, my own refusal to take money puts me under no obligation to talk with anyone when I don't want to? Or are you denigrating my diet on the grounds that what I eat is less healthy and sustaining than what you eat? Or that my food is harder to come by than yours, as being in scanter supply and more expensive? Or that your provisions are more enjoyable to you than mine are to me? Don't you know that for anyone the more he enjoys what he has to eat the less he needs any garnish, and the more he enjoys what he has to drink the less he feels the absence of any other beverage?

6 'As for clothing, you know that people who change their coats do so in response to cold or heat, and they wear shoes to avoid what hurts their feet and impedes their walking. Well, have you ever in the past known me to stay indoors any more than anyone else because of the cold, or to dispute a place in the shade with anyone because of the heat,

7 or to be prevented by sore feet from walking wherever I want? Don't you know that by training themselves people with the feeblest natural physique come to be better at what they are training for, and more tolerant of it, than the strongest of men who have neglected that training? That being so, don't you think that it is because of my constant training to endure any physical conditions presented to me that I can tolerate them all more easily than you can with your lack of training?

'As for not becoming a slave to food, sleep, or sexual excess, can you 8
think of anything more effective than having other occupations more
enjoyable than those, which not only give pleasure in their immediate
pursuit, but also afford hopes of permanent benefit? Another point is
this. As you will know, people who think they are not successful in
anything have nothing in which they can take pleasure, but when people
think that their business—farming, shipping, or whatever else it may
be—is going well for them, that feeling of success does give them
pleasure. Now, do you think that the pleasure derived from any of that 9
can compare with the pleasure of thinking that you are both bettering
yourself* and acquiring better friends? Well, for my part that is
always my constant thought.

'And if there is need to come to the aid of friends or city, which of
us has more time to devote to that—the man who lives as I do now, or
the one with your idea of the perfect lifestyle? Which of us would take
more easily to military service, the one who cannot live without his
expensive diet, or the one who is satisfied with whatever is to hand?
Which of us would more quickly succumb to a siege, the one who
craves the foodstuff which is most difficult to find, or the one who gets
along well enough with what is easiest to obtain?

'You come across, Antiphon, as someone who sees happiness as the 10
life of luxury and expense. My own view is that having no needs at all
belongs to the gods, but having as few needs as possible is the closest
we can get to that divine state: the divine is the ultimate ideal, and
closest to the divine is closest to the ideal.'

On another occasion in conversation with Socrates Antiphon said: 11
'You know, Socrates, I grant you honesty, but I can't credit you with
any wisdom at all, and I think you realize this yourself—at any rate
you don't charge anyone for your company. Yet if you thought that
your coat or your house or any other of your possessions had some
monetary value, so far from giving them away to anyone for free you
would accept not a bit less than their worth. Clearly, then, if you 12
thought that your company too had some value, you would charge for
that also at a rate no less than its worth. So that would make you
honest, for not swindling people for your own profit, but evidently
deficient in wisdom, because your knowledge has no value.'

This was Socrates' reply: 'Antiphon, in our circle it is generally 13
thought that the same distinction applies to the use made of one's
youthful beauty and of one's wisdom—in both cases there is an

honourable way and a shameful way. If someone sells his beauty to
any paying client, people call him a prostitute:* but if someone forms
a personal friendship with a lover whom he recognizes as a man of
quality, we think that shows good judgement. And it is the same with
wisdom. Those who sell it to any paying client are called sophists: but
we think that whoever makes a friend of someone in whom he recognizes inherent potential, by teaching him all the good he has to
impart, is carrying out what should be the duty of any citizen of qual-
14 ity. In my case, Antiphon, I take yet more delight in good friends than
others may take in a good horse, or a good dog, or a good bird: if
I have anything good to impart, I teach it to them, and I introduce
them to others from whom I think they will get some help in their
progress to moral virtue. And together with my friends I open and
search through those treasure houses which are the books* written
and bequeathed to us by the wise men of earlier times, picking out
whatever we see to be good. And we consider it a great gain to form
this shared friendship.'

As I listened to this, it certainly seemed to me that Socrates was
completely happy in himself, and was guiding those who heard him
towards a life of quality.

15   And there was another occasion when Antiphon asked him how, if
he was such an expert, he thought he was preparing others to be
politicians,* when he himself took no part in politics. Socrates replied:
'Which would be the greater contribution I could make to politics,
Antiphon? Would it be by taking part on my own, or by making it
my concern to ensure the largest number of people competent for
that role?'

7 LET us consider whether a further way in which he encouraged
his associates to cultivate virtue was by deterring them from empty
pretence.* He would always say that there was no better route to
reputation than that which leads to proficiency in the field in which
one wants to be thought proficient. And this was how he used to
2 demonstrate the truth of that. 'So let us think', he said, 'what would
have to be done by someone who wants to be thought a good pipe-
player* when he is not. Wouldn't he have to copy the good players in
the externals of their art? They have fine equipment and travel with
a numerous entourage, so first of all he must do the same. Then,
because they have large audiences to applaud them, he too must

provide himself with a large body of fans.* But of course he must never accept any actual engagement anywhere, or he will immediately be shown up as a laughing-stock, and not just a bad player but also an impostor. In the end, with huge expense for nothing gained, and a trashed reputation as well, he will surely live out a burdensome and profitless life as a figure of fun. Similarly, let's imagine what would *3* happen to someone who wanted to be seen as a good general or a good helmsman,* when he was not. Isn't it the case that if his earnest efforts to present himself as competent to undertake such duties failed to convince, that would be painful enough for him—but yet more calamitous if they did convince? It stands to reason that anyone appointed to such a post who didn't know how to control a ship or command an army would be the ruin of those on whom he would least wish it, and the result for himself would be disgrace and disaster.'

In the same way he demonstrated how pointless it was to present *4* oneself as rich or brave or strong when one was not. Such people, he said, were given tasks beyond their capacity, and when their inability to perform them gave the lie to their supposed competence, there would be no forgiveness. Even persuading someone to lend money or *5* a piece of equipment and then refusing to return it he would call a serious fraud: but for him by far the greatest fraud was committed when someone completely worthless had persuaded the city that he was competent to lead it.

So by talking like this, in my opinion Socrates also deterred his associates from any false pretension.

BOOK 2

1 HERE is another example of the sort of conversation by which it seemed to me that Socrates encouraged his associates to exercise control over their desires* for food and drink, sexual activity, and sleep. Aware that one of his associates was somewhat lax in such matters, he said, 'Tell me, Aristippus,* if you had to take charge of two young men and educate them so that one would be capable of governing* and the other would not even aspire to government, how would you educate each of them? If you agree, let's start with the basics, as it were, and consider the question of food.'

'Well, yes,' said Aristippus, 'I think food does come first—after all, one can't live without being fed.'

2 'So it's likely that a desire to take food will come over both of them at the usual times?'

'Yes, that's likely,' he said.

'So which of the two would we train to prioritize work on urgent business over satisfying his belly?'

'Good heavens, the one who is being educated for government*—so that state business doesn't go neglected on his watch.'

'It follows, then, that when both have a desire to drink, that same one must be given the ability to resist thirst?'

'Absolutely,' he said.

3 'And what about control over sleep—the ability to go to bed late, get up early, and go without sleep if need be? To which of the two would we give this further capacity?'

'To the same again,' he said.

'And what about control of the sexual urges, so they don't get in the way of taking action when action is needed?'

'The same again,' he said.

'And what about not shirking hard work, but tackling it with a will? To which of them would we also give this ability?'

'That too should go to the man being educated for government,' he said.

'And what about being taught the sort of knowledge which can be useful for the defeat of one's adversaries? Which of them would more appropriately be given this teaching?'

'Good heavens,' he said, 'the one who is being educated for government, by far: without such knowledge those other attributes are of no use.'

'So don't you think that the man with this education would be less 4 likely than other creatures to be caught by his adversaries? Some of them, as you know, are snared by their greed, and even the most timid of them are still lured to the bait by their desire for food, and so get caught: and some are trapped by the need to drink.'

'Absolutely,' he said.

'And aren't there others too who are snared by their sexual urge? Quails and partridges,* for example, are drawn to the cry of the female by their desire and hope for sex, and reckless of the danger rush headlong into the hunters' nets.'

Again he agreed.   5

'So don't you think it shaming that a man should be in the same state as the most mindless of wild creatures? I mean, adulterers make their way into the private quarters* of people's houses, knowing full well that committing adultery runs the double risk of incurring the penalties threatened by the law and also of walking into a trap, getting caught, and beaten up. When the adulterer has such serious disaster and humiliation hanging over him, and there are many innocuous ways of relieving his sexual urge, for him to head straight for danger even so—isn't this now something which only a completely possessed lunatic would do?'

'I think so,' he said.

'And when the majority of the most essential activities in this world 6 take place in the open air*—those to do with warfare and agriculture, for example, and others no less important—but most men do not train themselves to endure cold and heat, don't you think that this is gross negligence?'

Again he agreed.

'So don't you think that our prospective ruler should practise a ready tolerance of these conditions too?'

'Absolutely,' he said.

'Well then, if we put those with self-mastery in all these respects 7 into the category of potential rulers, shall we put those with no such ability into the category of men who will not even aspire to government?'

Again he agreed.

'What then? Now that you know the categories for each of these two types, have you perhaps considered into which of the categories you would be right to place yourself?'

8   'Yes, I have,' said Aristippus, 'and I certainly don't put myself in the category of those who want to govern. Given how much work it is to provide for one's own needs, it seems to me sheer madness not to stop at that, but to add the further burden of satisfying the needs of the rest of the citizen body as well. It is surely the height of folly for anyone to forgo much of what he wants for himself, and by taking on the leadership of his city to open himself to prosecution* if he doesn't

9   deliver all that the city wants. Cities expect to treat their rulers as I do my household slaves.* I expect my servants to provide me with a limitless supply of the necessaries, but not to touch any of them themselves, and cities likewise think that their rulers should bring them maximum benefit while keeping their own hands off any part of it. So I would class as potential rulers those who want to have a lot of trouble themselves and cause a lot of trouble to others, and I would have them educated as you suggest: but as for me personally, I class myself among those who want to lead as easy and enjoyable life* as they can.'

10   To which Socrates said, 'If you agree, shall we then consider which is the more enjoyable life, that lived by the rulers or by the ruled?'*

'By all means,' he said.

'Well then, let's look first at the nations known to us.* In Asia* the Persians are the rulers, and the Syrians, Phrygians, and Lydians the ruled; in Europe* the Scythians are the rulers and the Maeotians the ruled; in Africa* the Carthaginians are the rulers and the Libyans the ruled. Which of these two categories do you think has the more enjoyable life? Or take the Greeks, of whom you are one yourself: which seem to you to have the more enjoyable life, those who dominate or those who are dominated?'*

11   'But look,' said Aristippus, 'I'm not placing myself in the position of a slave* either. Rather it seems to me that there is a middle road,* and that is the path I try to tread—not the path of either rule or servitude, but the path of freedom, which is the surest way to happiness.'

12   'Well,' said Socrates, 'if this path of yours which avoids both rule and servitude also avoids the real world, you might perhaps have a point. But you live in the real world, and if you have no intention of either ruling or being ruled, and won't willingly be subservient to those who do rule, I imagine you can see that the stronger have ways of reducing the weaker

to both collective and individual misery, and treating them as slaves.* Or *13* are you unaware of the people who cut the corn* and fell the trees that others have sown and planted, and use every means of starving out the weaker folk who refuse them subservience, until they prevail on them to opt for slavery rather than a fight against the stronger? And then again in private life, don't you know that the bold and powerful first enslave the timid and powerless and then exploit them?

'Yes,' he said, 'but my way of avoiding this treatment is not to lock myself into any political system, but to remain a foreigner* wherever I go.'

To which Socrates said, 'Well now, that's very clever of you—that *14* trick will really throw them! Ever since Siris and Sciron and Procrustes* were killed, nobody now does any harm to foreigners! Yet nowadays people involved in the political system of their own countries pass laws to protect themselves against wrongdoing; they get themselves other friends to help them as well as those who can be said to have family obligations; they surround their cities with fortifications and get themselves weapons to keep off those who would do them wrong; and they equip themselves with external allies as well. With all these assets they still have crimes committed against them. So do you, without any of *15* this, who will spend so much time on the open road, where most crimes are committed, and, in whatever city you come to, will be less protected than all of its citizens and an obvious target for those with criminal intent—do you nevertheless think you will not be harmed because you are a foreigner? Is that because these cities give you a public guarantee of safe conduct when you enter or leave? Or is it because you realize that a man like you would be of no use as a slave* to any master? Who would want a man in his household who is averse to hard work and takes his pleasure in the most expensive living?

'And let's look at how masters treat slaves like that. Don't they *16* suppress their sexual urges by starving them, stop them from stealing by locking away anything they could take, and beat the laziness out of them with floggings? Or what action do you yourself take when you realize that you have a slave of that sort in your house?'

'I punish him hard in every way,' he said, 'until I force him to do *17* what a slave should. But given that, Socrates, what about those who are being educated for "the royal art of government",* which you seem to equate with happiness?* How do they differ from people compelled to hardship,* if they must willingly submit to hunger, thirst, cold, sleeplessness, and all those other tribulations? For my part I can't see any difference between a voluntary and an involuntary flogging—it's the same skin—or generally between submitting willingly or unwillingly to all such assaults on one's body: again, it's the same body. The only difference, is it not, is the added folly of the man who volunteers to endure the suffering?'

18 'Really, Aristippus?', said Socrates. 'Don't you think that the difference between the voluntary and involuntary* in all this is that the man who chooses of his own free will to go hungry or thirsty can eat or drink, or whatever else, whenever he wants, whereas the man compelled to this suffering cannot end it when he wants? And then people who voluntarily put themselves to hardship are kept cheerful by the hope of a good outcome for their labour: hunters, for example, gladly
19 wear themselves out in the hope of catching their game. Such rewards for labour are relatively trivial. But what of those who labour to acquire good friends, to overcome their enemies, to make themselves capable in both body and soul to manage their own household well, to do good to their friends and benefit to their country? Surely we can't deny that their labour to win rewards of this sort is happily undertaken and gladdens their life, bringing them personal satisfaction and
20 the praise and emulation of others? And what's more, lazy habits and the immediate gratification of pleasure, as the physical trainers tell us, cannot produce good condition in the body, nor do they instil any worthwhile knowledge in the soul, but it is practice through endurance which affords us the route to what is fine and good in the doing—and this is what the good men tell us. Hesiod* says somewhere:

> "Vice can be found in abundance, and easily yours for the taking:
> smooth is the road, and she lives very close, an immediate neighbour.
> Virtue, though, is remote, and before her the gods, the immortals,
> have put sweat in your path, long travel and arduous climbing,
> rocky at first: but once you have reached that ultimate summit,
> then it is easy to claim her, hard though she was to discover."

And Epicharmus* adds his testimony in the line:

> "Pain's the price the gods demand for all the goods we get from them."

And elsewhere he says:

> "You poor fool, don't look for comfort, or you'll find your bed is hard."

'And in the lecture* on Heracles* which the learned Prodicus*   *21*
gives to huge audiences he presents this same idea about virtue. As far
as I recall, his lecture goes like this:

'"When Heracles was at the transition from boy to young man, the
time when the young are already gaining their independence and
showing whether the path they will take in their approach to life will be
that of virtue or of vice, he went out to a quiet place and sat down to
ponder which path he should follow. There appeared two women of   *22*
great stature coming towards him. One was fine-looking,* with the
mark of good breeding, and her attractions were a clear complexion,
modestly lowered eyes, and a sober bearing: and she was dressed in
white. The other had been fed to corpulence and fleshiness;* she was
tricked out with cosmetic enhancement* to make her complexion look
whiter and pinker than it was, and artificial means to exaggerate her
height; she kept her eyes wide open, and was dressed in diaphanous
clothing for the maximum exposure of her charms. She was constantly
checking her appearance, and looking to see whether anyone else was
looking at her: and often she would glance at her own shadow.

'"When they came nearer to Heracles, the first of the women I have   *23*
described continued her even pace, but the other, wanting to get there
first, broke into a run, came up to Heracles, and said: 'Heracles, I can
see that you are pondering which path to take in life. Now if you make
me your friend and follow me, I'll lead you along the pleasantest and
easiest path,* and you'll go through life tasting all its pleasures and
untouched by any of its hardships. First, you won't have to bother   *24*
about wars or matters of state, but the only questions in your life will
be what food or drink you could find to take your fancy, what sight or
sound would give you pleasure, what things you would enjoy smelling
or touching, which boyfriend would delight you most with his company, how to ensure the softest bed—and how to come by all this with
the least effort. And if ever you have any misgiving about lack of the   *25*
means to support these pleasures, never fear that I shall lead you to any
tiresome effort of body or soul for their acquisition. No, you will enjoy
the fruits of other people's labours, and won't hold back from anything
that can bring you the possibility of gain. I give my followers the
licence to take advantage wherever it is to be found.'

'"After listening to this, Heracles asked, 'Lady, what is your name?'   *26*
She said, 'My friends call me Happiness: but those who hate me have
their own pet name for me—they call me Vice.'

27   ' "By now the other woman had approached Heracles. She said:
'I too have come to you, Heracles, because I know your parents* and
am well aware of the character you showed during your education.
This makes me hope that, if you take the path that leads to me, you
will become an exceptional agent of fine and noble deeds, and
I myself will be shown in a yet more honourable and prestigious light
as an influence for good. I shall not mislead you with overtures of
pleasure, but I'll explain to you in all honesty how things in this
28 world have been ordained by the gods. Nothing which is truly good
or fine has been granted to mankind by the gods without the need for
effort and application. If you want the gods to look kindly on you,
you must do the gods service; if you want the love of your friends,
you must do good to your friends; if you want to be honoured by
a city, you must benefit that city; if you expect the admiration of all
Greece* for your qualities, you must try to serve Greece well; if you
want your land to produce abundant crops, you must cultivate the
land; if you think that livestock should make you wealthy, you must
look after the livestock; if you aim to make your success in war and
want the power to liberate your friends and defeat your enemies, you
must learn the science of war from the experts and gain practice in
its proper use; and if you want bodily strength, you must train your
body to the dictates of your purpose, and put it through exercises
which require hard work and sweat.'

29   ' "And now", says Prodicus, "Vice cut in, saying, 'Do you see,
Heracles, what an arduous and long road to good cheer this woman is
mapping out for you? Whereas I shall lead you to happiness by a road
which is easy and short.'

30   ' "And Virtue said: 'You wretch, what good do you have to offer, or
what real pleasure do you know, when you refuse to do anything to
achieve them? Here you are, not even waiting on the desire for pleasant things before stuffing yourself with all of them in advance of any
desire. You eat before you are hungry and drink before you are thirsty.
For your pleasure in food you get professional chefs* to cook for you;
for your pleasure in drink you procure expensive wines and run
around looking for ice in summer; and for the pleasure of a deep sleep
you provide yourself not only with soft blankets but soft beds too and
cushioned bases. It's not work, but having nothing else to do, which
makes you want your sleep. You insist on sex when there is no call for
it, turning all the tricks and using men like women.* That's how you

educate those in your set of friends—debauching them at night, and
sending them to bed for the best part of the day.

'"'You may be immortal, but you have been rejected by the gods, *31*
and good men despise you. You have never heard the sweetest of all
sounds, words spoken in your own praise, and you have never seen the
sweetest of all sights—never yet have you been able to look on anything good of your own doing. Who would believe anything you say?
Who would comply with any demand you make? Or what sane man
would bring himself to join your devotees? When they are young their
bodies are devoid of strength, and when they grow older their souls
are devoid of sense. Kept plump and sleek in their carefree youth,
they are dry and withered as they journey on through a careworn old
age. They are ashamed of what they did before, and burdened by what
they have to do now: they ran through the pleasures in their youth,
and stored up the hardships for their old age.

'"'But I keep company with the gods, and likewise with good men. *32*
No fine action of god or man takes place without my involvement, and
I am held in the highest honour of all among both gods and men of
the right persuasion. I am a cherished co-worker for craftsmen,
a sympathetic advocate for slaves,* an excellent collaborator in the
tasks of peacetime, a firm ally in the conduct of war, and the very best
partner in friendship. For my friends the enjoyment of their food and *33*
drink is a pleasure without complication—they simply abstain until
they have the appetite. They enjoy a more grateful sleep than the idle,
and they don't resent having to abandon it, nor do they make sleep an
excuse for neglecting their duties. The young are glad to have the
approval of their elders, and the older folk delight in the respect
shown them by the young; they recall their past actions with pleasure,
and take equal pleasure in the good they do in the present; because of
me they are dear to the gods, cherished by their friends, and valued by
their country; and when their fated end comes on them, they do not
lie there forgotten and bereft of honour, but live on for all time, ever
fresh in memory and celebration.

'"'So then, Heracles, with your noble parentage this is the sort of
life to which you should direct your every effort: and if you succeed,
the prize awaiting you is the most blessed happiness of all.'"

'That is more or less how Prodicus related Virtue's lesson for *34*
Heracles, though he dressed up the thoughts in yet more elevated
language* than I have used just now. Anyway, Aristippus, you would

do well to take this to heart and try to show some concern for the future conduct of your life.'

2 THERE was one time when Socrates became aware that his eldest son Lamprocles* was angry with his mother.*

'Tell me, son,' he said, 'do you know that some people are called ungrateful?'*

'Sure,' said the young man.

'So have you realized what it is that people do to be called that?'

'Yes,' he said. 'Ungrateful is what people are called when they have received some benefit and don't show any gratitude in return when they could.'

'So in your view ingratitude should be reckoned as a form of injustice?'

'Yes,' he said.

2   'Now I wonder if you have ever considered this question. If it is thought unjust to enslave* one's friends, but justified to enslave one's enemies, is ingratitude perhaps a similar case—unjust when shown to one's friends, but justified when shown to one's enemies?'

'I have indeed thought about it,' he said, 'and in my view anyone who has received a benefit from whatever source, friend or enemy, and does not try to show his gratitude in return, is guilty of injustice.'

3   'Well, if that is so, ingratitude would be an injustice, pure and absolute?'

He agreed.

'So the greater the benefit someone receives, the greater the injustice would be if he fails to show gratitude in return?'

He admitted this too.

'Well, who could we find in receipt of greater benefits from anyone than children from their parents? It is their parents who brought children from non-being into being, and caused them to see all the beautiful sights and share in all the good things which are the gods' gifts to mankind—gifts which we regard as of such pre-eminent value that for all of us their loss is what we try to avoid more than anything: and cities have made death the penalty for the most serious crimes precisely because there is no greater fear which could have been an effective deterrent to crime.

4   'And then you don't suppose that people have children simply out of a desire for sex*—the streets and brothels are full of the means to relieve that need. In fact it is easy to see that we look carefully for the

sort of women who could bear us the best children,* and then form
a union with them for the production of those children. The man 5
supports the woman who will be his partner in procreation and
makes advance provision, to the greatest extent he can afford, of all
that he thinks will benefit his future children in their lives. Once she
has conceived, the woman carries this burden,* growing heavy with
the weight of it, risking her life, and nourishing it with its share of
her own food. And then after all she has suffered in carrying it to
term and giving birth, she feeds and cares for it, even though the
baby has done her no favour so far and has no notion of who is looking after it so well. It cannot even indicate what it wants, but the
mother has to guess at its needs and likes and try to supply them:
and she continues to feed it for a long time, putting up with that
labour by day and night, and not knowing what thanks she will get
for her efforts.

'And it does not stop at simply providing food. As soon as their 6
children seem capable of learning things, the parents teach them
whatever good lessons for life they themselves can offer, and if they
think there is more that someone else is better able to teach, they send
them to him at their expense, and take every care to have their children grow up in the best possible way.'

To this the young man replied: 'Yes, but even if she has done all this 7
and a whole lot more besides, no one could put up with her harsh
character.'

And Socrates said, 'Which sort of ferocity do you think is harder to
bear—an animal's or a mother's?'*

'I would say a mother's,' he said, 'at least if she is like mine.'

'Well, has she ever done you the sort of injury commonly inflicted
on people by animals? Has she ever bitten or kicked you?'

'No,' he said, 'but by god she says things which no one would want 8
to hear in the whole of his life.'

'But what about you?', said Socrates. 'How much tiresome trouble
do you think you gave her day and night with your peevish crying and
temper tantrums ever since you were a little boy? And how much distress you caused her when you were ill?'

'But I never said or did anything to embarrass her,' he said.

'Well now, do you think it is harder for you to have to hear what she 9
says than it is for actors in tragedies when they say the most terrible
things to one another?'

'But actors, I imagine, can take it all lightly because they don't think that the character pressing a case against them really wants to have them punished, or the character uttering threats really intends to do them harm.'

'And yet you take it hard, when you know full well that what your mother says to you is said not only without any malicious intent, but actually because she wants the best for you, more than for anyone else? Or do you think that your mother does bear you malice?'

'No, certainly not,' he said. 'I don't think that.'

10   'So,' said Socrates, 'this mother of yours is kindly disposed to you, she does her utmost to make you well and satisfy your every need when you are sick, and furthermore she constantly prays to the gods for your welfare and fulfils her vows on your behalf—and you call her harsh? I can only conclude that if you can't bear a mother of that character,

11   you can't bear anything that is good for you. Tell me, is there anyone else who you think deserving of your attention? Or are you dead set on not making any attempt to please anyone, and not following anyone's instructions,* either military commander or any other authority?'

'No, of course not,' he said.

12   'So in that case,' said Socrates, 'do you want to make yourself pleasant to your neighbour, for example, so that he will bring you light for your fire* when you need it, assist you in promoting your interest, and be close by with friendly help if you meet with some setback?'

'Yes, I do,' he said.

'And what about a fellow traveller on the road or at sea, or just anyone else you happen to meet? Would it make no difference to you whether they become friendly or hostile, or do you think you should make it your business to establish good relations with these too?'

'Yes, I do,' he said.

13   'So then you are prepared to cultivate relations with these people, but you don't think you have a duty to be attentive to your mother, who loves you more than anyone? Don't you know how the city itself regards this? With any other form of ingratitude it is unconcerned and prescribes no penalty, and takes no notice if people fail to return thanks for benefits received. But the city does penalize anyone who is failing to look after his parents,* and disqualifies him from holding any public office, on the grounds that sacrifices offered on behalf of the city would lack all due piety if he were presiding, and nothing else would be done in the right and proper way under his administration.

And this is by no means all: if after the death of his parents anyone fails to tend their graves, that too comes under investigation when the city is vetting candidates* for office.

'So, my boy, if you have any sense you will beg the gods for forgive- *14* ness if you have neglected your mother in any way: otherwise they too may consider you ungrateful, and refuse to do you any favours of their own. And you should go carefully with your fellow men, in case they all turn their backs on you if they see you neglecting your parents, and you could then find yourself devoid of friends: if people get the impression that you are ungrateful to your parents, no one would expect any thanks from you if they did you a favour.'

ON another occasion he became aware that two brothers well known **3** to him, Chaerephon and Chaerecrates,* were at odds. When he saw Chaerecrates, he said, 'Tell me, Chaerecrates, you are surely not one of those people who think that possessions are more useful to you than a brother?* And they think that even though possessions are insensible objects while a brother is a sentient being, possessions need you to look after them while a brother can look after you, and, what's more, there may be a lot of possessions but only one brother. It's strange, *2* too, that if someone regards his brothers as a liability because he doesn't possess their property as well as his own, he doesn't also regard his fellow citizens as a liability because their property is not his. In this latter case people can calculate that it is better to live in a community where they are safe and have enough for their own needs, rather than spend their time in isolation with precarious ownership of all their fellow citizens' property: but they fail to recognize that the same principle applies where brothers are concerned. Again, people who *3* can afford it buy slaves to assist them in the house, and acquire friends* for the help they can give, but ignore their brothers—as if they can develop friendships with their fellow citizens, but not with their brothers. And yet common parentage and growing up together *4* are powerful factors making for friendship, as can be seen in the instinctive sense of loss which even animals feel when they miss the siblings who shared their nurture. Besides, people in general are more respectful of those who have brothers as opposed to those who do not, and are less likely to target them.'

Chaerecrates replied, 'Well, Socrates, if the difference between us *5* was not all that great, perhaps I ought to put up with my brother and not let small things keep us apart: as you say, a brother who behaves like a proper brother is an asset. But when he fails on every count and is quite the opposite in every way, why attempt the impossible?'

6   'Tell me, Chaerecrates,' said Socrates, 'is there nobody to whom Chaerephon behaves pleasantly, as he evidently doesn't even to you, or are there some who find him perfectly pleasant?'

'That's exactly it, Socrates,' he said. 'That's why I feel justified in disliking him—he can be pleasant to others, but whenever he is around me, everything he does or says makes him more of a liability than an asset.'

7   'Well then,' said Socrates, 'a horse is a liability if you try to handle it without knowing how. Might it be the same with a brother—a liability if you try to handle him without knowing how to do it?'

8   'But how could I not know how to handle a brother?' said Chaerecrates. 'What I do know is how to reciprocate when someone speaks or acts kindly to me. But I couldn't speak or act kindly to someone who tries to annoy me with everything he says or does—and I won't try either.'

9   'I can hardly believe what you're saying, Chaerecrates,' said Socrates. 'If you had a dog that was good with sheep* and friendly to the shepherds, but growled whenever you came near it, you wouldn't think of getting angry with it, but would try to mollify it by showing kindness. You say that your brother would be a great asset if he behaved like a proper brother, and you agree that you know how to act and speak kindly—but you don't try to come up with a method of turning him into the best asset you could possibly have.'

10   Chaerecrates said, 'I'm afraid, Socrates, that I'm not enough of a genius to make Chaerephon treat me as he should!'

'And yet it seems to me', said Socrates, 'that there's no need to find any subtle or unusual method of dealing with him. I think he could be won over to a high regard for you if you simply apply the knowledge you already have.'

11   'I'm all ears', he said, 'to hear what magic power you have seen in me which I didn't know I possessed!'

'Then tell me,' he said, 'if you wanted to contrive an invitation to the dinner* whenever an acquaintance of yours was holding a sacrifice, what would you do?'

'Obviously my first move would be to invite him to any sacrifice I was holding myself.'

'And if you wanted to prevail on one of your friends to look after *12*
your affairs when you were abroad, what would you do?'

'Obviously I would first undertake to look after his affairs when he
was abroad.'

'And if you wanted to have a foreigner offer you hospitality* when- *13*
ever you visited his city, what would you do?'

'Obviously again I would first offer him hospitality whenever he
visited Athens. And if I wanted him to promote the business which
had brought me to his city, I would first have to do the same for him.'

'So after all you do know all the magic which works on people, and *14*
you have been keeping it hidden all this time! What is stopping you
from making the first move? Are you afraid that it may reflect badly
on you if you are ahead of your brother in showing good will? And yet
we think it highly laudable if a man is quick to do harm to his enemies*
and benefit to his friends. So if I thought Chaerephon better placed
than you to lead the way to this friendship, I would be trying to persuade him to initiate a reconciliation with you. But as things are,
I think this is more likely to be achieved with you in the lead.'

Chaerecrates replied, 'That's a strange suggestion, Socrates, and *15*
not at all like you to tell me to take the lead when I am the younger
brother—the universal convention is surely that the older should be
foremost in anything that needs to be done or said.'

'Really?' said Socrates. 'Isn't it also the custom everywhere that the *16*
younger man should make way for the older when they meet on the
road, should stand up to offer him a seat, give him the privilege of
a soft bed, and let him do the talking? My dear chap,' he continued,
'don't hang back, but set about mollifying the man, and in no time at
all he will respond to you. Don't you see how proud and generous he
is at heart? Some form of gift may be the only way likely to win over
the lower sorts of humanity, but with men of quality you will best
achieve it by behaving like a good friend.'

'And what', said Chaerecrates, 'if I do all this and there is no *17*
improvement from him?'

'Well at least that will give you the chance to have shown that you
are someone decent and brotherly, and he is a poor sort who doesn't
deserve any kindness. But I don't suppose any of that will happen.
I think that once he realizes that you are issuing this challenge, he will
try his utmost to win the contest by outdoing your benevolence in all
he says or does.

18   'You see, at the moment the way you two are behaving to each other
is like it would be if a pair of hands* were to abandon the collaboration
for which god designed them and turn to mutual obstruction, or if
a pair of feet were to ignore their god-given role of working together
19 and start to get in each other's way. Wouldn't it be gross stupidity and
pure madness to use what has been designed for our benefit to do
ourselves harm? And yet it seems to me that god made brothers to be
of greater benefit to each other than hands or feet or eyes or anything
else he created in us to work as a pair. If hands were required to deal
at one and the same time with things which are more than a couple of
yards apart, they couldn't do it; feet can't cover even that distance in
a single stride; and even though eyes clearly have the greatest range,
they can't simultaneously see both front and back of objects much
closer than that. But if two brothers are good friends, they work
together, at whatever physical distance from each other, for their
mutual benefit.'

4   I ONCE heard* him discussing friendship too in a way which I thought
would give anyone very helpful guidance in how to acquire friends
and how to treat them.
   He said that he often heard people saying that a good and true
friend was the best of all possessions,* but that he saw most people
paying less attention to the acquisition of friends than to anything
2 else. He saw them taking care when they were acquiring houses, fields,
slaves,* livestock, and equipment, and doing their best to preserve
what they had, but when it came to friends, which they claimed were
their greatest blessing, he saw most people giving no thought to how
they might acquire new friends or keep those they already had.
3 Indeed, if one of their friends or one of their household slaves* fell
sick, he saw some people summoning the doctor for the slave and
assiduously making all other provision for his return to health, but
ignoring the friend. And if both of them died, they were vexed by the
death of the slave and considered it a financial loss, but didn't think
they were in any way diminished by the death of the friend. They
wouldn't let any other of their possessions go without care and attention, but they had no thought for the equal need to take care of their
4 friends. And what's more, he said, he found that most people knew
how many other things they possessed, however great the number,
but when it came to friends, few as they were, they not only had no

idea how many they had, but when asked about this number their attempts to make a list of those they regarded as friends included some whom they would subsequently remove. That was how much thought they gave to their friends!

'And yet', he said, 'what other possession could compare with the 5 far superior worth* of a good friend? What horse, what pair of oxen is as useful as the friend who serves you well? What slave is so loyal and constant? Or what other possession is of such manifold service?* The 6 good friend takes on the job of addressing all that his friend lacks in private provision or public involvement. If there is need to do someone a favour, the friend adds his contribution. If the other is troubled by some anxiety, the friend comes to his assistance. At various times the friend will share expenses, join in action, add his voice in support, or use force as needed. A friend is foremost to congratulate the successful and set back on their feet those who have taken a fall. A benevolent 7 friend is as good to any man as the hands which do him service, the eyes which look out for him, the ears which catch what he needs to hear, the feet which carry him through to his purpose; and often friend has helped out friend when the other has not accomplished or seen or heard or carried through things for himself. But even so, while some put effort into cultivating trees for their fruit, most people are lazy and indifferent when it comes to the care of their most constantly fruitful possession—that which we call a friend.'

ON another occasion too I heard him talking in a way whose effect, it 5 seemed to me, was to stimulate anyone in the audience to self-examination* and an appraisal of how much he was worth to his friends. He had seen that one of his associates was neglecting a poverty-stricken friend. So in the presence of a large company including this neglectful associate he put some questions to Antisthenes.*

'Tell me, Antisthenes,' he said, 'do friends have various values in 2 the same way that domestic slaves do? One slave is worth perhaps two minas,* another not even half a mina, another five minas, and another ten: and they say that Nicias the son of Niceratus* paid a whole talent* for a manager of his silver mines.* So I'm interested in the answer to this—do friends vary in value in the same way as slaves?'

'Indeed they do,' said Antisthenes. 'In my case at any rate there are 3 some friends I would rather have than two minas, some I would value at less than half a mina, some I would choose to have at a cost of even ten minas, and some for whose friendship I would expend any amount of money and effort.'

4 'So if that is how things are,' said Socrates, 'everyone would do well to ask himself how much he is really worth to his friends, and try to make that value as much as possible, so that his friends will be less likely to abandon him. You see, I often hear people complaining that "a friend has abandoned me", or "someone I thought was a friend has

5 rejected me for the gain of a mina", and all that sort of thing, which makes me wonder whether, just as someone will put an unsatisfactory slave on the market for what he will fetch, so it may be tempting to sell an unsatisfactory friend when there is the possibility of gaining more than he is worth. But good slaves, I find, are definitely not for sale, and good friends are not abandoned.'

6 Iᴛ seemed to me that in this next conversation he also gave good advice on how to test* what sort of people were worth acquiring as friends.

'Tell me, Critobulus,'* he said, 'if we wanted a good friend, how would we set about the search? Should we first of all look for someone who is in control of his desires for food, drink, sex, sleep, and idleness? Anyone in subjection to these desires would not be capable of doing his duty either to himself or to a friend.'

'He certainly wouldn't,' he said.

'So you think that we should avoid anyone who is governed by these things?'

'Absolutely,' he said.

2 'Well then, what about the spendthrift who can't meet his own expenses, but is always begging off his neighbours, cannot repay them if they give him a loan, and resents them if they don't? Would you agree that he too would be problematic as a friend?'

'Certainly,' he said.

'So we must avoid him too?'

'We must indeed,' he said.

3 'Well then, what about the businessman* who is good at making money, but so keen to make a lot of it that he drives a hard bargain, and is happy enough to rake the money in but reluctant to pay any out?'

'In my view,' he said, 'this one is even worse than the last.'

'And what about the man who has such a passion for money- *4* making that he has no time for anything which doesn't offer the prospect of personal profit?'

'We must avoid him too, I think. There would be no benefit in having anything to do with him.'

'And what of the political agitator,* who is prepared to lumber his friends with a whole load of enemies?'

'Good god, we should run a mile from him!'

'And if there is someone without any of these faults who happily accepts a kindness with no thought of reciprocating?'*

'No benefit in him either. But what sort of person is it, Socrates, that we will try to make our friend?'

'Well, I suppose one who, in contrast to those others, has control *5* over the pleasures of the flesh, and turns out to be loyal, easy to do business with, and eager not to be outdone in matching kindness given with kindness received—in other words, good news for those familiar with him.'

'Then how can we test these qualities, Socrates, before starting that *6* familiarity ourselves?'

'With sculptors,'* he said, 'the test that we apply is not reliant on what they say, but we judge by previous examples of their work, and if we see that a sculptor has already produced some fine statues, we trust him to maintain that quality in his subsequent works.'

'You mean, then,' said Critobulus, 'that a man who can be shown to *7* have treated his earlier friends well is clearly likely to do well by his subsequent friends too?'

'Yes,' said Socrates, 'and it's the same with horses: when I find that someone has treated his horses well in the past, I think he will treat other horses equally well.'

'All right then,' he said. 'And when there is someone who seems worthy *8* of our friendship, how should we set about making him our friend?'

'The first thing is to seek divine guidance* and find out whether the gods will advise us to make him a friend.'

'And then?', he said. 'When we have decided on someone and there is no opposition from the gods, can you say how we should set about hunting him down?'

'Well, it's certainly not by chasing him on foot like a hare, or trap- *9* ping him with snares like a bird,* or using brute force on him as we would on an enemy. It is hard work to capture a friend against his will, and difficult to keep him tied up like a slave. That sort of treatment turns people into enemies rather than friends.'

10   'But how are people turned into friends?', he asked.

'They do say that there are some enchantments* which those who know them can use to enchant anyone they wish into becoming their friends: and there are love potions too, which those who know them can give to anyone whose love they want to win.'

11   'So how could we learn about these?', he asked.

'Well, you have heard from Homer the song the Sirens sang to enchant Odysseus,* which begins like this:

"Come to us now, most famous Odysseus, pride of Achaea." '

'Was this then, Socrates, the song that the Sirens sang to keep other people too under their spell, so those they bewitched would never leave them?'

12   'No, they only sang like that to those who prided themselves on their qualities.'

'You're saying in effect that any enchantment must be suited to the individual hearing it, so he won't think that the one singing his praises is actually mocking him?'

'Yes, because if you praise as handsome, tall, and strong someone who knows he is short, ugly, and feeble, you will only make him dislike you more, and cause others to keep their distance.'

'Do you know of any other enchantments?'

13   'No, but I have heard that Pericles* had a whole repertoire at his disposal, which he sang to the city to make it love him.'

'And how did Themistocles* make the city love him?'

'Certainly not by singing enchantments to it! But he did give it the all-round protection of an effective amulet.'*

14   'I think you are saying, Socrates, that if we are to acquire a good man as a friend, we ourselves must prove good men in all that we say and do.'*

'And did you imagine', said Socrates, 'that it was possible for a bad sort to acquire worthy friends?'

15   'Well, yes,' said Critobulus. 'I have seen poor public speakers friendly with excellent orators, and incompetent commanders keeping company with men of great strategic ability.'

16   'So—and this is the point in question—do you also know of any people who can make useful friends when they themselves are useless?'

'I certainly don't,' he said. 'But if it is impossible for a bad sort to acquire friends among the men of quality, what concerns me now is whether someone who has proved himself a man of quality can thereby automatically be a friend to others of that same character.'

'I know what's troubling you, Critobulus,' said Socrates. 'It's that *17* you often see men who act honourably, and have nothing to do with anything shameful, indulging in party strife rather than being friends, and treating one another worse than they would people of no worth whatsoever.'

'Yes,' said Critobulus, 'and this is not confined to individuals. *18* Cities* too which have the greatest concern for honourable behaviour and the least tendency to anything shameful are often at war with one another. These considerations make me really despondent about *19* acquiring friends. On the one hand I see that bad sorts cannot make friendships among themselves—how could you be friends with people who are ungrateful, slovenly, greedy, untrustworthy, or incapable of self-control? In fact I am convinced that bad sorts by their very nature are more enemies to one another than friends. But then *20* again, as you say, bad sorts could never be suited for friendship with honest men either—how could people who engage in criminality become friends with those who hate all such behaviour? And if indeed those who practise virtue are going to indulge in party strife for supremacy in our cities and let jealousy turn to hatred of one another, who will then be left for us to befriend, and where in society will we find goodwill and trust?'

'Well, Critobulus,' said Socrates, 'this is quite a complex issue. It is *21* in human nature to have friendly instincts: people need one another, they feel pity, they collaborate for the common good, and in recognition of this they show gratitude to one another. And there are hostile instincts too. Given that some things are universally regarded as fine and desirable things to acquire, people fight over them, take sides, and form opposing camps. Hostility also springs from rivalry and anger, resentment from the desire to gain the advantage, hatred from jealousy. But even so friendship finds its own way through all this and *22* unites the men of quality. As a matter of principle these men choose the untroubled possession of a moderate substance* rather than fighting for mastery of all there is. They can happily share their food and drink even when they themselves are hungry and thirsty; they can resist any pleasure in the sexual allure of the handsome young, so

23 as not to offend where offence should not be given; in money matters
too not only can they live with their lawful share without seeking
advantage at others' expense, but they can also help out one another;
they can settle any dispute not only painlessly but also to mutual
benefit, and they can prevent anger proceeding to a cause for regret;
they remove jealousy altogether by giving their friends free use of
their assets as if they were family, and regarding their friends' assets
as their own.

24   'So surely we can expect the men of quality to be the same when it
comes to political preferment—taking up their share not only without doing damage to one another but actually working together for
their common benefit. People who aim for position and power in their
cities so that they can be free to extort and oppress while living the life
of luxury will be unjust, immoral low types incapable of cooperation

25 with anyone else. But when a man wants preferment in his city so that
he can avoid injustice to himself and help his friends by securing
justice for them, and once in office tries to do some good for his country, why should someone of that character not be able to cooperate
with others like himself? Will his association with other men of quality reduce his ability to help his friends? Will he be less capable of
doing good to his city if he has other such men working with him?

26   'Consider too the athletic games.* If it were possible for the strongest competitors to form one team against the less good, clearly they
would win all the events and carry off all the prizes. Now that is not
allowed in the games, but in politics, when the men of quality are
dominant, there is no bar to joining up with whoever you want for the
benefit of the city. So it must be advantageous to acquire the best
possible friends before entering political life, and to have them as
partners and collaborators in your programme rather than competitors.

27 And then again if it does come to a power struggle, clearly a politician
will need allies, and more of them if he is ranged against men of quality. Potential allies must be treated well to make them enthusiastic for
the cause, and it is a much more effective strategy to apply that lar-
gesse to the best people, who are fewer in number, than to the more
numerous inferiors—the lower sorts want many more favours than
their betters.

28   'But don't lose heart, Critobulus, and try to make yourself a good
man. When you have done that, you can set about hunting the men of
quality. Perhaps I myself could use my expertise in matters of love* to

help you in that hunt for men of quality. When I want someone, it's quite something how completely I throw myself into getting him to reciprocate my love, my longing for him, my desire for his company. I see that you too will need this passion when you want to form *29* friendships. So don't hide from me the names of those you wish to make your friends. The care I take to please those who are pleasing to me has given me some experience as a hunter of men.'

And Critobulus said, 'Yes indeed, Socrates, I have long wished for *30* this sort of instruction, especially if the same technique will work for the bodies beautiful as well as the noble souls.'

'No, Critobulus,' said Socrates, 'my technique has nothing to do *31* with laying hands on beautiful people to make them submit. I'm in no doubt that men avoided Scylla* because she laid hands on them, whereas with the Sirens* the story is that everyone submitted and was bewitched by their song, because they always sang it from a distance and never laid their hands on anyone.'

And Critobulus said, 'Well, if I promise not to lay hands on anyone, *32* please teach me whatever good plan you have for acquiring friends.'

'So does that mean that you won't lay mouth on mouth either?' said Socrates.

'Don't worry!' said Critobulus. 'I won't put my lips to anyone either—unless he is beautiful!'

'That's you all over, Critobulus,' said Socrates. 'You have just negated your own best interest. Beautiful people don't submit to that sort of approach—it's only the ugly who actually welcome it, thinking that by "beautiful" you are speaking of their souls.'

'All right,' said Critobulus. 'I'll kiss the beautiful and smother the *33* good with kisses! So don't worry on that score, and teach me the ways of hunting down friends!'

'Well then, Critobulus,' said Socrates, 'when you want to become friends with someone, will you allow me to tell on you and say that you admire him and want to be his friend?'

'Tell on me all you like,' said Critobulus. 'I've never known anyone take against people who sing his praises.'

'And if I go on to allege that because of your admiration for him *34* you also feel warmly disposed towards him, you won't think that I'm misrepresenting you, will you?'

'No,' he said, 'because I too find myself warming to those I have reason to think are warmly disposed to me.'

35   'So then,' said Socrates, 'I shall be allowed to say this much about you to those you want to make your friends. Now if you give me further permission to say of you that you are someone who cares for his friends, and that you take more pleasure in good friends than in anything else; that your pride in your friends' achievements and your delight in their good fortune is as great as that in your own, and that you never tire of doing all you can think of to promote their welfare; and that you are firmly of the view that a man's best quality lies in outdoing his friends in generosity and his enemies in malice—if you let me say all that, I'm pretty sure you will find me a handy fellow huntsman in the chase for good friends.'

36   'So why are you asking me?' said Critobulus. 'It's not as if you can't decide for yourself whatever you want to say about me.'

'Oh no I can't,' said Socrates, 'according to what I once heard from Aspasia.* She said that good matchmakers have remarkable success at effecting marriage alliances because what they advertise about their clients' good qualities is true, and she had no time for those who presented a false picture—the couple thus misled would end up hating each other and the matchmaker as well. I am convinced that she was right about this, so I too think that I have no licence to say anything in your praise which I don't know to be true.'

37   'So that seems to be the extent of your friendship, Socrates,' said Critobulus. 'You will only support me if I myself have some quality conducive to the making of friends: otherwise you would not be prepared to make up some complimentary report which could work to my benefit.'

'And what do you think would be more beneficial for you on my part, Critobulus,' said Socrates, 'to pay you false compliments, or to
38   persuade you to try to become a good man? If the answer to that is not already clear to you, look at it this way. Suppose I wanted to establish a friendship between you and a shipowner and told him lies to your credit, saying that you were an excellent navigator, and suppose that he believed me and put his ship under your command, when you had no idea how to navigate—do you think it likely that you would avoid losing both the ship and your own life? Or suppose I persuaded the assembly to entrust the city to your charge, by falsely promoting you as the man with all the military, legal, and political qualities for the job—what do you think would happen to you yourself and the city

with you in charge? Or again, in private life, if I had persuaded some citizens to entrust their affairs to you, by falsely claiming that with you they would be in safe and financially competent hands, when you came to the test wouldn't you turn out to have ruined them and made a mockery of yourself?

'No, Critobulus, if you want to be thought good at anything, the *39* shortest, the safest, and the best route is to try actually to make yourself good at it. You'll find, if you think about it, that all the various qualities which people speak of as virtues are developed through study and practice.* So for my part, Critobulus, I think that we should do just that. But if you take some other view, tell me what it is.'

And Critobulus said, 'No, Socrates—I would be ashamed to argue against that: anything I said would be neither honourable nor true.'

AND now another subject. When his friends were in difficulty, if their **7** problem was not knowing what to do, he would try to solve it by offering advice, and if it was a question of lack of money, by teaching them all to help one another out to the best of their ability. I shall set out what I came to know of him in this context too.

One day he saw Aristarchus* looking morose, and said, 'It looks as if you have a burden on your mind, Aristarchus. You should share it with your friends, and perhaps we can help to lighten it for you.'

'Well, yes,' said Aristarchus. 'I am in dire straits. Since the civil *2* war* broke out and so many have left the city for the Piraeus,* a whole crowd of family womenfolk* have been left behind in Athens—sisters, nieces, and cousins—and have converged on my house: so we are now fourteen in the house, and that is only the free-born. We get no income from our land, because our opponents have seized it, and nothing from our properties either, because the resident population in town has fallen so low. Nobody is buying household goods, and it is impossible to borrow money anywhere—I reckon you would have a better chance of finding money in the street than of securing a loan. So it's painful, Socrates, to see one's family wasting away, but impossible to support such a large number at times like these.'

Socrates listened to him, and said, 'How come, then, that Ceramon,* *3* with many to support in his household, can not only provide for his own and their needs, but actually has so much surplus income that he is growing quite rich—whereas you, with your numbers to support, are afraid that you will all die of starvation?'

'An obvious reason, for heaven's sake,' he said. 'His dependants are slaves. Mine are free.'

4   'And which do you think are the better types, the free people with you or the slaves with Ceramon?'

'Well, in my opinion,' he said, 'the free people with me.'

'Isn't it shaming, then, that he, with that household of lower types, is comfortably well off, while you are in such straits with your much higher class of residents?'

'Not at all,' he said. 'Those he is feeding are workmen: I have to feed people brought up in gentility.'

5   'Would you say that workmen are people who know how to produce something useful?'

'Certainly,' he said.

'Is milled barley useful?'

'Very much so.'

'What about bread?'

'Just as much.'

'And what about men's and women's coats, and shirts, cloaks, jackets?'

'Yes, all these are very useful too.'

'Then don't those lodging with you know how to make any of these?'

'They know how to make them all, I think.'

6   'Then are you not aware that from one of these activities—the production of milled barley—Nausicydes* maintains not only himself and his household slaves, but large numbers of pigs and cattle too, and makes such a surplus that he is often called on by the city to sponsor public services?* That thanks to his bakeries Cyrebus* feeds his whole household well and lives the life of plenty, and Demeas of Collytus* earns a good living by making cloaks, Menon* by making blankets, and most of the Megarians* by making those jackets of theirs?'

'Of course I know that,' he said. 'That's because they buy in foreign slaves as a resident workforce, and so can make them produce whatever suits: but those in my household are free-born relatives.'

7   'Do you then think', said Socrates, 'that because they are free and related to you they should do nothing except eat and sleep? Look at other free people—do you see those who live that sort of life having a better time of it, and do you call them happier than those who apply themselves to the useful life-skills they have learnt? Or is it your perception that idleness and indifference are what is needed for people to

learn the skills they should have, to remember what they have learnt, to keep themselves healthy and physically strong, and to acquire and maintain what is useful for life—and industry and application are no use at all?

'When these women of yours learnt the skills you say they possess, *8* what was in their mind—that these were all things of no relevance to their life, and they had no intention of taking up any of them, or, on the contrary, that here were skills which would give them an occupation and bring some profit too? Which is the more sensible way to live one's life—idleness or useful occupation? And which is the more equitable way—to work, or to fuss about provisions without doing any work?

'But as things are at present, I imagine, you don't like them and *9* they don't like you. You think they are a burden on you, and they can see that you are annoyed at them. And the danger in this is that dislike will grow and what was once gratitude will correspondingly diminish. But if you take charge and get them working, you will become fond of them when you see them making a profit for you, and they will warm to you when they sense that you are pleased with them. You will all have happier memories of those past acts of kindness and feel more gratitude for them, and the result will be that you live together in a more friendly way and with a closer family bond. Now of course if *10* their proposed work was anything shameful,* they would have to regard that as a fate worse than death. But as it is, the skills they apparently possess are those considered the most honourable and decorous for women, and everyone works with the greatest ease, speed, efficiency, and pleasure at the skills they know. So don't hesitate', he concluded, 'to introduce an idea which will profit both you and them: and in all probability they will welcome your proposal.'

'Well, by all the gods, Socrates,' said Aristarchus, 'that seems to me *11* an excellent suggestion! Before now I was reluctant to take out a loan,* knowing that once I had spent whatever I borrowed I would not be able to pay it back. But now I think I'll bring myself to do just that, as capital for a start-up business!'

The result was that capital was forthcoming, and the wool pur- *12* chased. The women worked through their breakfast and only stopped when it was time for dinner. Happiness replaced gloomy faces, and the looks they exchanged were now open smiles rather than resentful glances. The women became fond of Aristarchus as their guardian, and he was happy with them for the productive work they were doing. Finally Aristarchus came to Socrates and joyfully told him the whole story, adding that the women were now complaining that he was the only member of the household not to work for his keep.

13   'Then why not tell them the fable of the dog?'* said Socrates. 'They say that in the time when the animals could speak, the sheep came to her master and said, "This is ridiculous! We provide you with wool and lambs and cheese, and you give us nothing more than we can crop from the land by ourselves: but you share your own food with the dog,

14   who doesn't provide you with anything like we do." The dog heard this, and said, "And quite right too! I am the one who protects you from being stolen by men or preyed on by wolves. On your own, without me there to keep guard over you, you wouldn't even be able to graze for fear of being killed." And so, it is said, even the sheep conceded the dog's right to preferential treatment. So you tell these women that you are their sheepdog and protector, and it is because of you that they can live and do their work in safety and happiness, with no one to harm them.'

8 MEETING another old friend one day after not having seen him for a long time, Socrates said, 'And where have you appeared from, Eutherus?'*

'I was abroad until the war ended, Socrates,' said Eutherus, 'but now I am back here. We lost our foreign property,* and my father left me nothing in Attica, so I am now forced to resume residence here and make my living by manual labour.* I think that's better than asking people for help, especially as I have nothing which could be security for a loan.'

2   'And for how long do you think you will have the physical strength to work as a hired labourer?' asked Socrates.

'Not very long, for sure,' he said.

'And then when you get older,' said Socrates, 'you will obviously have expenses to meet, and no one will want to hire you for manual labour.'

3   'True,' he said.

'Then your best course', said Socrates, 'would be to lose no time in taking up the sort of job which will still support you when you are older. You should apply to some wealthy landowner who needs an assistant manager.* You could serve him by supervising the work, helping to get in the harvest, and helping to take care of the property, with an appropriate return for your service.'

'I would find it hard, Socrates,' he said, 'to submit to the condition 4 of a slave.'

'And yet those who take charge of their cities and supervise public affairs are not regarded as thereby lowering themselves to the status of a slave, but rather as displaying more of the qualities of a free man.'

'To be honest, Socrates,' he said, 'I don't at all welcome the idea of 5 having someone holding me to account.'*

'And yet, Eutherus,' said Socrates, 'it's not at all easy to find a job in which you would not be held to account. It's difficult enough to do any job without making mistakes, and difficult too to escape inconsiderate criticism even if your performance has been impeccable—even in what you say is your present work I would be surprised if you find it easy to get through without any complaints being made. So you 6 should try to avoid overcritical employers and go for the considerate ones. Take on the duties you are capable of performing, steer clear of what is beyond you, and, in whatever you do, give it your best attention and put your heart into it. This way, I think, lies your best chance of avoiding criticism, finding a solution to your present difficulty, and being able to live your life in complete comfort and security, with ample provision into your old age.'

I KNOW that he once heard Crito* complaining that life in Athens was 9 difficult for a man who just wanted to get on with his own business.* 'At the moment,' said Crito, 'there are people bringing legal actions* against me, not because I have done them any wrong, but because they reckon I would sooner pay them off than have all that hassle.'

Socrates said, 'Tell me, Crito, do you keep dogs to defend your 2 sheep against wolves?'

'Certainly I do,' said Crito. 'It pays me to keep dogs.'

'Then why not keep a man who would be willing and able to defend you against the people trying to do you harm?'

'I would gladly do so,' he said, 'if I wasn't afraid that he might turn on me.'

'What? Don't you see that profiting from the gratitude of a man 3 like you is a much more attractive prospect than alienating him? I can assure you that there are qualified people here in Athens who would be honoured to have you as their friend.'

4   So after this conversation they lighted on one Archedemus,* who was an extremely capable advocate and fixer, but poor—he was not one to make money indiscriminately, but a passionate champion of honesty, and he said that it was very easy to sting these false accusers. So whenever Crito was bringing in stores of farm produce—corn, oil, wine, wool, or any of the other staples of life—he would set on one side a portion to give to Archedemus, and would invite him whenever he was holding a sacrifice, and generally showed him all care and atten-

5 tion. Archedemus came to regard Crito's house as his refuge, and was assiduous in paying his respects. Soon enough he found out that one of Crito's false accusers had a long history of criminality and a long list of enemies, and summoned him to appear for trial in a public court,

6 which would decide what punishment or fine to inflict. Conscious of the many misdeeds he would have to answer for, the man tried every means of shaking off Archedemus, but Archedemus would not let go until the man withdrew his charge against Crito and paid him compensation.

7   This and other such successes achieved by Archedemus now had the effect that many of Crito's friends begged him to lend them Archedemus as their protector too, just as it is when one shepherd has a good dog and the other shepherds want to keep their flocks near his,

8 to get the benefit of his dog. Archedemus was happy to oblige Crito, and so it was not only Crito but his friends too who were left in peace. If any of those whose enmity he had thereby incurred taunted Archedemus with toadying to Crito for the benefits he received from him, he would answer, 'So where lies the disgrace? In making friends of honest men by returning favours for favours received, and setting yourself in opposition to the criminal classes—or in making enemies of the men of quality by trying to do them harm, looking to make friends among the criminal classes by supporting their activities, and preferring their company to that of honest men?'

From then on Archedemus was counted as one of Crito's friends, and an honoured member of that circle.

10 I RECALL too a conversation he had with Diodorus,* one of his companions. It went like this.

'Tell me, Diodorus,' he said, 'if one of your household slaves runs away, are you concerned to get him back?'

2   'You bet I am,' said Diodorus, 'and I call in others to help by offering a reward for his recovery.'

'And what about this? If one of your household slaves falls ill,* are you concerned enough to call in doctors, to prevent him dying on you?'

'Certainly,' he said.

'And if one of your acquaintances—someone much more useful to you than your slaves—is in danger of dying for lack of subsistence, don't you think that merits a concern on your part to save him? Now *3* I'm sure you know that Hermogenes* is a sensitive man, who would be ashamed to take help from you without being able to return the favour. But I think a more valuable possession than any number of slaves is a willing, loyal, and reliable assistant who is not only well able to carry out instructions, but has the further capacity to act to your benefit on his own initiative, and to think and plan ahead. Good *4* accountants say that the time to buy is when high-value commodities can be had at a low price: and in the present situation good friends can be acquired at rock-bottom cost.'

'That is a good point, Socrates,' Diodorus said. 'Tell Hermogenes *5* to come and see me.'

'Oh no,' said Socrates, 'I'm not going to do that. I think you would do better to go and see him yourself rather than calling him in—and you have just as much to gain from this arrangement as he does.'

And so Diodorus went off to find Hermogenes, and at no great *6* expense he acquired a friend who made it his business to look for all he could say or do to be helpful to Diodorus and keep him happy.

BOOK 3

1 I SHALL now describe how Socrates used to help those who aspired to high office* by making them work at the requirements of the office to which they aspired.

There was one occasion when he had heard that Dionysodorus* had arrived in Athens advertising lessons in generalship,* and he was aware that one of his associates was keen to obtain office as one of the **2** city's generals. So he said to this young man, 'You know, young fellow, it would be a disgrace for someone who wants to be a general in the city to have passed up the opportunity to learn what is required, when that was open to him. The city would have good cause to treat such a man much more punitively* than someone who takes commissions **3** for statues without having learnt how to sculpt. That's because in the dangers of war the whole city is dependent on the general, and great good or great harm can come from his success or failure. So wouldn't it be right to penalize someone who puts himself up for election without bothering to learn how to do the job?'

This advice persuaded the young man to go and attend the lessons. **4** When he came back at the end of the course, Socrates began to poke fun at him. 'Well, gentlemen,' he said, 'Homer described Agamemnon* as "majestic", and don't you think that our friend here looks more "majestic" now that he has learnt how to be a general? Someone who has learnt to play the lyre is still a lyre-player even if he never performs, and someone who has studied medicine is still a doctor* even if he never practises. So from this moment on our man will always be a general, even if no one votes for him! But no one untrained is ever **5** a general or a doctor, even if he is elected unanimously. Be that as it may,' he went on, 'tell us what was the first lesson he taught you about generalship, so that if any of us find ourselves in charge of a company or a platoon under your command, we can be better informed about military science.'

'It was the same all the way through,' he said. 'He taught us about troop formations* and nothing else.'

6 'And yet that is only a very small part of generalship,' said Socrates. 'A general must also be able to procure the resources for war and arrange for the provisioning* of his troops; he must be inventive, energetic, focused, hardy, and quick-witted; capable of being both benign and brutal, both frank and devious, both watchman and thief,* both lavish and grasping,* both generous and greedy, equally good at defence and attack—and there are many other qualities, either natural or taught, which are needed by someone who wants to be a successful general. Still, a knowledge of troop formations is a good thing *7* too. There is a great difference between a properly ordered army and one in disarray, just as building materials*—stones, bricks, timbers, tiles—thrown together in a random heap are completely useless, but when the materials which do not rot or decay, the stones and the tiles, are given their proper place at the bottom and top, and the bricks and timbers are arranged in the middle, as in any construction, the result then is something of great value to the owner—a house.'

'That's a very good analogy, Socrates,' said the young man. 'In war *8* you should put your best troops at the front and in the rear, and the worst in the middle, so that they have a lead from the front and a push from behind.'

'That's all very well,' said Socrates, 'if he also taught you how to *9* distinguish the good and the bad troops: otherwise, what use have these lessons been to you? No more use than if he had told you to arrange a pile of coins with the best at the front and back and the worst in the middle, without teaching you how to distinguish true coin* from counterfeit.'

'No,' he said, 'he certainly didn't teach us that. So we would have to decide for ourselves who are the good and who the bad.'

'So shouldn't we consider how we might avoid misjudging them?' *10*
'Yes, please,' said the young man.

'Well then,' said Socrates, 'suppose we had to make a raid to plunder a load of money. Wouldn't it be good tactics to put in the front line the men with the greatest love of money?'

'I would think so,' he said.

'And what about when there is danger to be faced? Should our front ranks then be filled by the men with the greatest desire for glory?'

'Well yes,' he said. 'They are the ones who are ready to face danger in order to earn commendation. And in this case there's no doubt about who they are—you can tell them anywhere, so this would be an easy choice.'

11   'All right,' said Socrates, 'but did he only teach you how to arrange an army for battle, or did he go on to give instruction about where and how various formations should be used?'

'No, not at all,' he said.

'And yet there are many situations for which it is not appropriate to use just one and the same way of arranging the troops and taking them into battle.'

'Well,' he said, 'he certainly didn't explain that.'

'So please go back,' said Socrates, 'and put these further questions to him. If he knows his stuff and is not without conscience, he will be ashamed to have taken your money and sent you away ill-equipped.'

2 ONE day when he met a man who had been elected general, Socrates asked him, 'Why do you think Homer called Agamemnon "shepherd of the people"?* Is it because the shepherd must see to it that his sheep are safe and have what they need, so that the purpose for which they are kept is achieved? And in the same way must the general see to it that his troops are safe and have what they need, so that the purpose for which they campaign is achieved—that purpose being to win

2 a happier life by defeating the enemy? Or what can Homer have meant by praising Agamemnon as "both a good king and a strong fighter too"? Is it that he would not be "a strong fighter too" if he were the only one to distinguish himself in the battle against the enemy, but if he were the inspiration for the whole army to follow his example? And "a good king" not if he were solely concerned with the quality of his own life, but if he also ensured the happiness of his

3 subjects? A king is elected* not to take care of his own comfort, but to be responsible no less for the welfare of those who chose him. And all who go to war do so to secure the best possible life for themselves, and

4 elect generals to lead them to that end. So the general's duty is to deliver that outcome for those who elected him to his office: it is not easy to think of any achievement finer than that, or anything more shameful than its opposite.'

And so in this examination of what constitutes the particular virtue* of a leader he stripped away all else and left simply the ability to ensure the happiness of those under his leadership.

3 AGAIN, I know that he once held this conversation with a man who had been elected one of the cavalry commanders.*

'Could you tell us, young man,' he said, 'what it was that made you eager for a cavalry command? It can't, I presume, have been the desire to ride at the head of the cavalry, as that privilege goes to the mounted archers*—at any rate they ride ahead of all, including the commanders.'

'That is true,' he said.

'But it can't have been for public recognition either—madmen too are known to everyone.'

'Again, that's true,' he said.

'Well perhaps you think that you can improve the cavalry, and hand 2 it back to the city in better condition after your tenure, and that as commander you can do something for the good of the city, if need arises for the use of cavalry?'

'I do indeed,' he said.

'And that is certainly a fine thing,' said Socrates, 'if you can do that. I presume that this command to which you have been elected covers both horses and riders.'

'Yes, it does,' he said.

'Come then, tell us first how you intend to improve the horses.'   3

'But I don't think that is my job,' he said. 'Every man has to look after his own horse.'*

'So if your men present you with horses which have such problems 4 with their hooves or legs, or are so sick or underfed, that they can't keep up with the others, or are so unmanageable that they won't stay where you place them in line, or such bad kickers that it's impossible to get them into line at all—what use can you make of your cavalry? How will you be able to do anything for the good of the city if you are in command of horses like that?'

'That is a good point,' he said, 'and I shall try my best to look after the horses.'

'Right, and the men? Won't you also undertake to improve their 5 performance?'

'I will,' he said.

'So you will first make them better at mounting their horses?'

'Yes, I must: because then if any of them takes a fall, he'll be better able to rescue himself.'

'And what when you have to face the danger of an engagement 6 somewhere? Will your standing orders be to draw the enemy into the sandy ground familiar from your practice manoeuvres,* or will you try to carry out your training in the sort of terrain where wars are actually fought?'

'Yes, that would be better,' he said.

7   'Again, will a priority be to ensure the maximum number of hits scored from the saddle?'

'Yes, that would be a good idea too,' he said.

'And have you formed a plan for whetting the spirits of your men and whipping up their anger at the enemy, which can stiffen their courage?'

'If I haven't, I'll certainly try to do so now,' he said.

8   'And have you given any thought to what will make the men obey your orders?* Without that discipline the best and bravest horses and cavalrymen are useless.'

'That's true, Socrates,' he said, 'but what would be the best way of encouraging their obedience?'

9   'Well, I'm sure you know that in any sphere of activity people are most willing to obey those whom they consider to be the best. So in sickness they most readily follow the instructions of whoever they consider the most expert doctor, in travel by sea the most expert ship's captain, and in agriculture the most expert farmer.'*

'That is certainly the case,' he said.

'Then it's probably the case with cavalry operations too—whoever has the most expertise in how things should be done is most likely to have the others following him.'

10   'So then, Socrates,' he said, 'if I am obviously the best horseman among them, will that be enough to ensure their obedience?'

'Yes, provided that you also show them that following your orders will be the more honourable course for them to take and more likely to keep them safe.'

'How then shall I do that?' he asked.

'Much more easily, I can assure you,' said Socrates, 'than if you had to prove that bad is better than good,* and the more advantageous course!'

11   'Do you mean', he said, 'that as well as everything else the cavalry commander must also concern himself to become a good speaker?'*

'And did you suppose', said Socrates, 'that your command should be exercised in silence? Have you never reflected that all the finest lessons that tradition has taught us, the lessons which give us the knowledge of how to live our lives, have been learnt from the spoken word, that any other good lesson anyone learns is taught by word of mouth, that the best teachers use spoken argument as their main method, and that those with the best knowledge of the most important subjects are also the best at speaking on their subjects? Or have you never reflected *12* that whenever this city produces a chorus, like the one which is sent to Delos,* no chorus produced anywhere else can match it, and no other city can assemble such an impressive group of men as we do here?'

'That's true,' he said.

'And yet what distinguishes the Athenians from the others is not so *13* much the quality of their singing or their physical size and strength as their collective sense of pride,* which is the strongest incentive to fine performance and consequent honours.'

'That's true too,' he said.

'Then don't you think that if someone took the same trouble with *14* our cavalry, they too would be greatly superior to the rest in the quality of their equipment and horses, in their discipline, and in their readiness to face danger against the enemy, if they thought that by these means they would win praise and honour?'

'Probably, I grant you,' he said.   *15*

'Well don't hesitate, then,' said Socrates. 'Try to encourage this way of thinking in your men. You will reap the benefit yourself, and so, thanks to you, will your fellow citizens.'

'I'll certainly do my best,' he said.

ONE day he saw Nicomachides* coming back from the elections and **4** asked him, 'Who have been chosen as generals, Nicomachides?'

He replied, 'Isn't it typical of the Athenians, Socrates? They didn't choose me, when I've worn myself out with soldiering ever since my enlistment, commanding platoons and companies and taking so many wounds in action against the enemy'—and here he bared his body to show the scars—'but they did choose Antisthenes,* who has never served as a hoplite or achieved anything of note in the cavalry, and knows nothing except how to make piles of money.'

'Isn't that a point in his favour,' said Socrates, 'if at least he'll be *2* capable of funding supplies for the troops?'

'Merchants can make piles of money too,' said Nicomachides, 'but that doesn't mean that they could command an army.'

'But Antisthenes is also keen to win,' said Socrates, 'and that's *3* a useful quality in a general. Haven't you seen that whenever he has had to sponsor a chorus,* his chorus has always won?'

'Yes,' Nicomachides replied, 'but for heaven's sake there's no comparison between managing a chorus and managing an army.'

4 'And yet', said Socrates, 'with no experience of music or chorus-training Antisthenes was capable of finding the best people in the business.'

'And so in the army too,' said Nicomachides, 'he'll find others to do the organizing for him, and others to do the fighting.'

5 'Well,' said Socrates, 'if he applies to the business of war the same method of identifying and appointing the best people as he employs in his choral productions, there's a good chance that he could be victorious in war too: and it's likely that he'll be yet more willing to spend his money on winning a military victory which involves the entire city than on success for his own tribe* in a choral competition.'

6 'Are you saying, Socrates, that a successful impresario would equally well make a successful general?'

'What I'm saying', Socrates replied, 'is that in any management role the man who knows what is needed and can supply it will be a good manager—whether he's managing a chorus, an estate, a city, or an army.'*

7 Nicomachides exclaimed, 'Good heavens, Socrates, I would never have thought I would hear you saying that good estate-managers would make good generals!'

'All right, then,' said Socrates, 'let's examine their respective duties to see whether they are the same or differ in some way.'

'Yes, let's,' he said.

8 'Isn't it, for a start, the duty of both to make sure they get compliance and ready obedience from those under their command?'

'Very much so,' he said.

'And to assign the various tasks to the appropriate people?'

'That too,' he said.

'Then I imagine both should punish the bad and reward the good.'

'Most certainly,' he said.

9 'And of course both would do well to ensure the loyalty of their subordinates?'

'That too,' he said.

'And do you think it is in the interest of both to get allies and helpers on their side, or not?'

'It most certainly is,' he said.

'And shouldn't both keep a close guard on their property?'

'Absolutely,' he said.

'And both should be focused and painstaking in the performance of their own duties?'

'So far', he said, 'all these things are common to them both. But 10 fighting is not—that's something else.'

'But there'll be enemies for both of them, wouldn't you say?'

'Yes,' he said, 'no doubt of that!'

'So both have an interest in getting the better of their enemies?'

'Yes, indeed,' he said, 'but you're missing something out—when 11 it comes to fighting, what use will there be in having managed an estate?'

'That is in fact where it will have its greatest use. The good manager knows that there is nothing so profitable and gainful as taking on his enemies and winning, and nothing so profitless and punitive as losing. So he will be keen to look out for and equip himself with all that holds the promise of victory, and careful to assess and guard against all that could lead to defeat. And then he will launch vigorously into battle if he sees that he is equipped to win, but, just as important, he will avoid an engagement if he is not fully prepared.

'Don't underestimate the men who manage estates, Nicomachides. 12 The management of a private business differs only in scale* from the management of public affairs, and in other respects they are very similar, notably and most importantly in that neither can be done without the involvement of people, and there is no distinction between the people involved in private and public operations—those in charge of public affairs are dealing with just the same sort of people as private managers. And those who understand how to treat people make a success of their operation, whether private or public, and those who don't go wrong in both.'

ONE day Socrates was talking with Pericles, the son of the great 5 Pericles.* 'Let me tell you, Pericles,' he said, 'with you elected general I am hopeful that the city will recover its military success and reputation, and manage to defeat our enemies.'

'I wish it were so,' said Pericles, 'but I have no idea how this could happen.'

'So shall we talk about it,' said Socrates, 'and look to see where this possibility already exists?'

'Yes, please,' he said.

2   'Well,' said Socrates, 'you know that the Athenians are not numer-
     ically inferior to the Boeotians?'*

     'Yes, I know that,' he said.

     'And who do you think could field the larger elite force of men in
     prime physical condition—the Boeotians or the Athenians?'

     'Here too I would think that the Athenians are at no disadvantage.'

     'And which side do you think has the greater harmony among its
     people?'

     'I would say the Athenians. Many of the Boeotians resent their
     exploitation by the Thebans. I don't see anything like that in Athens.'

3   'And then the Athenians surpass all others in ambition and pride,
     which are powerful incentives to risk one's life for honour and
     country.'

     'One can't fault the Athenians in this respect either.'

     'And then again no other people have a greater or a longer history
     of fine achievements by their predecessors than the Athenians, and
     this inspiring memory encourages many to summon their courage
     and prove their worth in battle.'

4   'All this is true, Socrates. But you can see that after the disasters
     suffered by Tolmides and his thousand men at Lebadea,* and then
     under Hippocrates at Delium,* it has all changed in the conflict
     between Athens and Boeotia—Athenian prestige has been brought
     low, and Theban assertiveness raised high. The result is that the
     Boeotians, who previously didn't dare to face the Athenians even in
     their own country without support from the Spartans and the other
     Peloponnesians, are now threatening to invade Attica on their own:
     and the Athenians, who in earlier times used to overrun Boeotia, are
     now afraid that the Boeotians will ravage Attica.'

5   'Yes, I'm aware that this is how things are,' said Socrates. 'But it
     seems to me that the city is now more inclined to accept the leader-
     ship of a good man. Confidence induces carelessness, relaxation, and
     indiscipline, but fear makes people more attentive, more obedient,

6   and better disciplined. You can see proof of this in the way sailors
     behave. When they have nothing to fear it seems they are a hive of
     misrule, but as long as there is the threat of a storm or enemy action
     they not only comply with all their orders, but wait in silence for the
     next command like members of a chorus.'

7   'Well now,' said Pericles, 'if the Athenians are indeed more likely to
     follow a lead in the present circumstances, this would be a good time

for you to tell me how we could bring them to recover their love of the courage, the glory, and the prosperity of the old days.'*

'Well,' said Socrates, 'if we wanted them to lay claim to property 8 once owned by the Athenians of former times, the best way to incite them to execute their claim would be to show them that this was their fathers' property and rightly belonged to them. But now we want them to set their sights on pre-eminence won by courage, and here again we should show them that this has been a prerogative belonging to them from of old, and that if they put their minds to it they can beat anyone.'

'So how can we put this across?' 9

'I think by reminding them that the earliest of their ancestors* of whom we have heard tell were themselves said to be the best of men.'

'Are you referring to the judgement between the gods,* which was 10 given to Cecrops* and his people to decide in view of their qualities?'

'Yes, and also the birth and nurture of Erechtheus,* and the war waged in his day with the inhabitants of the whole adjacent mainland region, the war against the Peloponnesians in the time of the Heraclids,* and all the wars fought in Theseus' time*—all these wars are proof of the Athenians' pre-eminence among the men of those times. And you could add, if you like, the achievements of their 11 descendants in a generation not much earlier than ours, when entirely on their own* they resisted the masters of all Asia and Europe as far as Macedonia,* who had acquired more power and resources and accomplished greater things than ever before in their history; and then again when they shared the honours* with the Peloponnesians on both land and sea. These Athenians too are said to have been far superior to other men of their time.'

'Yes, that is what is said of them.'

'And that is why, despite all the migrations* there have been in 12 Greece, the Athenians always remained in their own land, and many others have entrusted to them arbitration in disputes over their rights, or found refuge* with them when oppressed by stronger powers.'

'Yes indeed, Socrates,' said Pericles, 'and that makes me wonder 13 what has led to our city's decline.'

'My own view,' Socrates replied, 'is that rather as it can happen with athletes who have been far ahead of the field and won everything—they can relax their efforts and fall behind the competition—in the same way the Athenians, after all that clear superiority, have neglected themselves and so fallen into decline.'

14   'So what now can they do to recover their old quality?'

'There's no mystery, it seems to me,' said Socrates. 'If they rediscover the practices followed by their ancestors* and follow them as well as they did, they would become just as good as their ancestors. Or else they could model themselves on those who are at present in the ascendant, and follow the same practices as they do—with equal application to the same methods they would be just as good as those others, and with greater application even better than them.'

15   'What you're saying', said Pericles, 'is that true quality of men now seems at a far remove from our city. For instance, will the Athenians ever be like the Spartans* in showing respect for their elders, when they despise all the old, beginning with their own fathers? Or in physical training, when they not only neglect their own fitness but ridicule

16 anyone who does take it seriously? Will they ever be so obedient to authority, when they actually take pride in their contempt for the authorities? Or will they ever be as united as the Spartans, when instead of working together for the common interest they are more abusive and spiteful to one another than to the rest of the world? They are exceptionally quarrelsome in any meeting, whether private or public, constantly in the courts, preferring litigation and a gain at others' expense to any concept of mutual assistance, disdainful of involvement in public affairs as not for them, while at the same time fighting over politics, and revelling in their powers to create all this

17 dissension. As a result a great madness and mischief is taking root in the city, and great enmity and mutual hatred developing among the citizens, which leaves me in constant dread that some disaster may come on the city beyond our ability to sustain it.'

18   'Oh no, Pericles,' said Socrates, 'you really mustn't think that the Athenians are suffering from a moral infection as hopeless as that! Don't you see how disciplined they are in the navy,* how disciplined in their obedience to the officials in the athletic contests, and how as members of a chorus* they follow their trainer's instructions as strictly as any?'

19   'Yes,' he said, 'and there's the remarkable thing—that people in these activities obey those in charge of them, but the hoplites and the cavalry, who are supposed to be the elite, selected as citizens of quality, are the most insubordinate of all.'

Socrates said, 'But what about the Council of the Areopagus,* 20
Pericles? Isn't that composed of men who have met the test of formal
scrutiny?'*

'Yes it is,' he said.

'Then do you know of any other body of men who decide the cases
brought before them and conduct all their other business in a way
which is more honourable, lawful, dignified, and just?'

'I have no criticism of the Areopagus,' he said.

'Well then,' said Socrates, you must not despair as if there were no
discipline in Athens.'

'But yet in the military at least,' he said, 'where self-control, good 21
discipline, and obedience under command are pre-eminently needed,
Athenians pay no attention to any of these.'

'Perhaps', said Socrates, 'that's because their commanders have
very little of the relevant expertise. You must have observed that no
one attempts to direct musicians, chorus-members, or dancers without the necessary expertise, and the same with wrestlers and pancratiasts too. All with authority in these fields are able to show where they
learnt the business which they now supervise—but most of our generals are starting from scratch.

'However I don't think this is the case with you. I imagine you can 22
just as easily say when you began to learn generalship as when you
began to learn how to wrestle. And I imagine that as well as retaining
a good number of strategic principles inherited from your father, you
have assimilated many others from every source which can offer some
useful lesson in generalship. I imagine too that you are constantly 23
alert to the possibility that you might be missing some such useful
information, and that if you become aware of such a gap in your
knowledge you seek out the experts in that field and spare no gift or
favour to learn from them what you don't know and secure the benefit
of their collaboration.'

And Pericles said, 'You can't fool me, Socrates! In saying this 24
you don't believe for a moment that I am applying myself to this
preparation, but you're trying to show me that anyone intending to
be a general does need to apply himself to all of this. And I agree
with you.'

'Have you noticed, Pericles,' said Socrates, 'that our country is 25
protected by high mountains extending across the border into
Boeotia, with only steep and narrow passes through them into our

territory, and that a belt of formidable mountains runs through the middle of Attica?'

'Yes, of course,' he said.

26   'Well now, have you not heard that the Mysians and Pisidians,* who occupy formidably rugged country in the Great King's domain and are only lightly armed, can nevertheless do great damage in their raids on the King's territory, and still preserve their independence?'

'Yes, I have heard that too,' he said.

27   'And don't you think that if some Athenians still in their active youth were more lightly armed* and took up occupation of those mountains screening our country, they would both prove damaging to the enemy and provide our citizens with a substantial defence against invasion?'

And Pericles said, 'I think, Socrates, there is merit in all these suggestions too.'

28   'Well then,' said Socrates, 'if they meet with your approval, try them out, my good man! Any success in them will be an honour to you and a good for the city. And if you can't manage them all, you will not be doing any harm to the city or discredit to yourself.'

6 WHEN Ariston's son Glaucon,* not yet twenty years old but ambitious for leadership of the city, kept trying to make speeches in the assembly, none of his family or friends could stop him, even though he was regularly dragged off the platform and greeted with derision. The only person who did manage to dissuade him was Socrates, who took a kindly interest in the young man because of Charmides,* son of the elder Glaucon, and Plato.*

2   Meeting him one day, Socrates ensured that he was ready to listen by beginning the conversation like this: 'So, Glaucon,' he said, 'you have made up your mind to be the city's leader?'

'I have indeed, Socrates,' he said.

'Well I do declare that's as fine an ambition as any man could have!' said Socrates. 'Because obviously if you do achieve that you will be able to satisfy all your own desires and have the means of helping your friends too; you will enhance your father's house and promote the fortunes of your fatherland; and you will make a name for yourself first in this city, then throughout Greece, and perhaps like Themistocles* in foreign lands also. Wherever you are, all eyes will be on you.'

This was enough to swell Glaucon's opinion of himself, and he *3* happily stayed on to hear more. So now Socrates continued, saying, 'Well, Glaucon, one obvious point is that if you want to win all that honour you must do some good to the city. Is that not so?'

'Absolutely,' he said.

'Well, come on then,' said Socrates, 'don't keep it to yourself, but tell us what will be the first thing you will do for the good of the city?'

When Glaucon fell silent, as if this was the first time he had had to *4* think about where to begin, Socrates said, 'If it was your aim to extend a friend's family holding, you would set about making him wealthier. Will you in the same way try to make the city wealthier?'

'Absolutely,' he said.

'And the city would be wealthier if it had more sources of revenue?' *5* 'I guess so,' he said.

'Tell me, then,' said Socrates, 'what the city's present sources of revenue* are, and how much they bring in. Obviously you will have looked into this, so that you can boost any that are failing and exploit any missed opportunities.'

'Well no, frankly,' said Glaucon, 'I haven't looked into that.'

'All right,' said Socrates, 'if you haven't got round to that, then tell *6* us at least about the city's expenditure*—obviously you have plans to cut back any excess.'

'Well, no again,' he said. 'Frankly I haven't yet had time for this either.'

'Then we'll postpone the question of making the city wealthier. Without knowing the facts about expenditure and income, how could anyone plan for either?'

'But, Socrates,' said Glaucon, 'a source of enrichment for the city *7* can also be reparations from its enemies.'

'Oh yes, no doubt of it,' said Socrates, 'if you are stronger than them; if weaker, though, you could further jeopardize what you start off with.'

'That's true,' he said.

'So anyone who will have to advise on where war should be declared *8* must know both the strength of the city and the strength of that enemy, so that if the city is stronger he can advise prosecution of the war, but if the enemy is stronger, he can advocate caution.'

'You are right,' he said.

'Then first tell us', said Socrates, 'what the city's land and naval *9* forces are, and then those of our enemies.'

'Frankly,' he said, 'I couldn't tell you that just off the top of my head.'

'Well, if you have some notes of it, please fetch them,' said Socrates. 'I would be really glad to hear what they say.'

'Frankly,' he said, 'I haven't yet made any notes either.'

10   'All right then, we'll put the advisability of war on hold too, at least for the present. We'll suppose that you're not long in power, and perhaps you haven't yet examined such weighty issues. But I'm sure that you have already thought about the defence of the country, and will know how many of our frontier-posts* are in the right place and how many are not, and how many of the garrisons are adequate and how many are not—and you will propose the strengthening of the well-positioned posts and the abolition of those which are surplus to requirements.'

11   'No,' said Glaucon. 'Frankly I would want to abolish the lot, as their so-called "protection" does nothing to stop the theft of our crops.'*

'But if the garrisons are removed don't you think that will be an open invitation to anyone intent on full-scale plunder? Anyway,' Socrates continued, 'have you been on a personal tour of inspection, or how do you know that there is poor protection?'

'I am guessing,' he said.

'Well on this question too,' said Socrates, 'shall we wait to make our proposals until we have moved on from guesswork to knowledge?'

'Perhaps that would be better,' said Glaucon.

12   'Now as for the silver mines,'* said Socrates, 'I'm sure that you haven't visited them, and so can't say why the revenue from them is now less than it was.'

'No, I haven't been there,' he said.

'Well frankly it's said to be an oppressive place,' said Socrates, 'so when you have to advise on the issue, you'll be able to rely on this excuse.'

'You're making fun of me,' said Glaucon.

13   'Oh, one more thing,' said Socrates, 'which I'm sure you haven't overlooked. You will have assessed for how long our home-produced grain* can feed the city, and how much more is needed each year, so that you are never caught unprepared if the city faces a shortage of food,* but can give informed advice on the supply of essentials, and so rescue the situation and see the city through.'

'You're talking about an immense task,' said Glaucon, 'if it really will require attention to matters like that too.'

'But surely', said Socrates, 'a man would never be able to run even *14* his own household properly, if he's not going to be aware of its needs and take care to supply them all. Given that the city consists of more than ten thousand houses,* and it is difficult to take care of so many households at once, how come you haven't made a start by trying to reform just one household—your uncle's?* It needs it. Then if you succeed with that one, you can try your hand at a larger number. But if you can't do any good for one household, how are you going to do it for many? It would be like someone who is unable to carry the weight of one talent—pretty obvious, isn't it, that he shouldn't even attempt to carry more than one?'

'Well, I could certainly make some improvement in my uncle's *15* household,' said Glaucon, 'if he would only listen to me!'

'So then,' said Socrates, 'you can't persuade your own uncle, and yet you think you can get all the people of Athens, including your uncle, to listen to you? Take care, Glaucon, that your desire for respect *16* doesn't lead you to the opposite. Or don't you see how risky it is for anyone to say or do things that they don't know about? Think of the others you know who are like that, people who turn out to be saying or doing things of which they have no knowledge. What do you see them getting for it—praise or blame, admiration or contempt? And think too of those who do know what they are saying or doing. *17* I think you will find that in every field of activity those who win respect and admiration are among the most knowledgeable, and those held in disregard are among the most ignorant. So if you are desirous *18* of public respect and admiration, try to ensure that you have the best possible knowledge of what will form your intended policy. If you set yourself on a political career with this advantage over the others, I would not be surprised if you found it quite easy to realize your ambition.'

SEEING that Charmides,* the son of the elder Glaucon, was a man of **7** distinction and far more capable than the politicians of the time, but reluctant to speak in the assembly or take any active part in politics, he said to him, 'Tell me, Charmides, what would you think of a man who was good enough to win the crown in the major athletic contests,* so bringing honour on himself and enhancing his country's reputation throughout Greece—but yet refused to compete?'

'Obviously I would think him a spineless coward,' he said.

2   'And what about someone who, if he engaged in public affairs, was
       capable of promoting the fortunes of his city and thereby winning
       honour for himself, but in fact shrank from doing so—wouldn't it be
       reasonable to think him a coward?'
            'Perhaps,' he said. 'But why are you asking me this?'
            'Because', said Socrates, 'I think you have the ability but shrink
       from applying it—and this in matters where it is your obligation as
       a citizen to play your part.'
3   'This so-called ability of mine,' said Charmides: 'where have you
       seen practical evidence of it to justify this criticism of me?'
            'In the meetings you have with the politicians,' said Socrates.
       'Whenever they confide in you I see you giving them good advice, and
       making sound objections whenever they are going wrong.'
4   Charmides replied, 'Conversation in private is not the same as
       debate in a crowded assembly,* Socrates.'
            'And yet', said Socrates, 'anyone who can count is able to count just
       as well in front of a crowd as on his own, and the best lyre-players in
       the privacy of their home are also the best in public performance.'
5   'But don't you see', said Charmides, 'that shyness and timidity are
       natural human emotions, which affect people much more when they
       have to face crowds rather than a private meeting?'*
            'Yes,' said Socrates, 'and in your case I hasten to point out that you
       are not shy in the most intelligent company or intimidated in talk with
       the very powerful, but you are too embarrassed to speak before an
6   audience of complete idiots and nobodies! Who are the people caus-
       ing you this embarrassment? Is it the fullers or the cobblers or the
       carpenters or the metalworkers or the farmers or the shopkeepers or
       the traders in the marketplace without a thought in their heads
       beyond what they can buy cheap and sell dear? Because the assembly
7   is made up of all these people. Do you think there is any difference
       between your behaviour and that of a man who can beat professional
       athletes but is afraid of amateurs? You have no difficulty talking with
       the leading men in the city, some of whom have made up their minds
       against you, and you are far superior to those who make it their business
       to address the public, and yet you shrink from speaking to an audience
       who have never given a thought to politics and have no preconceived
       bias against you—and all because you dread being laughed at.'
8   'Well,' he said, 'don't you think that the people in the assembly do
       often laugh at speakers who are talking good sense?'

'Yes, and so do those others,' said Socrates, 'and that's what puzzles me: you can easily out-argue the others when they do that to you, and yet you think there's no way that you will be able to handle the assembly-goers. My dear fellow, don't underestimate yourself! Don't 9 allow yourself to make the same mistake as most people—so many are quick to scrutinize other people's business without taking time to examine themselves. So don't shirk this duty, but make more effort to pay attention to yourself. And don't neglect public affairs, if there is any possibility that you could make a difference for the better. Good government will be a benefit not only to the other citizens, but also to your friends and, not least, to you yourself.'

ARISTIPPUS* was once trying to refute Socrates in the same way that 8 he himself had been refuted by Socrates in an earlier encounter. For the benefit of the company Socrates answered the questions with the air of someone confident that he was doing exactly what was required of him, rather than someone guarding against having the argument turned on its head.

Aristippus asked him if he knew of anything that was good,* 2 intending that if Socrates spoke of something like food, drink, money, health, strength, or courage, he could then demonstrate that it was sometimes bad. Socrates, knowing that if something irritates us we need a way to stop it, gave the answer which would be the killer. 'Are 3 you asking me', he said, 'if I know of anything which is good for a fever?'*

'No, I'm not,' Aristippus said.

'For ophthalmia, then?'

'Not that either.'

'For hunger, then?'

'Not hunger either.'

'Well then,' said Socrates, 'if you're asking me if I know of anything good which is not good for anything, I don't know and I don't want to know either.'

Again, Aristippus asked him if he knew anything beautiful. 'Yes, 4 many things,' he replied.

'And are they all like one another?' he asked.

'Well, some are as unlike* as can be,' Socrates said.

'How then', said Aristippus, 'can something which is unlike the beautiful be beautiful?'

'Because, of course,' said Socrates, 'there is a difference between someone who is a beautiful runner and another who is a beautiful wrestler:* and a shield which is beautiful for defence is utterly unlike a javelin which is beautiful for the speed and power of its trajectory.'

5   'That's the same sort of answer', he said, 'as you gave to my question whether you knew of anything that was good.'

'And do you think', said Socrates, 'that there is a difference between "good" and "beautiful"? Don't you know that, in relation to the same things, everything good is also beautiful? In the first place, excellence is not "good" in some relations and "beautiful" in others. And then the term "beautiful and good"* is applied to people without any difference of sense or relation. The human body is seen as both "beautiful" and "good" in relation to the same things, and everything else in human use is considered both "beautiful" and "good" in respect of whatever it may be for which it has effective utility.'

6   'So is even a dung-bucket* beautiful?' he said.

'Certainly,' said Socrates, 'and a golden shield is ugly, if the one is beautifully made for its purpose and the other is badly made.'

'Are you saying that the same things can be both beautiful and ugly?' he said.

7   'Certainly,' said Socrates, 'and both good and bad. Often what is good for hunger is bad for a fever, and what is good for a fever is bad for hunger. What is beautiful in running is often ugly in wrestling, and what is beautiful in wrestling is ugly in running. All things well suited to their purpose are good and beautiful, and all things badly suited are bad and ugly.'

8   Similar was his contention that the beauty of a house* was the same as its utility. His argument on this topic strikes me as a lesson in what sort of houses we should build. This is how he introduced the issue: 'If someone is going to have his ideal house, should he design it to be both as pleasant to live in and also as practical as he can make it?'

9   With this agreed, he asked, 'And is it pleasant to have a house which is cool in summer and warm in winter?'

When they agreed with this too, he went on, 'Now in houses which face south, in winter the sun sheds light through the verandas, and in summer passes over our heads and above the roof, giving us shade. So, assuming this is the way we like it to be, we should build our houses higher on the south side, to catch the winter sun, and closer to

10   the ground on the north, to keep out the cold winds. It would follow,

in short, that the most pleasant and at the same time the most beautiful house would be the one which at all seasons can give the owner the most pleasant retreat for himself and the safest storage for his property. Paintings and tapestries are more of a trouble than a pleasure.'

For temples and altars* he said that the most suitable location was a highly conspicuous site well off the beaten track, which pleasingly serves a double purpose: those who see it from afar can offer up a prayer, and those who make their way up to it can do so without contamination.

THEN on another occasion he was asked* whether courage was some- **9** thing that could be taught or was a natural gift.* 'I think', he said, 'that just as one body is by nature stronger than another for physical work, so one soul is in better natural condition than another when it comes to confronting danger. That is because I can see that people brought up under the same laws and in the same traditions differ widely in their capacity for bold action. But I also think that what *2* develops courage in anyone's nature is learning and practice.* For example, it's obvious that Scythians and Thracians would not be fool-hardy enough to take up heavy shields and spears and enter a battle with Spartans,* and equally clear that Spartans would not be pre-pared to fight Thracians with light shields and javelins, or Scythians with bows. And I see the same in all other areas too—people differing *3* from one another by nature, but greatly improving themselves by application. It clearly follows from this that everyone, whatever their natural endowment, talented or not so sharp, should both study and work at what they want to be noted for.'

He did not distinguish between wisdom and self-control,* but *4* would judge a man to be both wise and self-controlled on the twin criteria of his recognition and consequent adoption of what is beauti-ful and good, and his knowledge and consequent avoidance of what is demeaning. When asked further whether he thought that in those who knew what they should do, but did the opposite, there was a com-bination of wisdom and lack of control, he replied, 'No, more than that—it's a combination of lack of wisdom as well as lack of control. I suppose that when they have various possibilities of action people make a deliberate choice of the course which they think is in their best interest: and so I consider that those who act wrongly* are neither wise nor self-controlled.'

5   He also said that justice, and every other form of virtue, is wisdom,* because both just actions and all other actions informed by virtue are beautiful and good, and those who know what is beautiful and good would never choose to do anything other, while those without that knowledge are incapable of such action—and even if they try, they get it wrong. In the same way, he said, it is the wise who do what is beautiful and good, while those who lack wisdom are incapable of such action—and even if they try, they get it wrong. Since then just actions and all other actions which are beautiful and good are informed by wisdom, it is clear that justice and all other forms of virtue are wisdom.

6   Then madness,* he said, was the opposite of wisdom, though he did not think that pure lack of knowledge was madness. What he did reckon pretty close to madness was ignorance of oneself—holding opinions and thinking one knows about things which one doesn't know. He said that most people do not regard as mad those who are deluded about matters of which the general public are ignorant too, but what they do call madness is delusion about matters of common

7   knowledge. For example, if someone thinks he is so tall that he has to stoop to go through the gates in the city, or so strong that he tries to lift houses or attempts anything else which everyone knows is obviously impossible, they say that he is mad. Minor delusions are generally not thought to be madness, but just as people call a powerful desire 'love', so a major derangement of the mind is called madness.

8   Considering a definition of envy,* he found that it was a kind of pain, though not the same as that arising from the misfortunes of friends or the good fortunes of enemies—the emotion of envy, he said, was only experienced by those who were distressed by their friends' successes. When some expressed surprise that anyone friendly with another would be pained by his success, he reminded them that many people were like this in their social relationships—incapable of ignoring others in trouble, and helping them out when they were down on their luck, but pained when they saw them doing well. Though this, he said, would not be the case with anyone of good sense—it was an affliction of the foolish.

9   Considering a definition of leisure,* he said that he found that most people did have some form of occupation. Even gamblers and comedians had an occupation, but all these were in a sense at leisure, because it was open to them to go and do something better. But nobody

was at leisure to move from better to worse: if anyone took that route, he said, it was the lack of leisure which made him go wrong.

Kings and rulers,* he used to say, were not those who hold the 10 sceptres, nor those elected by all-comers, nor those chosen by lot, nor those who have gained their position by force or fraud—but those who have the expertise to rule. Whenever he had agreement that it 11 was for the ruler to lay down what must be done and for the ruled to obey him, he would point out that on a ship it is the expert who rules, and the shipowner and all the others on board who obey the expert; and that in agricultural matters the landowners, in sickness the patients, in physical training those on a training regime, and all others who have something that needs attention, take care of it themselves if they think they know how, but otherwise obey the experts, and not only when they are at hand—they even send for them if they are away, so that they can do what is needed under expert instruction. Again, he would point out that in wool-spinning* the women rule the men, because they know how to spin wool and the men do not.

If anyone objected that a tyrant* can refuse to follow good advice, 12 he would say, 'And how could he refuse, when there is a penalty for ignoring good advice? In any situation where someone rejects the good advice he is given, he is bound to go wrong, and then will pay the penalty for his error.'

And if anyone said that a tyrant can actually have a well-intentioned 13 adviser killed, he would say, 'And do you think that anyone who has killed the best of his supporters will go unpunished, or pay only a trifling penalty? Which do you think the more likely—that someone who acts like that will survive, or simply accelerate his own downfall?'

When someone asked him what he thought was the best pursuit for 14 a man, he answered, 'Successful action.'* To the next question, whether he thought that good fortune was also a pursuit, his reply was, 'No, in my view fortune and action are complete opposites. To chance on something you need without looking for it I consider good fortune, but I think that successful action consists in doing something well after study and practice, and in my observation those who make this their pursuit do meet with success.' And he used to say that in any field the 15 best men and the most favoured by the gods were those who did their job well—in agriculture the good farmers, in medicine the good doctors, in public affairs the good politicians. Anyone who did nothing well, he said, was of no use and enjoyed no favour from the gods.

10 THEN again, whenever he talked with any of those who possessed an artistic skill and used it professionally,* his conversation was equally useful to them too. For example, one day he visited Parrhasius* the painter, and in the course of their conversation he asked, 'Would you say, Parrhasius, that painting is a representation of the things we can see? At any rate, you painters use your colours to imitate* and reproduce the appearance of valleys and heights, features in light or shade, things hard or soft, rough or smooth, and human bodies young or old.'

'That's true,' he said.

2   'And in your portrayal of beautiful figures, since it's not easy to find complete perfection in any one model, you combine the best features* from each of several models to create the appearance of bodies which are beautiful in every aspect.'

3   'Yes, that is how we work,' he said.

'Well now, what about that aspect which is the most compelling, delightful, affectionate, desirable, and lovely of all—the character of a soul?* Do you portray that? Or is it something beyond portrayal?'

'How could it be portrayed, Socrates,' he said, 'when it has no shape or colour or any of those features you just spoke of, and is not even visible at all?'

4   'Tell me, then,' said Socrates, 'is it human experience that the way we look at others can convey either friendliness or hostility?'

'Yes, I think so,' he said.

'So can that be depicted in the eyes?'

'Certainly,' he said.

'Do you think that in response to friends' good or bad fortune those who care about them have the same facial expressions as those who do not?'

'Goodness me, no,' he said. 'Those who care look radiant at their friends' good fortune and depressed at their misfortunes.'

'And is it possible to represent these expressions too?'

'Certainly,' he said.

5   'And then noble and free-spirited or cringing and servile, controlled and intelligent or abusive and vulgar—all these characteristics are reflected in people's faces and the way they hold their bodies at rest or in motion.'

'That's true,' he said.

'And can these be depicted too?'

'Certainly,' he said.

'Now do you think', said Socrates, 'that it's more agreeable to look at portrayals of people which reveal a beautiful, good, and lovely character, or one which is ugly, depraved, and hateful?'

'No doubt at all, Socrates,' he said. 'There is a huge difference there.'

On another occasion he visited Clito the sculptor,* and in the 6 course of that conversation he said, 'Clito, I can see for myself and already know that the figures you create of runners, wrestlers, boxers, and pancratiasts* are beautiful. But the quality which viewers find most intriguing is that they seem alive—how do you produce that in your statues?'

Clito could not come up with an immediate answer, so Socrates 7 continued, 'Is it by modelling your work on living examples that you make your statues seem more lifelike?'

'Yes, certainly,' he said.

'So it's by modelling the effects on the body of various poses—crouched or stretched, closed or open, tense or relaxed—that you make your statues seem more convincingly like the real thing?'

'Absolutely,' he said.

'And don't viewers also appreciate a representation of the emotions 8 when bodies are in action?'

'I imagine so,' he said.

'So you should reproduce the threatening look in the eyes of fight-ers, and portray the satisfied expression on a victor's face?'

'Most certainly,' he said.

'It follows, then,' said Socrates, 'that the sculptor must make his figures represent the condition of the soul.'*

When he visited Pistias the armourer,* and Pistias showed him some 9 well-made breastplates, Socrates said, 'By Hera, Pistias, the breast-plate is a wonderful invention! It covers the parts of a man which need protection without impeding the use of his arms. But tell me, 10 Pistias,' he added, 'how come you charge more for your breastplates than others do? Yours aren't stronger or more expensive to make.'

'Because the ones I make, Socrates, are better shaped,' he said.

'And how do you explain the higher price you ask for this shaping—is that by weight or by dimensions? I don't suppose you make them all in one and the same size—if, that is, you make them to fit.'*

'Well of course I make them to fit!' he said. 'Without that a breast-plate is useless.'

11 'Isn't it the case', said Socrates, 'that some men's bodies are well proportioned and others ill proportioned?'

'Certainly,' he said.

'How then do you make a breastplate well-shaped if it is to fit an ill-proportioned body?'

'Exactly by making it fit,' he said. 'A good fit is a good shape.'

12 'It seems to me', said Socrates, 'that you are using "well-shaped" not in any absolute sense, but as relative to the wearer, just as you might call a shield or a greatcoat "well-shaped" for the man it fits—and probably on your usage the same applies to everything

13 else. But perhaps there is another quite important advantage in the good fit.'

'Do tell me what you have in mind, Socrates,' he said.

'Well-fitting breastplates', said Socrates, 'feel less oppressively heavy on the body than those which fit badly, even though they are of the same weight. The misfits prove uncomfortable and troublesome, either because their whole weight hangs on the shoulders or because they press hard on some other part of the body. But the good fits, with their weight evenly distributed and variously supported by collarbones and shoulder-blades, then shoulders, chest, back, and abdomen, seem more like an extension of the body than any external burden.'

14 'You have hit on the precise reason why I think my products represent the best value,' he said. 'But some prefer to buy decorated or gilded breastplates.'

'Well,' said Socrates, 'if that means they are buying ill-fitting breastplates, it seems to me that they are spending their money on

15 decorated and gilded rubbish. One more thing, though: given that the wearer's body is not static, but sometimes bent and sometimes upright, how can tightly fitted breastplates allow for that?'

'They can't,' he said.

'You mean', said Socrates, 'that the good fit is not the tight fit, but the one that causes no discomfort in actual use?'

'That's exactly what I do mean, Socrates,' he said, 'and you have got the point absolutely right!'

11 AT one time there was a beautiful woman in Athens called Theodote,* the sort of woman who could be persuaded to keep a man company.* One of the group with Socrates had mentioned her name and said that the beauty of this woman was beyond description—artists, he

said, visited her to paint her picture, and she let them see as much of herself as was decent. 'We had better go and take a look at her,' said Socrates: 'if something is beyond description, just hearing about it won't tell us what we want to know.'

'Come with me right now,' said the informant. So they set off to 2 Theodote's house, and found her posing for a painter. They looked on.

When the painter had finished, Socrates said, 'Gentlemen, should we be more grateful to Theodote for letting us see her beauty, or she to us for being the spectators?* Could it be that if she has more to gain from the display of her beauty, she ought to thank us, and if we have more to gain from the sight of it, we should thank her?'

When someone said that this was a fair point, Socrates continued, 3 'Well now: she has already gained our appreciation, and when we spread the word more widely she will benefit yet more. As for us, we are already longing to touch what we have seen, we will go away in a state of some excitement, and when we are gone we will yearn for her. It's reasonable to conclude that the direction of service rendered is from us to her.'

At this Theodote said, 'Well, goodness me! If that is so, I ought to be grateful to you for coming to look at me!'

Socrates could see that Theodote herself was expensively decked 4 out, that her mother there with her was dressed and presented uncommonly well, that the many good-looking maids* in attendance were smartly turned out too, and that generally no expense had been spared on the amenities of the house. So he said, 'Tell me, Theodote, do you own land?'

'No, I don't,' she said.

'Well, perhaps a property that brings you an income?'

'Not that either,' she said.

'Perhaps a workforce, then?'

'No workforce either,' she said.

'How then', asked Socrates, 'do you support yourself?'

'If a man makes friends* with me and wants to see me right,' she said, 'that's my livelihood.'

'By Hera, Theodote,' said Socrates, 'it's a fine thing to have a flock 5 of friends—a much better investment than a herd of sheep or goats or cattle! But do you leave it to chance whether some friend will settle on you like a fly, or do you have some scheme of your own to attract them?'

6   'And how could I come up with a scheme for that?' she asked.

'Oh, it would be much more specific to you than what the spiders do,' said Socrates. 'You know how they hunt for their livelihood—they weave fine webs and feed on whatever falls into them.'

7   'Are you advising me that I too should weave some sort of trap?' she said.

'Oh no, you mustn't think it's going to be that simple to hunt friends, the most valuable prey there is! Don't you see that even those

8 who hunt low-value hares* use a variety of techniques? Hares feed at night, so the hunters get themselves dogs specially trained for night hunting; then since after feeding the hares run back when day comes, the hunters have another pack of dogs which can sniff them out by following the scent from their feeding-grounds to their beds; and since hares are quick enough to escape even when running in the open, the hunters are equipped with yet more dogs, fast ones this time, to run the hares down; and since some hares escape even these dogs, the hunters set nets on the tracks which the hares use for their escape, so the hares run into them and get entangled.'

9   'So what technique like that could I use to hunt friends?' she asked.

'I'll tell you,' he said. 'You can do it if you substitute for the dogs someone who can track down* and find for you men of wealth and good taste, and when he's found them can devise a means of driving them into your nets.'

10   'Nets?' she said. 'What sort of nets* do I have?'

'Well, one is obvious—and a very effective catch-all it is—your body! But in your body you have a soul, and that is how you know what looks will charm and what words will delight; that is what tells you that you should warmly welcome in the serious suitor and shut your door on the playboy, that if your friend falls sick you should show your concern by visiting him, that if he achieves some success you should be effusive in your congratulation, and that if someone is really keen on you, you should put heart and soul into meeting his every wish. As for actual love, I'm sure you know how to combine submission and friendly support: and I'm sure too that you convince your friends of your affection by how you behave to them, not just what you say.'

'But honestly,' said Theodote, 'I don't use any of these methods.'

11   'And yet', said Socrates, 'it's very important to use the right approach which suits the nature of the human species! You can't catch

or keep a friend by force—it's by showing kindness and giving pleasure that this particular prey is caught and kept constant.'

'That's true,' she said.

'So with men who are keen on you,' Socrates said, 'at first you *12* should only ask them for such favours as they will grant with hardly a second thought: and then you should repay them with your own favours on the same scale. That is the surest way to make them love you, with the most lasting love and the greatest generosity. And you *13* will gratify them most if you present them with what you have to offer only when they are in need of it. The most delicious foods, you see, are unwelcome if served before an appetite has been worked up, and can actually induce nausea in those who have already had their fill. But even inferior fare seems delicious when served to someone who has been left to grow hungry.'

'So how can I make people hungry for what I can serve up?' she *14* asked.

'I'll tell you how,' said Socrates. 'First, don't keep on offering or teasing when they have had their fill: wait until they have recovered from their surfeit and start asking for more. Then when the desire is on them tease them by starting the most innocuous conversation, conveying the impression that you're not willing to give them what they want, and leaving the room until their desire is at its height. And what you give them then will be so much better than the same thing before their appetite was aroused.'

And Theodote said, 'Why then, Socrates, haven't you been my *15* partner all along in the hunt for friends?'

'I'll certainly join you,' he said, 'if you can persuade me.'

'And how could I persuade you?' she asked.

'You'll work that out for yourself,' he said, 'and find a way if you want some help from me.'

'Come and see me often, then,' she said.

'Well, Theodote,' said Socrates, with a playful dig at his own inactivity, *16* 'it's not that easy for me to find the time. There's a lot of private and public business that keeps me fully occupied, and there are girlfriends* who won't let me leave them day or night—I'm teaching them about love potions and spells.'*

'So you know about those too, Socrates?' she said.   *17*

'Well,' he said, 'why do you think that Apollodorus here and Antisthenes* never leave me? And why do Cebes and Simmias* come to me from Thebes? I can tell you that this doesn't happen without a good number of potions and spells and magic wheels.'

18   'Then lend me your magic wheel,' she said, 'so I can spin it first to attract you.'

'Oh no,' he said, 'I don't want me to be attracted to you, but you to come to me.'

'Then I'll come,' she said, 'but be sure to let me in!'

'Oh yes,' he said, 'I'll let you in all right—as long as I don't have a girlfriend I like better already with me!'

12   WHEN he saw that Epigenes,* one of his associates, was in poor physical shape* for a young man, he said to him, 'You have a rather individual way of looking after your body, Epigenes.'

And he said, 'That's because I am an individual, Socrates.'

'And so are those who will be contestants in the Olympic Games!' said Socrates. 'Or do you think there is nothing to worry about in the life-and-death contest with their enemies which the Athenians will

2   enter sooner or later?* And yet in the perils of war many men lose their lives through lack of fitness, or only survive with dishonour. And many for the same reason are captured alive, and once taken prisoner either spend the rest of their lives in slavery, perhaps in the harshest conditions, or else are reduced to the most desperate straits and, after paying a ransom sometimes greater than all they possess, live out the rest of their lives in destitution and misery. For many too their physical weakness earns them a bad reputation, and they are thought cowards.

3   'Or do you make light of these penalties inherent in poor physical condition, and think that you could easily tolerate such consequences? Well, in my view anything that has to be endured by the man who takes care to keep his body in good condition is far easier and far more pleasant than what you face. Or do you consider that being unfit is somehow healthier and generally better for you than being fit? Do you think nothing of the benefits resulting from good physical condition?

4   And yet in every way those who keep their bodies in good condition* experience the opposite of those who don't. Those in good condition are healthy and strong. This is what enables many to survive the trials of war with their honour intact and escape all its dangers. This is how many can help their friends and do good to their country, for which they earn gratitude, gain great glory, and win the highest honours:

and on that account they live a better and more pleasant life for the rest of their time, and leave their children better resources for their own lives.

'The fact that the city does not provide military training at public 5 expense* is no excuse for neglecting it as a private individual—in fact it's all the more reason for taking it up yourself. Let me tell you that, quite apart from war, there is no other contest in life, indeed no activity whatsoever, in which having got your body into better shape will be any disadvantage. The body has its use in all human activity, and in all the uses to which it is put having one's body in the best possible condition makes all the difference. Even in the workings of the mind, 6 where you may think the body has minimal use, everyone knows that here too many people go badly wrong for lack of a healthy body. It often happens that because of their poor physical condition loss of memory, depression, bad temper, or insanity invade many people's minds so completely as to drive out whatever sound knowledge they had. But those who keep their bodies in good condition are well 7 insured, and at least there is no danger of them suffering any of these disabilities for lack of physical well-being. In fact it is more likely that their good condition will serve them for the direct opposite of the effects of poor condition. And what man of sense would not submit to anything to achieve that opposite state?

'Besides, it reflects badly on a man if he lets himself grow old 8 through neglect of his person, before seeing just how handsome and strong his body could become. Neglect denies him that sight, because these things won't come about of their own accord.'

WHEN someone was angry because the greeting he gave to another **13** was not reciprocated, Socrates said, 'You wouldn't be angry if you met someone whose body was in worse condition than yours, so it's absurd to be annoyed because you have come across someone with a soul less politely attuned.'

Someone else said that he took no pleasure in eating. 'Acumenus* 2 prescribes a good cure for that,' said Socrates. 'And what's that?' asked the other. 'To give up eating,' he said: 'and when you've done that, you'll find life more pleasant, and cheaper and healthier too.'

Then again someone complained that the drinking water at his 3 house was too warm. 'So whenever you want a warm bath,' said Socrates, 'it'll be there ready for you.'

'But it's too cold to wash in,' said the other.

'So tell me,' said Socrates, 'are your household slaves bothered by using the same source of water for drinking and washing?'

'No, they are not,' he said, 'and in fact I've often been surprised at how content they are to use it for both purposes.'

'Which water is warmer to drink,' asked Socrates, 'yours or the water at the temple of Asclepius?'*

'The water at the temple of Asclepius,' he said.

'And which water is colder for bathing, yours or the water at the shrine of Amphiaraus?'*

'The water at the shrine of Amphiaraus,' he said.

'So think about it,' said Socrates: 'it looks as if you are harder to please than your slaves and the invalids.'

4   When someone had punished his servant severely, Socrates asked him why he was angry with the man.

'Because', he said, 'he's as greedy and lazy as they come, likes his money and shirks his work.'

'So have you ever considered which of you deserves the worse beating—you or your servant?'

5   When someone was fearful of making the journey to Olympia,* Socrates said, 'Why are you afraid of the distance? Even when you're at home don't you spend most of the day walking about? So on that journey too you'll do some walking before breakfast, then do some more before dinner, and then go to bed. Don't you see that if you put together end to end all the walking you do in five or six days, you could easily get from Athens to Olympia? And it's more comfortable to set off a day earlier, rather than find yourself pressed for time. If you're forced to extend each stage unduly far, that makes it hard going: but to take one more day over the journey gives you a very easy time of it. Better, then, to hurry over the start than when you're already on the road.'

6   When someone else said that he was worn out after a long journey, Socrates asked him if he had been carrying a load.

'Oh, good heavens, no,' he said, 'only my coat.'

'Were you alone on this journey,' asked Socrates, 'or did you have an attendant with you?'

'I did,' he said.

'And this attendant—was he empty-handed or carrying something?'

'Well of course,' he said, 'he was carrying my bedding and all the other gear.'

'And in what shape was he after this journey?'

'I would say in better shape than me!' he said.

'Oh yes?', said Socrates. 'And how do you think you would have managed, if you had to carry his load?'

'Badly, for sure,' he said: 'or rather I wouldn't even have been able to do it.'

'So how do you think it appropriate for a fit adult to be so much less capable of hard work than a boy slave?'

WHENEVER there was a meeting of a dining club* to which some **14** members brought larger quantities of their own prepared food than others, Socrates would tell the attendant slave to pool the smaller contributions, or else share them out equally among all the diners. So those who had brought the larger quantities could not decently take their share of the pooled food* without putting their own food into the pool in return—and so they pooled their own food too. And since that meant that they got no more than those who brought little to the party, they gave up spending a lot of money on food.

On one occasion he noticed that one of the company at dinner had *2* abandoned the bread and was eating the cooked dishes* unaccompanied. The talk at table happened to be about names—what name was appropriate for any given activity. 'Gentlemen,' said Socrates, 'are we able to say for what sort of activity the term "guzzler"* is applied to someone? All of us, I presume, eat some cooked dish with our bread when it is on offer, but I don't think this is yet sufficient reason to call us "guzzlers".'

'Of course not,' said one of the company.

'Well then,' said Socrates, 'what if someone eats just the dishes *3* without any bread, and this is not some training regime but pure self-gratification? Would you regard him as a "guzzler"—or not?'

'It's hard to think of anyone more of a guzzler than that,' he said.

Here another of the company said, 'And what of someone who takes just a little bread with a large helping from the dishes?'

'In my view,' said Socrates, 'he too deserves to be called a guzzler. And probably when everyone else is praying to the gods for a plentiful harvest, he will be praying for a plentiful kitchen!'

The young man in question realized that what Socrates had been *4* saying was aimed at him: he did not stop eating the dishes, but now took some bread with them too. Socrates noticed this, and said, 'If you're sitting next to this one, keep an eye on him to see whether he'll be using the bread to help with the dish or the dish to help with the bread!'

5   On another occasion he saw one of his fellow diners tasting several of the prepared dishes* all together on just the one piece of bread. 'Could there be any cuisine more extravagant,' he asked, 'or more ruinous to the individual dishes, than that adopted by someone who eats a combination of several dishes at once, and puts a whole variety of sauces into his mouth at one go? By mixing together more ingredients than the cooks would do he pushes up the cost: and he is combining flavours which the cooks do not combine—because they don't go

6 well together—and so destroying the cooks' art. And yet how ridiculous can it be for someone to engage the most highly skilled cooks, and then, without the slightest claim to any personal knowledge of the art of cookery, to interfere with what they produce for him? And there is a further consequence for anyone in the habit of eating a variety of dishes all mixed together. If that variety is not provided, he could miss his usual indulgence and feel cheated: whereas someone accustomed to dipping his bread into the dishes one at a time can be quite happy with just a single dish when a variety is not on offer.'

7   He used to say too that 'having good cheer' was a local Athenian expression for 'eating'. The 'good' in that phrase, he claimed, implied the eating of only those foods which would do no harm to body or soul, and were not difficult to come by. So 'good cheer' was one more benefit which he attributed to the life of moderation.

BOOK 4

SOCRATES conferred such benefit in all matters and in every way that 1
any observer taking a balanced view can plainly see that nothing was
more beneficial than associating with Socrates and spending time
with him, no matter where or in what context. The very memory of
him* when he was gone brought no small benefit to those who were
his familiar associates and followed his teaching. And any who spent
time with him had no less to gain from his playful talk* than when he
was in earnest.

He would often say that he was in love* with someone, but it was 2
obvious that the objects of his affection were not those naturally
endowed with a body well formed for youthful beauty, but rather
those endowed with a soul well formed for the practice of virtue.
And he recognized this natural quality* in people by their alacrity
to learn whatever they studied, their ability to remember whatever
they had learnt, and their desire to be taught every lesson which
makes for the good management of household or city, and generally
for proper conduct towards other people and in all human affairs. He
thought that with education those of this quality would not only be
happy in themselves and manage their own households well, but also
had the capacity to bring happiness to other people, and to whole
cities too.

But he did not approach everyone in the same way. To those who 3
thought that nature had already given them good qualities, and any
further instruction was beneath them, he would explain that what are
regarded as the best natural talents are precisely those most in need of
education. He illustrated this by analogy with thoroughbred horses,
spirited and mettlesome creatures which develop to their full value
and quality if they are broken in as colts, but if left unbroken prove
completely unmanageable and valueless. And the same with pedigree
dogs:* those which are well trained prove their great worth as first-
class hunters, but untrained dogs turn out useless, skittish, and
utterly disobedient. So it is, he said, with the best breed of men,* 4
those with the greatest strength of soul and determination to achieve
whatever they set their hand to. If educated and taught where

their duty lies, they develop into people of the highest quality and value—they do a great deal of very great good. But if left uneducated and ignorant, they turn out the worst and most harmful of all: not knowing how to decide where their duty lies they often turn to immoral activities, and their self-importance and headstrong nature makes them hard to control and hard to discourage. And so *they* do a great deal of very great harm.

5   With those who prided themselves on their wealth and thought they had no further call for education, reckoning that wealth was all they would need to achieve anything they wanted and win general respect, he tried to put sense into their heads by arguing like this. 'Only a fool', he would say, 'would think it possible to distinguish between what is beneficial and what is harmful without previous instruction; and without the ability to make that distinction, only a fool thinks that by using his wealth to get all he wants he will be able to act in his own interest. Anyone without the ability to act in his own interest is stupid to think that he is doing well and has set himself up nicely or adequately for life; stupid too to think that when he knows nothing his wealth will make it appear that he has some talent, or that he will be well respected when there is no evidence of any talent at all.'

2 I SHALL now describe his way of dealing with those who thought they had received the best education, and prided themselves on their acquired knowledge. He had been told that Euthydemus (the handsome one)* had made a large collection of the writings* of the most celebrated poets and professors, and was now thinking that this made him better informed than others of his age, with high hopes of surpassing them all as a capable public speaker and politician. First of all, then, aware that Euthydemus was still too young to venture into the marketplace,* and conducted any business he had in mind from his perch in a saddler's shop* near the marketplace, Socrates went there himself with some of his companions.

2   At this first stage someone raised a question about Themistocles*— was it by constant attendance on one of the wise men of the time, or through natural ability, that he became so pre-eminent among his fellow citizens that the city always looked to him when it needed the service of a man of serious worth? Socrates wanted to provoke a reaction from Euthydemus, so he replied that it was silly to think that while the minor arts could not be developed to any serious degree

without competent teachers, political leadership, the most important accomplishment of all, just comes to men ready made.

Then on another occasion when Euthydemus was present, Socrates 3 noticed that he was holding back from the circle, and taking care not to let it seem that he admired Socrates for his wisdom. 'Gentlemen,' he said, 'it's clear from his habits that when he comes of age our friend Euthydemus here will not be reluctant to offer his advice when something comes up for debate in the assembly. I imagine that he has already prepared an elegant preamble* to the speeches he will give, designed to dispel any impression that he owes any of his knowledge to anyone else. No doubt when he begins to speak he will preface his remarks like this: "Men of Athens, I have never learnt anything from 4 anyone. When told of people who are competent in speech and action I have made no attempt to meet them. I have not taken the trouble to find any expert to give me instruction. In fact quite the contrary: I have resolutely avoided taking any lesson from anyone, or even the appearance of it. Nevertheless, I shall now give you as my advice whatever comes unbidden into my head."

'Such a preamble could be adapted for candidates seeking appoint- 5 ment as public physicians.* They would do well to begin their presentations like this: "Men of Athens, I have never studied medicine under anyone, and I have never tried to find a doctor to teach me. I have resolutely been careful to avoid learning anything from doctors, or even the appearance of having learnt the art. Nevertheless, please appoint me to this medical position: I shall do my best to learn on the job by experimenting on you."'

Everyone present laughed at this mock preamble.

When it became apparent that Euthydemus was now paying atten- 6 tion to what Socrates was saying, but was still careful not to say a word himself, in the evident belief that silence invested him with the semblance of restraint, Socrates now determined to put a stop to this behaviour. 'Here's a strange thing,' he said. 'People who want to become competent at playing the lyre or the pipes, or at horsemanship or anything else like that, try to practise whatever it is they want to master as constantly as they can, and not just by themselves but under the instruction* of the best acknowledged experts: they will do anything and submit to anything to make sure that they never deviate from their teachers' guidance, as that is the only way to achieve any serious proficiency. So why on earth do some of those who want to

become capable public speakers and politicians think they will auto-
matically acquire this capability straight off, without any preparation

7 or application? And yet the measure of how much harder it is to master these skills than those others lies in the fact that many more dabble
in politics and many fewer succeed. Clearly, then, those who harbour
this sort of ambition need to apply themselves for longer, and more
intensely, than aspiring practitioners of the other arts.'

8   At first, then, Euthydemus turned a deaf ear as Socrates kept up
this line of talk. But when Socrates sensed that Euthydemus was
showing a readier acceptance of what he had to say, and giving
him a more attentive hearing, he went alone to the saddler's shop.
When Euthydemus sat down next to him, Socrates said, 'Tell me,
Euthydemus, is it true, as I am told, that you have a large collection of
works by the reputed wise men of the past?'

      'Yes, by Zeus, I certainly do!' said Euthydemus. 'And I'm still
adding to the collection, until it's as complete as I can make it.'

9   'Well, by Hera,'* said Socrates, 'I do admire you for choosing
to build up a treasury of wisdom rather than silver and gold!
Obviously you think that silver and gold do nothing to make people
better, but the thoughts of the wise enrich their possessors with
good qualities.'

      Euthydemus was delighted to hear this, believing it meant that
10 Socrates thought he was taking the right road to wisdom. And now
Socrates, realizing that he was feeling pleased with this commendation, went on to say, 'And what exactly is it, Euthydemus, that you
want your collection of books to make you good at?'

      When Euthydemus fell silent, wondering what answer to give,
Socrates pressed on. 'Perhaps you want to be a doctor?' he said.
'Doctors too have written many treatises.'

      'Oh no,' said Euthydemus, 'certainly not that.'

      'Well, perhaps an architect then? This is another profession that
requires a precise mind.'

      'No, that's not for me,' he said.

      'Well, perhaps you're keen to become good at geometry,* like
Theodorus?'*

      'Not that either,' he said.

      'Well, perhaps you want to become an astronomer?'*

      And as he once again said no, 'A rhapsode,* then?' said Socrates.
'They say that you possess the complete poems of Homer.'

'Good heavens, no,' he said. 'What I know of these rhapsodes is that they may have the lines off by heart, but they have precious little intelligence of their own.'

So then Socrates said, 'Don't tell me, Euthydemus, that the quality *11* you are after is that which makes good politicians and good managers, men capable of exercising command and bringing benefit to people in general as well as themselves?'

'Yes, Socrates,' said Euthydemus, 'that is the quality I am very keen to acquire.'

'Well I do declare', said Socrates, 'that you have set yourself at the finest of all qualities and the most important skill there is! This is the skill of kings, and we call it "the royal art".* But tell me,' he went on, 'have you considered whether it is possible to become good at this sort of thing without also being just?'

'I have indeed,' he said, 'and I consider that it's not possible to be a good citizen either without justice.'

'All right,' said Socrates, 'and have you yourself achieved that *12* qualification?'

'I think, Socrates,' he said, 'that I can be shown to be as just as any other man.'

'So then,' said Socrates, 'do just people produce things* in the same way that carpenters have their products?'

'Yes, they do,' he said.

'So just as carpenters can point to their own products, can just people likewise give an account of theirs?'

'You're not suggesting, are you,' said Euthydemus, 'that I can't describe the products of justice? I most certainly can, and the products of injustice too—there are enough of those that we can see and hear about every day!'

'Would you agree, then,' said Socrates, 'that we should write down *13* a J on this side here, and an I on that side there, and then list* under the J whatever we think is a product of justice, and under the I whatever we think is a product of injustice?'

'Go ahead,' he said, 'if you think there's any need for that.'

Socrates wrote down the letters as he had proposed, and then said, *14* 'Right then: is lying something that happens in the world?'

'It is,' he said.

'So on which side should I put that?'

'Clearly under the heading of Injustice,' he said.

'And deception happens too, does it not?'

'Certainly,' he said.

'So where should I put that?'

'Clearly under Injustice again,' he said.

'What about theft?'

'That too,' he said.

'And enslavement?'

'That too.'

'So, Euthydemus, we won't have any of these listed under Justice?'

'No, that would be monstrous,' he said.

15　'Well then, suppose that someone who has been elected general captures an unjust and hostile city and enslaves its people, will we say that he is acting unjustly?'

'Certainly not,' he said.

'Will we not say that he is acting justly?'

'Very much so.'

'And what if he practises deception* on the enemy when he is at war?'

'That too is just,' he said.

'And if he steals and plunders their goods, will he not be acting justly?'

'Yes indeed,' he said, 'but at first I took your questions to have reference only to friends.'

'So everything we have listed under Injustice should also be listed under Justice?'

'It would seem so,' he said.

16　'So now that we have done that, do you agree that we should make a further distinction, namely that such behaviour towards enemies is just, but unjust towards friends, and that we should treat our friends with complete honesty?'

'Agreed, certainly,' said Euthydemus.

17　'Well now,' said Socrates, 'suppose that a general, aware of low morale in his army, falsely tells the men that reinforcements are on the way, and by that falsehood restores their morale—under which heading shall we place this deception?'

'Under Justice, I think,' he said.

'And suppose that someone's son refuses to take the medicine* which he needs, and the father manages to administer it by pretending that it is food, and makes his son well by means of this trick—where again should we put this deception?'

'This too in the same category, I think,' he said.

'All right,' said Socrates, 'and what if someone is afraid that a friend suffering from depression might do away with himself, and steals or removes any sword or other lethal weapon* available to his friend—under which heading again should we put this action?'

'This too belongs under Justice, no doubt at all,' he said.

'You're saying, then,' said Socrates, 'that we shouldn't always be *18* straightforward even with our friends?'

'No, we shouldn't—that's for sure,' he said. 'And with your permission I retract what I said earlier.'

'Permission granted!' said Socrates. 'That's much better than getting our lists wrong. But to leave nothing unexamined we should also *19* consider those cases where practising deception on friends causes them harm—which sort of harmful deception is the more unjust, the deliberate or the unintentional?'

'Oh dear, Socrates, I've now lost all confidence in my answers! All those previous questions now look different from what I first thought. Still, let me have a go: I would say that in those cases the deliberate harm is more unjust than the unintentional.'

'Do you think that justice can be taught* and learnt like reading *20* and writing?'

'Yes, I do.'

'Which would you judge the more literate, the man who deliberately makes mistakes in his writing or reading, or the one who can't help it?'

'The deliberate one, in my view: he could always get it right when he wants to.'

'So the man who deliberately makes mistakes in writing would be literate, and the one who can't help it would be illiterate?'

'Yes, of course.'

'And which of these knows what is just—the man who deliberately lies and deceives, or the one who does so unintentionally?'*

'Clearly the deliberate one.'

'So then you're saying that the man who knows his letters is more literate than the one who doesn't?'

'Yes.'

'And the man who knows what is just is more just than the one who doesn't?'

'That appears to be what I'm saying—but here again I'm conscious of rather flailing about.'

21   'Well now, what would you think of someone who wants to tell the truth, but is never consistent in what he says—asked to give directions, he sometimes describes the same road as going east, and sometimes west, and when adding up the same numbers makes the total figure now more, now less?'

'Pretty clearly, he doesn't know what he thought he knew.'

22   'You know that some people are called slavish?'*

'Yes.'

'Is that because of their wisdom, or their ignorance?'

'Because of their ignorance, obviously.'

'So is it ignorance of metalwork which earns them that description?'

'Certainly not.'

'Well, ignorance of carpentry, perhaps?'

'Not that either.'

'Of cobbling, then?'

'No, none of these. In fact quite the contrary: it is those with knowledge of trades like that who are for the most part slavish.'

'So does this description apply to those who are ignorant of what has the quality of being fine and good and just?'

'I think so,' he said.

23   'It follows, then, that we must exert every effort to avoid the condition of slaves.'

'Oh, good heavens, Socrates,' he said. 'I was confident that I was following a programme of study which, so I thought, would educate me in all that is appropriate for someone hoping for recognition as a man of that quality. But now imagine my despair when I realize that I can't even answer questions about the most important knowledge I should have, and there is no other route I could follow to self-improvement.'

24   Here Socrates said, 'Tell me, Euthydemus, have you ever been to Delphi?'

'Oh yes, twice,' he said.

'So did you notice somewhere on the temple that inscription "Know yourself"?'*

'I did.'

'And did you pay no attention to the inscription—or did you take it to heart and embark on some self-examination to discover who you are?'

'No, I did not!' he said. 'That at least was something I thought I did already know well. I could hardly have known anything else if I didn't even know myself!'

'And who would you say knows himself? The man who simply 25 knows his own name, or the man who takes the same approach as people who buy horses?* They don't think that they know an animal in which they are interested until they have examined whether it is obedient or stubborn, strong or weak, fast or slow, and generally how it suits or does not suit the function* they look for in a horse. In the same way the man who examines how he himself functions as a human being comes to know his own capability.'

'Put that way,' he said, 'it seems to me that the man who does not know his own capability is ignorant of himself.'

'And isn't it clear too,' said Socrates, 'that most of the good things 26 in people's experience are the result of self-knowledge, and most of the bad things the result of self-deception?* People who know themselves know what is right for them, and can tell what they can do and what they can't. By doing what they know they can do they supply all their needs and lead a successful life: and by staying clear of what they don't know, they keep themselves free from error and escape failure. Self-knowledge gives them the ability to appraise other people too, and so they can make use of others to help them in the procurement of what is to their good and the avoidance of what would be to their harm. Those who don't know themselves and have a mistaken view of 27 their own capabilities are in that same state of ignorance about other people and human affairs in general: they do not know what they need, or what they are doing, or who they are dealing with, and this compound error deprives them of anything good and sends them headlong into bad trouble.

'And people who know what they are doing gain admiration and 28 respect when they achieve what they set out to do. People of the same type are glad to associate with them, and those who are unsuccessful in their affairs are eager for the advice they can give, take them as their models, rest their hopes on them for good things to come, and for all these reasons hold them in the highest regard. But those who don't 29 know what they are doing make bad choices and fail in anything they attempt: as well as the loss or punishment directly resulting from what they have done, their failures ruin their reputation, make laughing-stocks of them, and leave them to a life of contempt and dishonour.

'And you can see the same with cities. Any city which goes to war against a more powerful enemy without knowing its own capability* is either devastated or forced to exchange freedom for slavery.'

30 Euthydemus now said, 'I can assure you, Socrates, that I fully realize how very important it is to know oneself. But where to begin the process of self-examination? Here I look to you for guidance, if that's all right with you.'

31 'Well,' said Socrates, 'I presume that you are perfectly well aware of what things are good and what are bad.'

'Of course I am,' he said. 'If I don't know even that, I would be more worthless than a slave!'

'Come on then, list them for me.'

'That's easy enough,' he said. 'I think, first of all, that health is an absolute good, and sickness is bad. And then the factors which result in either condition, such as drink and food and habits, are good when they lead to health and bad when they lead to sickness.'

32 'So then,' said Socrates, 'both health and sickness would be good when they result in something good, and bad when they result in something bad?'

'But when could health possibly result in something bad, or sickness in something good?'

'I'll tell you,' said Socrates. 'When in a bungled campaign or a doomed voyage, or many other such cases, those who are able-bodied enough to take part are lost, but the infirm are left behind and saved.'

'True,' he said, 'but, you see, the same applies to profitable ventures too—the able-bodied get to take part, and the infirm are excluded.'

'So then,' said Socrates, 'when things are sometimes profitable and sometimes harmful, are they any more good than bad?'

33 'Apparently not, dash it, at least on this argument! But take wisdom, Socrates—that at any rate is indisputably a good thing. Is there any circumstance in which a wise man would not be better off than a fool?'

'What? Haven't you heard of Daedalus,'* said Socrates, 'how he was captured by Minos* because of his wisdom and forced to be his slave, so he was robbed of both his country and his freedom? And how when he tried to escape with his son he lost the boy and couldn't save himself, but was carried off to a barbarian land and became a slave again there?'

'That is certainly the story,' he said.

'And haven't you heard of the fate of Palamedes? All the poets tell of how Odysseus* resented his cleverness and did away with him.'

'That too is the story,' he said.

'And how many others do you think have been dragged off to the Great King's court* because of their skills, to live there as his slaves?'

'It looks, Socrates, as if the most unambiguous good will be happiness,'* he said.   *34*

'That could be, Euthydemus, as long as people don't take ambiguous goods* as its constituent elements.'

'But what could be ambiguous about the elements that make for happiness?'

'Nothing,' said Socrates, 'as long as we won't include beauty or strength or wealth or fame or anything else like that.'

'But surely we'll include them!' he said. 'How could anyone be happy without them?'

'Then no less surely,' said Socrates, 'we'll be including the sources   *35* of much consequent human misery. Because of their beauty many are corrupted by men who are excited by pretty boys;* because of their strength many attempt feats beyond their ability and come to serious harm; because of their wealth many meet their end through their own excesses or schemes laid by others; and for many their fame and political power has been the cause of great suffering in their downfall.'

'Well really,' he said, 'if I can't get it right even when speaking up   *36* for happiness, I have to admit that I don't have any idea either what we should be asking the gods for in our prayers!'

'Well,' said Socrates, 'perhaps you were so confident that you knew the answer that you didn't even consider the question! But here's another question: since you are preparing yourself to lead a city under a democratic government, clearly you know what democracy is?'

'Absolutely, of course,' he said.

'Then do you think it is possible to know what democracy is with-   *37* out knowing what is meant by "the people"?'*

'I would say certainly not.'

'And do you know what is meant by "the people"?'

'I think I do.'

'And what do you think "the people" means?'

'I would say the poorer class of citizens.'

'You know the poor, then?'

'Of course.'

'Then do you know the rich* also?"

'Yes, just as well as the poor.'

'What sort of people do you call poor, and what sort rich?'

'I think I would call poor those who don't have enough to pay for their needs, and rich those who have more than enough.'

38   'But then have you noticed that some who have very little not only make do with that, but even manage to save something out of it, whereas some who have a great deal find themselves short?'

'Yes, indeed I have,' said Euthydemus, 'and thank you for reminding me of that. In fact there are even some tyrants* I know of who are driven to crime by lack of money, just like the most destitute.'

39   'Well then,' said Socrates, 'if that is so, we shall class the tyrants among "the people", and those of small means, if they husband them well, among the rich.'

And now Euthydemus said, 'I'm forced to agree once more, clearly because of my own inadequacy. I'm thinking it would be better for me to keep my mouth shut: it looks as if I simply know nothing at all.' And he went away profoundly depressed, kicking himself, and convinced that he was indeed a slave.*

40   Now many of those brought to this state by Socrates broke off all further contact with him, which made him think them yet more stupid. But Euthydemus appreciated that the only way he could become someone to be reckoned with was to spend as much time as he could in Socrates' company. So from then on he was never away from him, unless there was some pressing need, and he even began to adopt some of his practical habits. And when Socrates saw this new frame of mind in Euthydemus, he stopped reducing him to confusion* and began to explain in the simplest and clearest terms what he thought Euthydemus should know and what was the best practice for him to follow.

3   For Socrates the priority was not that his associates should become good speakers or capable men of affairs or subtle operators, but before any of that he thought that their first need was to have moderation* instilled in them. It was his view that people with those abilities who lacked moderation were more likely to act unjustly and more capable of doing harm.

2   In the first place, then, he tried to make his associates think seriously about the gods.* Others who were present on other occasions

when Socrates discoursed on this subject have given their own accounts:* but I myself was there* when Socrates had this following conversation with Euthydemus.

'Tell me, Euthydemus,' he said, 'has it ever occurred to you to 3 reflect on the care* the gods have taken to provide for the needs of human beings?'

'Actually, I can't say that it has,' he said.

'Well at least you must know that our first need is for light,* and the gods provide it for us?'

'Of course,' he said. 'If we didn't have light we might as well be blind, for all the use our eyes would be to us.'

'And then again we need rest, and the gods give us night as the perfect time for rest.'

'Yes, indeed,' he said, 'and we should be grateful for that too.'

'And since the sun is bright and gives us a clear view of the time of 4 day as well as everything else, but in its darkness night obscures that view, have the gods not made stars to shine in the night to mark the hours of night and so allow us to continue much of what we need to do?'

'Yes, that's so,' he said.

'And then again the moon* displays to us not only the divisions of the night but those of the month too.'

'Yes, indeed,' he said.

'And think of this too, that, since we need food,* the gods make the 5 earth produce it for us, arranging seasons appropriate for its production: and these seasons supply us with a whole variety of produce not only to meet our needs but to give us enjoyment also.'

'That too', he said, 'is a great kindness to humanity.'*

'And then there's the provision of water, such an invaluable 6 resource. It helps the earth and the seasons to germinate and grow everything useful for us, it plays its part in our own nourishment, and its combination with all that feeds us makes that food more digestible, more beneficial, and more agreeable. And since we need so much of it, the gods provide it for us in the greatest abundance.'

'That too shows their providence,' he said.

'And then there's the gift of fire,* as our defence against cold and 7 darkness, and our assistant in every craft and all that men produce for their benefit. In fact, to put it shortly, there is nothing of any significance for life which men can produce without the aid of fire.'

'This too', he said, ' is an outstanding kindness to humanity.'

8   'And then think of the sun, how after the winter solstice it approaches again, ripening some crops and withering others whose season is over; and when it has done that task it doesn't come closer still, but turns back, careful not to harm us with excessive heat; and then again when it reaches the point in this retreat where even we can see that any further distance would have us frozen with cold, it turns once more and comes nearer again, to take its course at just the right height in the sky to give us most benefit.'

      'Yes, indeed,' he said, 'all this looks very much like something created for the sake of mankind.'

9   'And then, since it's equally clear that we couldn't endure either the heat or the cold if they came on suddenly, think how the sun approaches and recedes so gradually that we hardly notice the progression from one extreme to the other.'

      'For my part,' said Euthydemus, 'I'm beginning to wonder whether in fact the gods have any other function besides being of service to mankind! My only difficulty is that the other living creatures* also enjoy these benefits.'

10   'Yes,' said Socrates, 'because isn't it clear too that these other animals are created and sustained for the sake of mankind? What other creature makes such good use of goats, sheep, cattle, horses, donkeys, and all the other animals as man does? In fact I would say that they are of greater use to us than crops. At any rate animals are used for food and commerce at least as much as crops. And there are many peoples who don't use what grows in the earth as their food, but subsist on the milk, cheese, and meat from their herds. And all people tame and domesticate those animals which are suitable for assisting them in war and for many other purposes.'

      'Here again I agree with you,' he said, 'seeing that even those animals which are much stronger than us become so amenable to human control that people can put them to whatever use they want.'

11   'And then think how, with so many beautiful and beneficial things of different kinds in the world, the gods have endowed men with senses* which answer to this variety and enable us to enjoy all these good things. And then how they have implanted in us the faculty of reason, by which we think about and remember what we have perceived through our senses, so coming to know where our advantage lies in each case, and inventing many means to enjoy the good and pro-

12   tect ourselves against the bad. And then think of their gift of verbal

expression, by means of which we pool information about all that is good, share it in the community, establish laws, and form governments.'

'It does seem, Socrates, that the gods take great care of mankind in every way.'

'And then, if we are incapable of foreseeing what will be to our benefit in the future, think how they assist us through divination, by revealing to enquirers what will come to pass, and telling them how to ensure the best outcome.'

'And they seem to be even more friendly to you,* Socrates, than to the rest of us, if without you even asking them they send you signs indicating in advance what you should or shouldn't do.'

'You too will come to realize for yourself the truth of what I am 13 saying, if rather than waiting to see the gods in physical shape you are content to worship and honour them on the evidence before your eyes of what they do for us. And notice that the gods themselves prompt this way of thinking. No gods ever appear in plain sight when giving us any of the good things they have in their gift, and this is especially so of the god who arranges and holds together the entire universe, in which all things are beautiful and good, and he provides them for our use ever fresh, untainted, and ageless, and unfailingly at our service even faster than thought. We can see the huge scale of his working, but as he organizes it all he himself is invisible to us.

'Note too that the sun, which we think of as entirely visible, does 14 not allow people to look at it directly, but anyone brazenly attempting a direct look is blinded. And you'll find that the agents serving the gods are invisible too. For example, it's clear enough that the thunderbolt is hurled from above and overwhelms everything where it lands, but we cannot see it as it comes, strikes, and leaves. And the winds are themselves invisible, but their effects are clear to us, and we can feel them coming. And then there is the human soul as well—if anything human partakes of divinity, it is the soul: it manifestly reigns within us, and yet it cannot be seen either.

'With all this in mind you should not belittle the things we cannot see, but understand the power they have from their resulting effects, and pay due honour to the divine.'

'For myself, Socrates,' said Euthydemus, 'I am quite clear in my 15 mind that I shall not for one minute ignore the divine. But what troubles me is the thought that no human being at all can return adequate thanks for the gods' benefactions.'

16   'No, don't let that trouble you, Euthydemus,' said Socrates. 'You
      must know that whenever someone asks the god at Delphi how he
      could gratify the gods, the response is "by following the customary
      practice of your city", and I imagine it is the custom everywhere to
      propitiate the gods with sacrificial offerings according to one's means.
      How then could one pay better and more reverent honour to the gods
17   than by doing what they themselves direct? But it is important not to
      be sparing of one's means: when anyone holds back like that, it is
      surely evident that he is not honouring the gods. So if one honours
      the gods to the full extent of one's means, one should be confident
      and hope for the greatest blessings, because anyone in his right mind
      would not hope for greater benefits from any other source than from
      those who have it in their power to do us the greatest good, or by any
      better means than by pleasing them. And how better to please them
      than by showing them the greatest possible obedience?'
18   So by talking to his associates like this, and practising himself what
      he told them, he sought to make them more reverent towards the gods
      and more serious in their thinking.

4   AND then on the subject of justice* he didn't keep his thinking to
     himself, but made it clear by his actions too. In his private life he was
     law-abiding and helpful to all, and in public life he obeyed the author-
     ities in all that the laws required of him, both at home and on military
     service, so scrupulously that he became known for his exceptional
2   discipline.* In particular, on the occasion when he was president of
     the assembly he would not let the people hold an illegal vote, but took
     his stand with the laws against such strong popular pressure that
3   I doubt any other man would have been able to resist it. And when the
     Thirty gave him illegal orders he refused to obey them. This was so
     when they tried to debar him from holding conversations with the
     young men; and when they ordered him and some other citizens to
     arrest a man* on a capital charge, he was the only one to refuse, on the
4   grounds that their order was illegal. And so again at his trial on the
     charge brought by Meletus.* Other defendants in the courts would
     commonly curry favour in their addresses to the jury, and resort to
     flattery and illegal appeals, and many had often secured the jury's
     acquittal by such means, but Socrates refused to employ any of these
     familiar but illegal courtroom gambits: he chose to abide by the law
     and die rather than break the law and live.

Among the many other occasions on which he expressed such 5
views, I know of one in particular when he had a conversation about
justice with Hippias of Elis.* It went like this. Hippias had arrived in
Athens for the first time after a long while, and came across Socrates
when he was talking to a group of people. Socrates was saying that if
you want to have someone taught to be a cobbler or a carpenter or
a metalworker or a horseman, it was easy enough to find where you
could send him for that purpose—and he had heard it said that even
if you wanted to get a horse or an ox to behave as it should, potential
trainers were thick on the ground. How strange, then, that anyone
wanting to learn justice for himself, or have it taught to his son or
household slave, should not know where to turn for that purpose.

When he heard this, Hippias said in a joshing way, 'Still talking 6
the same old stuff,* then, Socrates, that I heard from you all that
time ago?'

And Socrates said, 'Yes, Hippias, not only the same old stuff,
but—worse still—on the same old subjects too! But I imagine that
you, with all that wide learning of yours, don't ever say the same
things on the same subjects.'

'Well yes,' he said, 'I do try to say something new* every time.'

'Does that also apply to things that you know for sure?' asked 7
Socrates. 'For example, spelling: if someone asks you how many letters there are in the name "Socrates", and how it is spelt, do you try
to give a different answer now than you did previously? Or take numbers: if people ask you if twice five is ten, don't you answer now in the
same way you did before?'

'In those contexts, Socrates,' he said, 'I always say the same, just as
you do. But on the subject of justice, I'm quite confident that I now
have something to say which neither you nor anyone else could
contradict.'

'By Hera,' said Socrates, 'that means that you have made a hugely 8
beneficial discovery, if juries will now stop disagreeing about their
verdicts, citizens will stop arguing, going to court, and creating dissension over their rights, and cities will stop making claims and coun-
terclaims and going to war. Speaking for myself, I don't see how
I could tear myself away from you before hearing all about something
of such great benefit from the man who discovered it!'

'Oh no,' he said, 'you won't hear about it until you reveal your own 9
thought* on the definition of justice. You are content to ridicule

everyone else with your questions and refutations, but are never prepared to submit your own account or let anyone know what you think
about anything.'

10   'What, Hippias?' said Socrates. 'Haven't you noticed that I never
stop demonstrating my own view of what justice is?'

'And what form does this account of yours take?'

'Not so much a verbal definition,' he said, 'but rather a practical
demonstration in my own conduct. Or don't you think that actions
are more reliable evidence than words?'

'Oh yes, very much so,' he said. 'Many people profess justice and
act unjustly, but no one who acts justly can be unjust.'

11   'So have you ever known me bear false witness or bring vexatious
lawsuits or create dissension among my friends or the public, or commit any other unjust act?'

'No, I haven't,' he said.

'And don't you think that refraining from anything unjust amounts
to justice?'

'Socrates,' he said, 'you are clearly still trying to avoid expressing
any opinion on how you would define justice. You're not talking about
what just people do, but what they don't do.'

12   'Well, I had thought that refusal to act unjustly was sufficient evidence of justice,' said Socrates. 'But if you don't agree, see whether
this is more to your liking. I say that whatever is lawful is just.'

'Are you saying, Socrates, that "lawful" and "just" are the same?'*

13   'I am indeed.'

'I ask because I don't have a sense of what you mean by "lawful" or
what you mean by "just".'

'You accept that cities have laws?'

'I do.'

'And what do you think they are?'

'Prescriptions agreed and enacted by the citizen body setting out
what should be done and what should not be done.'

'So any citizen living his life in accordance with these prescriptions
would be acting lawfully, and anyone contravening them would be
acting unlawfully?'

'Certainly,' he said.

'And so anyone obeying these prescriptions would be acting justly,
and anyone disobeying them would be acting unjustly?'

'Certainly.'

'Wouldn't then the man who acts justly be just, and the man who acts unjustly be unjust?'

'Of course.'

'It follows then that lawful is just, and unlawful is unjust.'

Here Hippias said, 'Laws, Socrates, or conformity with them, can *14* hardly be thought a big deal when the very people who passed the laws often repeal them* and put new laws in their place.'

'Yes,' said Socrates, 'and cities which have gone to war often make peace again.'

'Very true,' he said.

'So do you think there is any difference between your belittling of those who obey the laws, on the grounds that the laws might be repealed, and finding fault with those who observe good discipline in times of war, on the grounds that peace might be made? Or do you actually blame those who readily support their countries in times of war?'

'No, of course I don't,' he said.   *15*

'And take the Spartan Lycurgus,'* Socrates continued. 'Have you noted that he would not have made Sparta any superior to any other city if he had not entrenched there complete obedience to the laws? And don't you know that in general the best city authorities are those who are most successful in ensuring obedience to the laws from their citizens, and that a city in which the people are most obedient to the laws has the best life in peace and cannot be resisted in war?

'Then again unity* is thought the greatest good in a city, and in *16* city after city their councils of elders and their most distinguished men are constantly impressing on their citizens the need for unity. Throughout Greece it is an established law that citizens must take an oath* to maintain unity, and everywhere they do swear this oath. I take it that the purpose of this is not to have the citizens agreeing on the same choruses to get their vote, the same pipe-players to cele-brate, the same poets to prefer, or the same pleasures to enjoy, but to ensure their obedience to the laws. Because the cities whose people abide by the laws prove the strongest and the most prosperous. Without unity there can be no good government of a city or good management of a household.

'And as for the individual,* what better way for him to reduce the *17* risk of penalty and increase the likelihood of honour from his city than by obeying the laws? How else could he be less exposed to defeat in the courts and more assured of victory? Who else would inspire more confidence as trustee for one's property or sons or daughters? Who else would the entire city think more trustworthy than the law-abiding citizen? Who else would be more likely to do right by parents, relations, household slaves, friends, fellow citizens, and foreigners? Who would be more trusted by enemies when it comes to a truce or a treaty or terms of peace? To whom would others more readily ally themselves than to the man who abides by the laws? And to whom would those allies be more likely to entrust leadership of the alliance, or command of a garrison, or the safety of their cities? From whom would anyone more confidently expect gratitude for a favour conferred* than from the law-abiding man? Or on whom would anyone more readily confer a favour than on someone he has reason to think will make him a grateful return? What other sort of person would one want most as a friend or least as an enemy? And on whom would anyone be less likely to make war than on the man whom he himself most wants as a friend and least as an enemy, and who has the largest number of others wanting to be his friends and allies, and the fewest who would want to be enemies or at war with him?

18   'So for my part, Hippias, I do maintain that "lawful" and "just" are the same. But if you take a contrary view, do explain it to me.'

And Hippias said, 'Oh no, Socrates, I don't think my view is at all contrary to what you have said about justice.'

19   'Do you know that there are some "unwritten laws",* Hippias?' asked Socrates.

'Yes,' he said, 'those that are equally observed on the same matters in every country.'

'So could you say that it was men who laid down these laws?'

'How could that be possible,' he said, 'when they couldn't all meet together and don't speak the same language either?'

'So who do think did make these laws?'

'I would say that gods laid down these laws for mankind: after all, the prime observance common to all men is worship of the gods.'*

20   'Isn't a duty of honouring one's parents* universally observed also?'

'Yes, that too,' he said.

'And a prohibition on parents having sex with their children or children with their parents?'

'I wouldn't say, Socrates, that this last is one of the god-given laws.'

'Why so?'

'Because I'm aware that some people break it.'

'And they break a good many other laws too!' said Socrates. 'But my 21 point is that those who break the god-ordained laws pay a penalty which no human being can in any way escape—unlike some transgressors of man-made laws who avoid punishment by escaping detection or using force.'

'And what sort of penalty is it, Socrates, that can't be escaped by 22 parents who have sex with their children* or children with their parents?'

'The very worst, let me tell you,' said Socrates. 'For people producing children what greater calamity could there be than the production of poor specimens?'*

'So why should anything go wrong with the children in such cases, 23 when it's perfectly possible that both the fathers and the mothers involved are good specimens themselves?'

'Because of course it's not enough for the partners in the production of children to be good specimens: they must also be in their physical prime. Or do you think that there is no difference between the sperm* of men in the prime of their life and that of those who have not yet reached their prime or have already gone past it?'

'No,' he said, 'very likely there is a difference.'

'So which is the better sperm?'

'Obviously that of the men in their prime,' he said.

'So it follows that those who are not in their prime do not produce high-quality sperm?'

'Probably they don't,' he said.

'So people in that condition should not procreate children?'

'Evidently not,' he said.

'So people in that condition who do procreate children are doing what they should not?'

'I would say so,' he said.

'Who else then is going to produce poor specimens, if not these people?'

'I'm with you there too,' he said.

'Well now, isn't it the accepted rule everywhere that favours* 24 received should be answered with favours in return?'

'The rule, yes,' he said, 'but this too is broken.'

'And don't those who break this rule too pay a penalty in the increasing loss of good friends and the consequent need to try to recapture people who now dislike them? Or isn't it the case that those who do favours to their associates are good friends to them, but those who don't return favours to these good friends find that friendship turned to dislike because of their ingratitude, and then have to do their utmost to recover an association which was of such great benefit to them?'

'I must say, Socrates,' said Hippias, 'that all this does look like the work of the gods. That these laws carry with them automatic punishments* for transgressors suggests to me a lawgiver of more than human ability.'*

25 'So how do you see the god-given laws, Hippias—are they just, or something other than just?'

'They can't be other than just,' he said. 'There could hardly be justice in any other legislation if god's laws are not just!'

'It follows then, Hippias, that the gods too are content to identify "just" and "lawful".'

It was by this sort of talk, and his own practice in conformity with it, that Socrates sought to instil a greater sense of justice in those who came into contact with him.

5 I SHALL now show how he also sought to make his associates more capable as men of affairs. He believed that self-mastery* was of fundamental benefit to anyone who would go on to some worthwhile achievement, and so first of all he let it be obvious to his associates that he himself had exercised it to a greater extent than any other man, and then in his discussions with them he encouraged them to 2 aim for self-mastery above all else. In fact he was always mindful himself of the factors which contribute to moral virtue,* and constantly put all his associates in mind of them too. I know, for example, that he once had a conversation about self-mastery with Euthydemus, which went like this.

'Tell me, Euthydemus, do you think that freedom* is a fine and splendid thing to possess, for an individual as much as for a city?'*

'Yes, as fine as can be,' he said.

3 'So take someone who is ruled by the pleasures of the body, and because of them is unable to do what is best—do you think that he is free?'*

'Not at all,' he said.

'Perhaps that's because you see doing what is best as the mark of the free man, and so think that having masters who will prevent that* means lack of freedom?'

'Absolutely,' he said.

'So no less absolutely in your opinion those who aren't masters of 4 themselves* have no freedom?'

'Yes, that certainly seems to follow.'

'Do you think that those without self-mastery are simply prevented from doing what is most honourable, or are they actually compelled to do what is most disgraceful?'

'In my view,' he said, 'they are just as much compelled to that course as prevented from the other.'

'And how would you describe masters who prevent what is best and 5 enforce what is worst?'

'The worst possible masters,'* he said, 'without doubt.'

'And what sort of slavery do you think is the worst?'

'I would say slavery under the worst masters,' he said.

'Does it follow, then, that those without self-mastery endure the worst form of slavery?'

'I think it does,' he said.

'And don't you think that lack of self-mastery precludes wisdom, 6 which is the greatest good, and drives people into its opposite? Or do you not think that it prevents them from looking to their own best interests and understanding where they lie, by diverting their attention to what gives them pleasure, and often makes them choose the worse over the better by skewing their perception of good and bad?'

'That does happen,' he said.

'And what of moderation? Can we think of anyone with less claim 7 to it than the man who is not master of himself? Because of course the effects of moderation and lack of self-mastery are the very opposites of each other.'

'I agree with that too,' he said.

'And do you think there is anything more likely to prevent application to one's proper business than lack of self-mastery?'

'No, I don't,' he said.

'And do you think there is anything worse for a man than that which causes him to choose what harms him rather than what does him good, persuades him to pursue the harmful and neglect the beneficial, and forces him to do the opposite of what sensible men of moderation would do?'

'I can think of nothing worse,' he said.

8   'So isn't it probably the case that self-mastery produces in people effects which are the opposite of those caused by its lack?'

'Certainly,' he said.

'So presumably also this cause of the opposite effects is a very good thing?'

'Presumably, yes,' he said.

'So, Euthydemus, doesn't it look as if self-mastery is the best thing a man can have?'

'Yes, it does seem so, Socrates,' he said.

9   'And I wonder if this other thought has ever occurred to you, Euthydemus?'

'What thought?' he said.

'The fact that, although pleasure* is evidently the only goal to which people are driven by their lack of self-mastery, it cannot actually take them there: it is self-mastery above all which gives us the enjoyment of pleasure.'

'How so?' he said.

'The difference is this. Failure to be master of themselves doesn't allow people to resist hunger or thirst or sexual desire or lack of sleep, without which there can be no pleasure in eating or drinking or having sex, and no pleasure either in rest and sleep. It doesn't allow them to wait and hold back until the time when maximum enjoyment of these things is to be had, and so prevents them from taking any appreciable pleasure in the most essential activities of everyday life. But only self-mastery can make us resist the urges I have mentioned, and so it is only self-mastery which gives us any pleasure worth the name in their satisfaction.'

'What you say is absolutely true,' he said.

10   'And then the same is true of learning anything fine and good, and of applying oneself to any of the practices which enable one to maintain one's own body in good shape, manage one's own household well, prove useful to one's friends and city, and get the better of one's enemies—practices which bring not only the greatest advantages but also the greatest pleasures. Those with self-mastery do all this and enjoy the benefits, but those without don't come near any of it. Who could we say has less claim to such things than the man who is least

capable of putting them into effect, consumed as he is by his pursuit of the most immediate pleasures?'

And Euthydemus said, 'I think you are saying, Socrates, that the *11* man who is dominated by the pleasures of the flesh has no claim whatsoever to any sort of virtue.'

'Yes, Euthydemus—because how can a man without self-mastery be any different from the most stupid animal? If someone won't consider the most important questions, but looks for every means of taking the most pleasant option, how does he differ from completely mindless cattle? Only those who are masters of themselves can consider the most important issues in life, use their reason and practical experience to divide them into their categories,* and then choose the good and reject the bad.'

And this, he said, was the discipline which produces the best and *12* happiest men, with the greatest facility for discussion.* The very word 'discussion', he maintained, derives from the notion of people coming together for joint debate on the division of things into their categories. And so, he said, we should try our utmost to get ourselves in shape for self-mastery, and practise it above all else: because this is what produces the best men with the greatest potential for leadership and the greatest dialectical skill.*

I SHALL try now to show how he also sought to make his associates **6** better equipped for dialectical argument.* Socrates held that those who know what any given entity is could also explain it to others, whereas it was hardly surprising that those who don't know both go astray themselves and mislead others. For this reason he never stopped involving his associates in enquiries into the meaning of any given entity.

To go through all his definitions* would be a substantial task, so I shall confine myself to giving a few examples which I think will illustrate his method of enquiry.

First, then, his consideration of piety* went something like this. *2* 'Tell me, Euthydemus,' he said, 'what sort of thing do you think piety is?'

'A very fine thing, for sure,' Euthydemus replied.

'So can you say what sort of person the pious man is?'

'One who honours the gods, it seems to me,' he said.

'Is it open to someone to honour the gods in whatever way he wants?'

'No—there are laws* which regulate how this should be done.'

3   'So anyone knowing these laws would know how he should honour the gods?'

'Yes, I think so,' he said.

'Then someone who knows how he should honour the gods thinks he should not do so in any way other than that which he knows?'

'Obviously not,' he said.

'And does anyone honour the gods in some way other than how he thinks he should?'

4   'I don't think so,' he said.

'So the man who knows what is lawful* concerning the gods will honour the gods lawfully?'

'Absolutely.'

'So the man who honours them lawfully is honouring them as he should?'

'Of course.'

'Yes, and the man who honours them as he should is pious?'

'Certainly,' he said.

'So would we be right to define the pious man as the one who knows what is lawful concerning the gods?'

'Yes,' he said, 'as far as I can see.'

5   'And what about people?* Is it open to someone to treat people in whatever way he wants?'

'No—here too there are laws regulating how we should treat one another.'

'So those who treat other people according to these laws are treating them as they should?'

'Of course.'

'And are those who treat people as they should treating them well?'

'Certainly,' he said.

'And so are those who treat people well conducting their human affairs well?'

'Presumably,' he said.

'Are those who obey the laws doing what is just?'

'Certainly,' he said.

6   'And do you know what sort of things are called just?'

'The things commanded by the laws,' he said.

'So those who do what the laws command are doing both what is just and what they should?'

'Of course.'

'And those who do what is just—are they themselves just?'

'I think so,' he said.

'Do you think, then, that any people obey the laws without knowing what the laws command?'

'No, I don't,' he said.

'And when they know what they should do, do you suppose that any people think they should not do it?'

'I think not,' he said.

'Do you know of any people who do something other than what they think they should do?'

'No, I don't,' he said.

'So those who know what is lawful concerning other people are those who do what is just?'

'Certainly,' he said.

'Yes, but aren't those who do what is just themselves just people?'

'Yes—who else could be?' he said.

'So now at last a potential definition—would we be right to define just people as those who know what is lawful concerning other people?'

'Yes, I think we would,' he said.

'And wisdom—what shall we say that wisdom is? Tell me, do you 7 think that wise people are wise in respect of what they know, or are there some people who are wise in respect of what they don't know?'

'Obviously in respect of what they know,' he said. 'How could anyone be wise about what he doesn't know?'

'So are wise people wise because of their knowledge?'*

'Yes,' he said. 'How else could anyone be wise except through knowledge?'

'And do you think that wisdom is anything other than that which makes wise people wise?'

'No, I don't.'

'It follows, then, that wisdom is knowledge?'

'I think so.'

'Now do you think it possible for a man to know all things that exist?'

'Good heavens no, not even the smallest fraction of them.'

'So there can't be any man who is wise in respect of all things?'*

'Most certainly not,' he said.

'Does it follow, then, that in every case a man is only wise in respect of that which he knows?'

'Yes, I think it does.'

8   'Now let's take the concept of "the good",* Euthydemus. Would this be the way to investigate it?'

'What way do you mean?' he said.

'Do you think that the same thing is beneficial to everyone?'*

'No, I don't.'

'What then? Don't you think that what is beneficial to one person is sometimes harmful to another?'

'Yes, indeed,' he said.

'Would you say that "the good" is something other than "the beneficial"?'

'No,' he said.

'Does it follow, then, that what is beneficial is good for anyone to whom it is beneficial?'

'I think so,' he said.

9   'And mustn't we take the same approach when speaking of "the beautiful"?* Or when you call anything beautiful—a body, a utensil, or anything else whatsoever—do you know it to be beautiful for all purposes?'

'No, certainly not,' he said.

'So is what is beautiful in anything's use relative to the specific purpose for which that thing is useful?'

'Absolutely,' he said.

'And is any given thing beautiful for any purpose other than that for which its use is beautiful?'

'No—for no other purpose,' he said.

'Does it follow, then, that what is useful is beautiful for whatever purpose it is useful?'

'I think so,' he said.

10   'And now courage,* Euthydemus. Do you think there is beauty in courage?'

'I would say supreme beauty,' he said.

'So do you think that the purposes for which courage has its use are not mere trivialities?'

'Far from it,' he said; 'they are the most important of all.'

'Now would you say that in fearful and dangerous situations it is useful not to realize the danger?'

'Not at all,' he said.

'So those who feel no fear in such situations, because they don't recognize them for what they are, are not courageous?'

'Certainly not,' he said, 'because in that case many madmen* and cowards would be courageous.'

'What about those who are afraid when there is no cause for fear?'

'Still less courageous, surely,' he said.

'So is it your opinion that those who are good at facing fearful and dangerous situations are courageous, and those who are bad at it are cowardly?'

'Absolutely,' he said.

'And do you think that anyone else is good at facing such situations *11* other than those who are capable of handling them well?'

'No—just those,' he said.

'And so those who are bad at it are those liable to handle the situations badly?'

'Who else?' he said.

'Now do each of these two types handle things as they think they should?'

'Yes—how else?' he said.

'So do those incapable of handling things well know how they should handle them?'

'Evidently not,' he said.

'Does it follow, then, that those who know how they should handle things are also the ones capable of doing so?'

'Yes, only those,' he said.

'Well then. Do those who have not got it wrong handle such situations badly?'

'No, I don't think so,' he said.

'So those who handle them badly are the ones who have got it wrong?'

'Probably,' he said.

'Does it follow, then, that those who know how to handle it well when faced with fearful and dangerous situations are courageous, and those who get it wrong are the cowards?'

'I think so,' he said.

Socrates held that kingship and tyranny* were both forms of gov- *12* ernment, but considered that there was a difference between them. Kingship he thought was government over a consenting population and a city subject to the rule of law, whereas authority exercised without the consent of the people, and observing no laws other than what the ruler chose to dictate, was tyranny. And he considered that a constitution* in which the qualification for public office was adherence to the traditional order was an aristocracy; a plutocracy, if based on property valuation; and a democracy if open to all.

13   If anyone challenged Socrates' opinion of some person without clear grounds for doing so, simply asserting on no evidence that someone he named was more intelligent or the abler politician or the braver man or anything else like that, Socrates would bring the whole discussion back to the underlying premise in some such way as this.

14   'Are you saying that the man whose praises you sing is a better citizen than the one I speak of?'

'Yes, I am saying that.'

'Why then didn't we first examine what the function of a good citizen is?'*

'All right, let's do that.'

'Well then, in financial management wouldn't the better man be the one who makes the city better off financially?'

'Certainly.'

'And in war the one who gives the city the upper hand over its opponents?'

'Of course.'

'And in diplomacy the one who wins friends rather than creating enemies?'

'Probably so.'

'And then in public speaking too the one who puts an end to party strife and engenders unity?'

'Yes, I would say so.'

When questions under discussion were brought back in this way to the basic premises, the truth of the matter became clear even to the very people taking a contrary position.

15   Whenever he himself was developing an argument, he would proceed by a series of steps which met with general agreement,* thinking that this was what gave an argument solid conviction. Consequently he had by far the greatest ability of anyone I have known to bring his audience round to agreement with whatever his argument was on any occasion. He used to say too that Homer attributed to Odysseus the quality of being a 'convincing speaker'* because he was able to build his arguments on what people already thought to be true.

7   I THINK it clear from the foregoing that Socrates declared his own opinion* quite straightforwardly to those who associated with him.

I shall now speak of the care he also took that they should be self-sufficient* in the activities of their choice. Of all those I have known he was the most diligent in finding out what particular expertise any of his associates might have, and keener than any to teach them what he possessed of the knowledge appropriate to a man of quality—and for any subjects outside his own competence he took them to the relevant experts.*

He also taught them how far a properly educated person should be familiar with any given subject.* For example, he said that geometry* should be studied only up to the point at which one was competent to measure a plot of land accurately, should that ever be needed for purposes of inheritance, conveyance, division, or proof of yield: and this was so easy to learn that anyone who applied his mind to the computation required would at one visit discover the size of the plot and come back from it knowing how it was measured. But he was not in favour of pursuing the study as far as those abstruse geometrical figures in which he said he could see no practical use. He was not actually unfamiliar with them, but he said they were capable of consuming a man's life to the exclusion of many other useful subjects.

He also told them to acquire some knowledge of astronomy, but here again only up to the point of being able to identify the appropriate time of the night or the month or the year for a journey by land or sea, or for setting sentry-duties, and to have ready to hand for all other activities which take place at night, or at a particular time of the month or the year, a clear means of telling the various stages of the period in question. And he said that this knowledge was easily acquired from night-hunters* and ships' captains and many others for whom it was a professional concern. But he strongly discouraged them from taking their study of astronomy to the point of understanding the bodies in irregular orbits, such as the planets and the variable stars,* and wearing themselves out with attempts to discover their distance from the earth, the nature of their circuits, and what causes those circuits. He said he could see no benefit in this sort of enquiry either (though once again he was not without some knowledge of it), and he repeated that this was capable of consuming a man's whole life to the exclusion of much that was more useful.

In fact he discouraged any speculation* at all about god's scheme for the various celestial phenomena. He thought that none of it could

be discovered by humans, and considered that anyone trying to find out what the gods had chosen not to reveal would incur their displeasure. And he said that anyone theorizing about these matters would risk going as mad as Anaxagoras* was in being so mightily pleased
7 with himself for his explanation of the gods' machinery. When Anaxagoras asserted that fire and the sun were the same thing, he was ignoring the fact that men look at fire without any problem, but cannot gaze directly at the sun, and that their skin is darkened by the sun's rays, but not by fire; and he also ignored the fact that no vegetation can make healthy growth without the light of the sun, but the heat of fire destroys it all. And when he claimed that the sun was a red-hot stone* he was ignoring another fact, that a stone heated in a fire does not glow or last very long, whereas the sun keeps shining for ever with the brightest light there is.

8   He also told them to study arithmetic: but here again, as with the other subjects of study, he told them to avoid taking it to pointless lengths. He himself would always join his associates in their investigation and detailed exploration of any subject up to the limit of its practical use.

9   He also strongly encouraged his associates to take care of their physical health. They should learn all they could from the experts, and then throughout his life each individual should monitor for himself what food or drink and what sort of exercise is best for him, and how to manage his regime to stay as healthy as possible. He said that anyone who looked after himself in this way would be hard put to find any doctor better able than himself to diagnose what is good for his health.

10   And if any of them wanted help beyond the reach of human wisdom, he would recommend that they turn to divination.* He said that anyone with knowledge of the means by which the gods give men indications about their concerns would never be bereft of divine advice.

8 IF any people think that the fact of his condemnation to death by the jury at his trial proved that he was lying in his claim to have a 'divine sign'* which forewarned him of what he should and should not do, they need to take account of two considerations. Firstly, that he had already reached such an advanced age that if his life had not ended then it would have done so not much later. And secondly, that he escaped the most burdensome time of life, when all begin to lose their mental capacity, and instead won for himself yet more renown for the inner strength he displayed in making the most honest, dignified, and scrupulously legal speech in his defence that any man has ever given, and in accepting his death sentence with the utmost calm and fortitude.

It is generally agreed that there was no record of any man ever yet *2* bearing his death more nobly. He was obliged to live on for thirty days after the verdict, because this was the month of the Delian festival,* and the law did not allow any judicial execution until the formal mission had returned from Delos: and throughout this time all his familiar friends could plainly see that he was continuing to live as he had before, with no change in his manner—and before then he had been admired more than any other for his cheerful and good-natured way of life. How then could anyone die more nobly than this? What death *3* could be nobler than a death most nobly borne? What death could be happier than the most noble death? And what death could be more blessed by the gods than the happiest death?

I shall also relate what I heard about him from Hermogenes* the *4* son of Hipponicus. Hermogenes said that even after the indictment had been laid against him by Meletus,* he personally heard Socrates talking on about every subject other than the trial, and told him that he ought to be thinking about his defence. Socrates' first comment was 'Don't you think I have spent my whole life preparing it?' When Hermogenes asked him how, Socrates said that throughout his life his only activity had been the analysis of right and wrong, and then the practice of what was right and the avoidance of what was wrong, and that he thought this was the best preparation he could have made for his defence.

Hermogenes came back with 'Don't you see, Socrates, that there *5* have been many cases before now when Athenian juries have been talked into condemning the innocent to death or acquitting the guilty?'

'Yes indeed, Hermogenes,' Socrates replied, 'but when I was just putting my mind to think about the defence I should make to the jury, my divine sign indicated its opposition.'

'I find that astonishing,' Hermogenes said.

'Are you astonished,' said Socrates, 'if the god thinks it better that *6* I should end my life now? Don't you know that to this day I would not

concede to anyone a better or more enjoyable life than that which
I have lived? I think that the best lives are lived by those who take the
greatest care to make themselves as good as they can be, and the most
enjoyable lives by those who are most conscious of becoming better
7 people. And to this day this has been my own experience of myself,
and in comparing myself to the other people I have encountered
I have always maintained this opinion of myself. And this is not just
my own opinion, but what my friends too have always thought about
me—not simply out of friendship (as anyone would feel that way
about the friends he cherishes), but because they believe that being in
8 my company will make them as good as they can be. But if I am to live
longer, I may well be obliged to pay the full penalty of old age—sight,
hearing, and mental capacity all deteriorating, becoming slower on
the uptake and quicker to forget, and finding myself left behind by
those who were once my inferiors. Now in that case life would not be
worth living* at all, if I was unconscious of that decline: and if I was
conscious of it, would it not inevitably be a worse life and a less enjoyable one?

9   'But if I am to die unjustly, the shame of it will be on those who will
have killed me unjustly. Because if injustice is shameful, then how can
any unjust act whatsoever not bring shame on the man who commits
it? For me, though, what shame can there be if others fail to decide or
10 act justly in my case? I'm aware also that the reputation left to posterity
by the men of previous generations is very different for the perpet-
rators and the victims of injustice. I know that men will remember me
too, and that if I am to die now, there will be a very different memory
of those who will have brought about my death. That is because
I think that it will stand as an enduring testimony to me that I never
wronged or corrupted anyone in my life, but my constant endeavour
was to make those who associated with me better people.'

That was how he talked with Hermogenes and with the others.

11   Of those who knew Socrates the man, all who were intent on pursuing moral virtue still miss him more than anyone even now,* as he
was their best guide to its cultivation. As for me,* I found him just as
I have described—a man so pious that he did nothing without the
approval of the gods; so just in his dealings with others that he never
did even the slightest harm to anyone, but was of the greatest benefit
to all who had contact with him; so self-disciplined* that he never
took the more pleasant option in preference to the better course; so

clear-minded that he was never wrong in the distinctions he drew between better and worse, and had no need to rely on anyone other than himself for his grasp of these issues. And he had the gift of using conversation to expound and define such matters, to put others under scrutiny, to expose their errors, and to encourage them to virtue and a life of quality.

To me, then, he seemed the perfect example of the best and happiest that a man could be. If anyone objects to this view, let him compare other people's characters and then make his judgement.

APOLOGY

APOLOGY

I THINK it is also worth putting on record how Socrates addressed the *1*
question of his defence and the end of his life once he had been summoned to trial. Now others too* have written about the trial,* and all
of them have captured the boastfulness* of his manner, so it is evident
enough that he did indeed speak in that way. But what these others did
not make clear is that he had already come to think that for him death
was preferable to life, and so his boastfulness is made to appear rather
foolish. However, Hermogenes the son of Hipponicus, a close friend *2*
of Socrates, has revealed details which go to show that this boastful
tone of his was in keeping with the decision he had reached.

This is what Hermogenes* reported. When he saw that Socrates
kept talking about every subject rather than the trial, he said to him,
'But Socrates, shouldn't you also be thinking about your defence?'
Socrates' immediate reply was, 'So don't you think that I have spent *3*
my whole life in preparation for my defence?' When Hermogenes
asked him 'How so?', he said, 'Because I have lived all my life without
doing any wrong, and I consider that the best preparation I could
have made for my defence.' Hermogenes came back with 'Don't you *4*
see that there have been many cases when Athenian juries* have been
talked into condemning the innocent to death, and many too when
they have acquitted the guilty after a speech which either excites their
pity or flatters them?' 'Yes indeed,' said Socrates, 'and twice already
I've set my mind to thinking about the speech in my defence, but my
divine sign* opposes me.'

Hermogenes said, 'I find that astonishing,'* to which Socrates *5*
replied, 'Are you astonished that the god too thinks it better that
I should end my life now? Don't you know that to this day I would not
concede to anyone that he has lived a better life than I have? Because
what has been most enjoyable in my life is the knowledge that it has
been lived in piety and justice throughout. This has been a source of
strong personal pride, and I have found that those who associated
with me formed this same opinion of me.

'But as things are now, I know that if my years are to be prolonged *6*
I shall have to pay the full penalty of old age*—sight deteriorating,

hearing impaired, slower on the uptake, and quicker to forget what I once knew. And if I am aware of my decline and find fault with

7 myself, how could I continue to take any pleasure in life? Perhaps, though,' he went on, 'the god in his kindness is looking after my interest* by arranging for me a release from life not only at just the right age, but in the easiest way as well. Because if the verdict goes against me now, clearly it will be open to me to avail myself of what the authorities have judged the easiest way to die, a death which causes the least distress to someone's friends as he comes to his end, and gives them the most poignant sense of loss. Because when a man leaves behind him nothing ugly or distasteful in the minds of those present at his death, but simply fades away with his body intact and his spirit as cheerful as ever, his loss will inevitably be poignantly felt, will it not?

8 'The gods were right', he continued, 'to oppose any consideration by me of the speech I might make in my defence, when we were think- ing that we should look into every possible means of securing my acquittal. If I had managed that, it's clear that instead of an immedi- ate cessation of life I would have destined myself to a painful death from disease or old age—which is a reservoir of all that is trouble-

9 some and utterly joyless. Good heavens, Hermogenes,' he went on, 'there's no way I shall wish that on myself! But if I alienate the jury by listing all the blessings I think it has been my good fortune to receive from both gods and men, and letting them know my own opinion of myself, then I shall be choosing to die rather than beg slav- ishly* to keep on living—which would gain me, instead of death, a much worse form of life.'

10 This, Hermogenes said, was what Socrates had decided when he came forward to speak after his opponents* had made their accusa- tions that he did not recognize the gods traditionally recognized by the city, but introduced other novel divinities, and that he corrupted

11 the young men. 'Well, gentlemen,' he said, 'the first thing that puz- zles me about Meletus* is what possible grounds he has for saying that I don't recognize the gods traditionally recognized by the city: because others who happened to be there at the time saw me sacri- ficing during the communal festivals and at the public altars—and

12 Meletus himself could have seen me if he so wished. And how could it be "introducing novel divinities" for me to say that I am made aware of a voice from god which tells me what I should do? People

who make use of divination* from the cries of birds or the random utterances of men are evidently taking "voices" as their guide. Will anyone dispute that thunder has a "voice", and is the most significant omen of all? And doesn't the very priestess who sits on the tripod at Pytho* use her voice as the mouthpiece for the god's pronouncements? The point I am making is this, that everyone both says and *13* believes that god has foreknowledge of the future and reveals it in advance to those he wishes. The only difference is that whereas others speak of this revelation coming from birds, significant utterances, chance encounters, or prophets, I call it my "divine sign", and I think that in so doing I am speaking more accurately and with greater reverence than those who attribute the gods' power to birds. And as further evidence that I am not taking god's name in vain I can add the fact that before now I have told many of my friends* what the god has advised, and on no occasion has this advice proved mistaken.'

At this, Hermogenes reported, there was uproar* from the jurors: *14* some of them did not believe his claims, and others resented it if he was getting greater favours from the very gods than they were. So Socrates continued: 'All right, then, let me tell you something else, to give yet further ammunition to those of you determined to disbelieve my claim to divine privilege. Chaerephon* once asked a question about me at Delphi, and Apollo's oracular response, delivered in the presence of many witnesses, was that there was no man superior to me in freedom of spirit, justice, or self-control.'

Hermogenes said that when this statement not surprisingly caused *15* yet greater uproar from the jurors, Socrates continued once more, saying, 'But, gentlemen, what the god said about me does not compare with his response to Lycurgus the Spartan lawgiver.* They say that when Lycurgus entered the temple the god greeted him with "I am wondering whether I should call you a god or a man". Well, Apollo did not liken me to a god, but he did give it as his judgement that I was by some way pre-eminent among men. Nevertheless, you should not simply take the god's word for it in my case either, but I invite you to examine each part of his pronouncement. So then, do *16* you know anyone who is less of a slave to the bodily appetites* than I am? Do you know any other man with greater freedom of spirit, seeing that I don't accept any gifts or payment from anyone? Who could you with any good reason consider more just towards others than the man who is so attuned to his own circumstances that he has no further need for anything that does not belong to him? And how could there be any good reason not to describe as "wise" someone like me, when ever since I first began to understand speech I have never ceased seeking out for myself or learning from others every good thing I could?

17 'And don't you see evidence that my labour was not in vain in the fact that many of our citizens who aspire to virtue, and many from abroad too, choose to associate with me rather than anyone else? And how shall we account for the fact that so many would dearly like to make me some gift,* even though everyone knows that I would be the least able to make any financial repayment? Or that I am never asked by anyone at all for a return favour, but there are many who acknow-

18 ledge the debt of gratitude they owe me for favours received? Or that during the blockade,* when everyone else was full of self-pity, my lifestyle was such that I could continue to subsist on a diet no more impoverished than it had been anyway when the city was at its height of prosperity? Or that while others get their delicacies from the marketplace at great expense, I can at no cost resource from my own soul delicacies more delightful than theirs? But if no one can prove me wrong in anything I have said about myself, how can it not be clear by now that I do deserve the praise of both gods and men?

19 'Despite all that, Meletus, do you still claim* that by such conduct I corrupt the young men? I think we all know what forms corruption of the young can take. So you tell me if you know of anyone who has been turned under my influence from piety to irreverence, or from decency to loutishness, or from sensible living to extravagance, or from moderate drinking to habitual drunkenness, or from physical exercise to flabbiness—or has fallen victim to any other degenerate indulgence.'

20 'Well, by god,' said Meletus, 'I certainly know of those you have persuaded to pay attention to you rather than their parents.'*

'That I admit,' Socrates said, 'at least as regards their education, which they know has been my particular study. On any question of health people pay more attention to the doctors than to their parents; and I imagine that all Athenians pay more attention to those who speak the best sense in the assemblies than they do to members of their family. And when you are electing generals, don't you choose—above your fathers or brothers or indeed your own people—those who you think have the best understanding of military affairs?'

'Yes,' said Meletus, 'because that works for the best and is the way we do things.'

'Well then,' said Socrates, 'don't you think that this is another 21 strange anomaly—that in all other fields the best practitioners not only meet with no disadvantage but are actually given preferential treatment, yet I am being prosecuted by you on a capital charge because there are some people who judge me the best expert on education, and there is no greater human good than that?'

Now obviously more than this was said both by Socrates himself 22 and by the friends who spoke in his support, but I did not set out to give a complete account of the trial. My limited purpose has been to demonstrate firstly that Socrates' overriding concern was to prevent it appearing that he had been guilty either of any irreverence towards the gods or of any injustice to men, and secondly that he regarded 23 begging to keep his life as out of the question—he had in fact already concluded that it was time for him to die. That this was how his mind was made up became more obvious after the verdict had been reached. Firstly, when invited to propose an alternative penalty* he refused to do so himself, and would not let his friends propose one either, maintaining that any such proposal would amount to an admission of guilt. And later, when his companions were ready to spring him from prison,* he would not go along with them, and even seemed to make a joke of it, asking if perhaps they knew of some place outside Attica which was inaccessible to death.

When the trial came to its end, Hermogenes reports that Socrates 24 made this final address to the jury. 'Well, gentlemen, where any guilty conscience of committing gross impiety and injustice must reside is in the minds of those who schooled the witnesses to perjure themselves and give false testimony against me, and of the witnesses themselves who agreed to do so. But as for me, why should I think any less of myself than I did before my condemnation, if I was not proved to have done anything of which I was accused in their indictment? Because it has not been shown that I sacrifice to any sort of "novel divinities" in place of Zeus and Hera and their associated pantheon, or that I swear by and name any gods other than those. And how could I be "corrupt- 25 ing the young men" by instilling in them the habits of physical endurance and frugal living? Death is the penalty laid down for crimes such as temple-robbing, housebreaking, kidnapping, or treason, but even the prosecutors themselves do not allege against me that I have

committed any of these: so what astonishes me is how you ever formed
the view that anything I had done deserved the death penalty.

26   'But being unjustly sentenced to death is no reason either for me to
think any less of myself: the shame of that belongs not to me but to
those who condemned me. And I take some comfort too from the
story of Palamedes,* who met a death similar to mine: because still to
this day he provides poets* with much nobler material for celebration
than Odysseus, the man who had him unjustly killed. And I know that
in my case too the future as well as the past will bear me witness that
I never wronged or corrupted anyone in my life, but always tried to be
of benefit to those who talked with me by teaching them, free of
charge, every good lesson in my power.'

27   The manner in which he then left the court was wholly in keeping
with the tone of these final words—there was a radiant quality in the
expression on his face, the way he held himself, the way he walked.
When he saw that those accompanying him were in tears, we are told
that he said to them, 'What's this? Have you kept your tears until now?
Haven't you known all along that from the moment of my birth nature
had condemned me to death? Well, if I am dying before my time while
my life is still being flooded with good things, that would clearly be
a sadness to me and those who wish me well: but if I am being released
from life when only hardships are in prospect, in my view you should
all be happy for the successful management of my life!'

28   There was with him one Apollodorus,* a fervent devotee of Socrates,
but otherwise rather naïve. He now exclaimed, 'But, Socrates, what
I find hardest to bear is the sight of you being put to death unjustly!'
We are told that Socrates stroked* the man's head and replied, 'But,
my dear Apollodorus, would you have preferred to see me put to death
justly rather than unjustly?'—and he said this with a smile.

29   We are told* also that as he saw Anytus* passing by he said, 'There
goes a man in his triumph, thinking that he has achieved something
great and noble by sending me to my death—and all because when
I saw that the city thought him worthy of its highest honours I told
him that he ought not to be educating his son in the tanning of hides.
Miserable creature that he is, he doesn't seem to realize that between
us the real victor is the one with the more valuable and nobler achievements to his everlasting credit.

30   'But I tell you something else,' he went on. 'Homer* attributed
foreknowledge of the future to some men when their life was at its last

ebb, and I too want to make a prophecy. I was once briefly associated with Anytus' son, and I thought him not without some strength of spirit. And so I predict that he will not stay long in the servile occupation* which his father has arranged for him, but for the lack of a responsible mentor he will fall into some shameful addiction, and the progress he makes will only be yet further into depravity.'

This prediction of his was not wide of the mark. The young man *31* became hooked on wine,* and never stopped drinking by night or day: he ended up good for nothing to his city, his friends, and himself. And so Anytus, even after his death, is still reviled for the poor upbringing of his son and his own bigotry.

As for Socrates, by singing his own praises in court he invited the *32* resentment of the jury and made them more inclined to convict him. It seems to me, though, that he won for himself the fate which the gods reserve for their favourites—he escaped the hardest time of life, and met the easiest of deaths. And he demonstrated the strength of *33* his spirit: once he had decided that it was better for him to die than to live on, unwilling as always to oppose anything which he thought to his good, he did not weaken in the face of death, but gladly accepted it and saw it through.

For myself, then, when I think of the man's wisdom and nobility, *34* I cannot help remembering him, or fail to applaud him in my memories. If anyone of those who aspire to virtue has met any more helpful guide than Socrates, I can only regard him as quite exceptionally blessed by fortune.

EXPLANATORY NOTES

MEMORABILIA

BOOK I

Chapter 1.1

Xenophon opens by questioning how Socrates' accusers persuaded the Athenians to convict him. He starts by examining the charge that Socrates did not recognize the city's gods, and goes on to portray Socrates as a man of conventional religious practice, who deferred to oracles in complex situations, and whose interactions with the young encouraged them to self-improvement. He concludes with a brief look at potential political motivations for the charges.

1.1.1 *I have often wondered*: expressions of wonder and astonishment (*thauma*) are a standard rhetorical device for opening speeches or emphasizing key points (cf. Isocrates *Areopagiticus, Panegyricus*; Demosthenes *On the Trierarchic Crown*). Wonder is also evoked in closing this dialogue (1.1.20), and opening the next (1.2.1).

city: the *polis* or city is the basic unit of Greek political organization. Cities are self-governing independent entities in which individual citizens (especially the male elite, the focus of Xenophon's attention) can expect to play a part in decision-making, military service, and contributing funds (although non-citizens pay more taxes).

not recognizing the gods: the first of the two charges made by Socrates' accusers covers his religious behaviour, and is presumed to refer to his 'divine sign', spirit guide or *daimonion* (see notes on 1.1.2).

corrupting the young men: the second of the charges relates to Socrates' teaching practice; it is widely held to refer to the political activities of his followers who were among the leaders of the 404/3 oligarchy which ended in a brutal civil war before democracy was restored.

1.1.2 *divination*: the gods' opinions could be discerned through a range of signs and omens: Xenophon lists a range of occurrences which could be treated as significant: sightings of birds, words spoken, chance meetings, and the state or quality of sacrificial victims. Throughout the *Anabasis* Xenophon portrays himself and others as careful observer of such omens as guides to action; Socrates sends him to Delphi and criticizes the way he uses the oracle (*Anab.* 3.1.5–8). Socrates' emphasis on divination features again at the end of *Memorabilia*, in 4.7.

'divine sign': Socrates is represented by Plato and Xenophon as receiving direct divine guidance from an inner voice or *daimonion* (literally 'little spirit') which warned him against taking certain courses of action. Such personal

communication from the divine was seen as unusual; Xenophon is at pains to show that Socrates' religious behaviour was otherwise entirely correct and that he did believe in the usual gods of the city; see also 4.3 and 4.8.

1.1.4 *encouraged*: the Greek verb here (*protrepesthai*) is also used to describe speeches encouraging the young to turn to philosophy ('protreptics'), an important mode of argumentation for Xenophon's Socrates.

his associates: Xenophon's language for those who spent time with Socrates suggests casual association rather than any formal teaching relationship.

1.1.6 *ask the oracle*: consulting an oracle was one way in which ancient Greeks, as individuals or as cities, hoped to understand the will of the gods and assess whether a planned action had divine support or not. There were many oracular sites across the Greek world, each with its own processes for consulting a specific god, but the oracle of Apollo at Delphi was perhaps the most significant and prestigious site in mainland Greece.

1.1.7 *To acquire skill in carpentry*: Xenophon lists a number of skills (identified by Greek adjectives ending in *-ikos*), which are standard examples in philosophical argument, as well as encompassing typical roles undertaken by politically active citizens.

1.1.10 *in public*: Xenophon presents Socrates as engaging in philosophical conversation in public places, such as the Athenian marketplace (*agora*) and the colonnades or porches which surrounded it and housed administrative offices, as well as in semi-private spaces such as exercise grounds and gymnasia, and occasionally in private homes. Plato's dialogues tend to feature Socrates speaking in semi-private and private settings, although the *Apology* and the *Euthyphro* are both set in public spaces.

1.1.11 *the nature of the universe*: Xenophon seeks to differentiate Socrates from other thinkers of his time, for whom this was a predominant topic of enquiry; Plato does the same in the *Phaedo* (see note on 1.1.15). Aristophanes' depiction of Socrates observing the heavens in the *Clouds* may well have captured an earlier phase of Socrates' intellectual career, although the ideas he attributes to Socrates have much in common with those of other philosophers of Socrates' time.

what the sophists call the 'cosmos': note the use of 'sophist' in a sense more parallel to 'philosopher' than the pejorative sense it takes in Plato. The use of the term *cosmos* was significant; originally it signified military order, the arrangement of troops for battle, but it came to mean the divine and orderly arrangement of heavenly bodies, and by analogy the arrangement of society.

celestial phenomena: observing the movements of the sun, moon, and planets ('wanderers') in the sky was of particular interest to ancient thinkers as they sought to construct a reliable calendar based on observations of repeated patterns of their movements. These celestial phenomena and the seasonal movement of constellations also played important roles in establishing the timing of key festivals, and thus in the organization of civic life.

1.1.14 *a crowd*: the Greek word used here, *ochlos*, often has a derisive sense of 'mob' when used in political discourse, but can also denote any gathering of the public. The Cynics would later be renowned for transgressing the norms of acceptable behaviour in public.

stones, odd bits of wood, or wild animals: although Xenophon here lists these as objects worshipped by mad people, some ancient cult statues kept in temples were pieces of wood not carved into a representative form (*xoana*).

a single indivisible entity: Xenophon points to Socrates' interest in metaphysics, which drew on his Presocratic predecessors such as the radical monist Parmenides of Elea, who thought that the universe was a single undifferentiated and inseparable entity, with human perception of movement and change an illusion. Other Eleatic philosophers included Zeno of Elea (author of the famous paradox of motion) and Melissus of Samos. Underlying tenets of Eleatic philosophy, such as the unchangeability of reality, greatly influenced Plato's metaphysics. In passages such as this, Xenophon demonstrates a greater awareness of contemporary trends in philosophy than some critics have ascribed to him.

an infinity of separate components: Xenophon completes his survey of key positions taken by Presocratic thinkers with a brief nod to the atomists. Atomists such as Democritus of Abdera thought that everything was made from multiple indivisible units or 'atoms'; their metaphysical thought attempts to define unity, multiplicity, and the infinite. The opposition between one and many also appears in other ancient summaries of Presocratic thought such as the first book of Aristotle's *Metaphysics* (A.3.983b19), although it is a frequent rhetorical opposition too. Like Socrates, however, Democritus was also interested in ethical and social questions.

perpetual motion: the idea that all matter was in constant motion, in the sense of changing and coming to be, was held by the Presocratic philosopher Heraclitus, in his doctrine of flux, and followed by many thinkers and poets, as Plato notes in the *Theaetetus* (152e). Plato presents this and the opposing view of Parmenides of Elea, that all that exists is still, in more detail at 179d–180e.

generation and extinction: associated with the idea of matter in spatial motion was the idea of change over time, that living creatures have a life course. Again, this view was opposed by Parmenides and the Eleatics, who saw the totality of being as a single unchanging and unmoving entity.

1.1.15 *winds, waters, seasons*: here Xenophon nods to the interest of Presocratic thinkers in natural phenomena. Plato reports that Socrates himself began his career pursuing these interests (*Phd.* 97b–99c).

1.1.16 *on human subjects*: Xenophon here lists definitional questions in the form *ti esti* 'What is *x*?', a form of philosophical enquiry also associated with Socrates by Plato. Plato represents questions about ethical topics as Socrates' mature interest or 'second voyage' (*Phd.* 99d); many Socratic dialogues take the form of an unsuccessful search for a definition for a specific quality or virtue, such as those listed here; Xenophon does likewise in some chapters of the *Memorabilia*, notably 3.9 and 4.6, in both of which he appears to be responding to specific passages from Plato's works.

men of quality: Xenophon uses the phrase *kalos kagathos* (literally 'fine and good' or 'beautiful and good') to describe men of exemplary character who display virtuous characteristics in their lives. For Xenophon, there is an aesthetic component to excellence, although Socrates questions this elsewhere (*Oec.* 6.13–17); Xenophon himself is described as such in the ancient biographical tradition (DL 2.48).

slaves: one way in which 'men of quality' are defined is in the difference between them and the enslaved. The contrast between the slave and the *kalos kagathos* runs throughout the *Memorabilia*; the enslaved are represented as ineducable and incapable of developing the moral capacities of self-management and restraint. Xenophon's representation of the enslaved differs from that of Plato, who shows Socrates demonstrating the innate knowledge of humans by leading a young slave owned by Meno to understand the geometry of triangles (Pl. *Meno* 82a–86b).

1.1.18 *member of the Council*: all Athenian citizens could attend the assembly, but each year 500 were selected by lot to be part of the Council (*boulē*), a decision-making body which prepared the agenda for the larger Assembly (*ekklēsia*). Fifty citizens were selected from each of the ten tribes into which citizens were grouped; each month one tribe held a rotating presidency, and a randomly selected councillor from that tribe would chair meetings.

the execution of nine generals: Socrates was said to have chaired the Assembly, by virtue of his role as a member of the Council in the tribe that then held the presidency or 'prytany', on the day when it voted, illegally, to hold a single trial, with one vote to convict all the accused, for the generals involved in the disastrous aftermath of the naval victory at Arginusae (406 BCE); despite his opposition, they were convicted and later executed. At Arginusae, a sudden storm had prevented the victorious Athenians from retrieving their dead and still living sailors from sinking ships. Xenophon narrates the story of the battle and trial in more detail in *Hell.* 1.6–7; see also 4.4.2.

Thrasyllus and Erasinides: two of the generals involved in the Arginusae trial; Thrasyllus was first elected general by the fleet during the oligarchy of the Four Hundred in 411 BCE (Thuc. 8.76.2). Another of the Arginusae generals was Pericles Jr, son of the famous general Pericles, who appears as Socrates' interlocutor in 3.5.

Chapter 1.2

The second accusation was that Socrates corrupted the young. This chapter explains the origins of that accusation and begins the process of rebutting the underlying political complaint, that Socrates' teaching had encouraged opponents of democracy to overthrow the Athenian constitution.

1.2.1 *control over his appetites*: Xenophon values self-control over physical appetites, *enkrateia*. This is paralleled by and a subsidiary part of control over mental states and emotions, *sōphrosunē*, one of the core virtues.

exceptional endurance: Plato too depicts this aspect of Socrates, as reported by Alcibiades in his account of Socrates' military service (*Smp.* 220b).

physical hardships: Xenophon regards undertaking labour as virtuous activity, but this applies to specific forms of voluntary activity—working for pay does not count as 'labour' and cannot be virtuous.

1.2.3 *his example*: Xenophon shares a common Greek view that students learn by imitating examples (*mimēsis*), whether the example of the teacher himself (as Socrates is presented by Plato and Xenophon) or of case studies provided by the teacher (an approach favoured by the writer and educator Isocrates).

1.2.4 *excessive eating*: Xenophon regards the control of appetite as a key element of virtue, especially for those living in conditions of luxury and plenty, and as vital preparation for life on campaign. He returns to this topic in 3.12–14; see also the description of Cyrus' use of hunting expeditions for physical training (*Cyr.* 1.2.9-10, 7.5.80, 8.1.34–6, 8.1.44).

care of the soul: *epimeleia*, oversight or care, is a key concept for Xenophon, who regards proper oversight of and attention to others as key tasks for rulers, leaders, and managers in a variety of contexts (see the Introduction). *Epimeleia* can describe the supervision of troops, or of members of the household, but in Xenophon's time began to be used, as it is here, to describe an individual's conscious surveillance of his own character and actions.

1.2.5 *love of money*: Socrates' training reduces his students' desire for material goods and so their need for money, here expressed as an erotic desire. The desire for money was a specific target of fourth-century thinkers; Aristotle treats handling money as a problematic form of acquisitiveness (*Pol.* 1.10.1258a37–b8).

1.2.6 *making no charge*: Socrates' refusal to accept fees is presented as an aspect of his self-care, his protection of his personal freedom (*eleutheria*); rather than enter into the bonds of obligation which would be implied in a client relationship with students (or their parents), he chooses to give up the pay conventionally given to teachers.

1.2.7 *teach virtue*: the question of whether excellence or virtue (*aretē*) could be taught to individuals, either by their family or by professional teachers, features in many of Plato's dialogues focused on education (*Meno*, *Protagoras*, *Laches*). Socrates argues that it cannot be acquired passively.

a good friend: making friends and maintaining friendship (*philia*) is a major theme of the *Memorabilia* (see the Introduction). In the world of the Greek polis, *philia* encompasses a much broader set of relations than modern ideas of friendship, including community and business relationships as well as personal and familial ones. Whether friendship is a reciprocal and equal relationship, or one through which social inequalities can be managed, is a key question for Xenophon.

1.2.9 *his accuser*: there are two main explanations for Xenophon's use of the singular to refer to one of Socrates' accusers here. One possibility is that, in dividing the different charges made in court, he treats each as made by one accuser individually. Another attractive suggestion is that this is a reference to a written version of the accusation of Socrates; such texts circulated in Athens in the decade after Socrates' death. Diogenes Laertius notes an accusation of Socrates by Polycrates cited by other authors (DL 2.39–40) but notes that due to anachronistic details it cannot be the speech from the trial. Polycrates was a sophist known for such speeches: Isocrates' *Busiris*, defending the legendary king of Egypt, is a response to another rhetorical work of accusation aimed at a mythical figure.

appoint state officials by lot: most administrative roles in Athens were held by citizens appointed by lot, who had to undergo scrutiny for suitability before taking up such posts. This aspect of Athenian democratic practice made it harder for the wealthy and the traditional elite to sustain networks of power and influence.

established constitution: the constitution or *politeia* of a city can mean its political and administrative arrangements (as here), its citizenship criteria, or its political culture more broadly.

to violence: moving from debate and disagreement to violence is a key step in civil conflict (*stasis*). Xenophon goes on to explore how some of Socrates' students were linked to political violence in Athens and to the overthrow of the city's democratic constitution.

1.2.10 *rational thought*: Xenophon identifies *phronēsis*, sometimes translated 'practical wisdom' when it appears in the work of Aristotle (e.g. *NE* book 6), as an acquired habit, and the capacity to use philosophical training to manage everyday activity.

persuasion... violence: the contrast between physical force (or other forms of compulsion) and verbal persuasion is a commonplace of Greek rhetoric, activated by Plato in the *Laws*. Committing physical violence against a fellow citizen was strongly deprecated in Athenian democratic culture. Xenophon uses the contrast to lead into the case study of Critias and Alcibiades, two Athenians who transgressed conventions regarding the use of force among citizens.

1.2.12 *Critias*: the Athenian politician who became one of the Thirty Tyrants of the 404/3 BCE oligarchy, and died in the battle in which it was overthrown (see note on 1.2.32). It has been argued that the Athenian prosecution of Socrates was due to the role of his former students in the oligarchy, though carefully couched in terms which did not breach the official amnesty against prosecution for actions during that time (see Lysias 12). Critias was a relative of Plato, and wrote both verse and prose *politeia* texts critical of conventional ideas and political arrangements, although the attribution of surviving fragments to him is far from secure. He appears as a speaker in Plato's *Charmides*, seeking a definition of moderation, and also in Plato's *Timaeus* and *Critias*.

Alcibiades: Athenian politician and student of Socrates, died 404 BCE. Alcibiades was the ward of the Athenian general Pericles (see below), a charismatic and glamorous member of the elite. Thucydides represents him as encouraging the Athenians to invade Sicily, being given and then stripped of command as he was caught up in religious scandal, before fleeing to Sparta to evade Athenian justice. Xenophon depicts his later return to Athens with a nuanced assessment of divided opinion about him (*Hell*. 1.4.8–20); he does not shy from considering the negative.

1.2.14 *self-sufficient*: being self-sufficient increased the likelihood of both the individual and the city achieving happiness, later identified by Aristotle as the chief good of human life. Xenophon mentions it again when summarizing the practical benefits of Socratic education at 4.7.1.

1.2.17 *an example in his own person*: Xenophon here presents Socrates, in contrast to Critias and Alcibiades, as an example of the *kalos kagathos*. Given Socrates' eccentricities and lack of physical beauty, this is a somewhat paradoxical presentation, and one which is called into question in the *Symposium*.

1.2.20 *training*: Xenophon argues that constant training in both physical and mental skills can lead to excellence, prefiguring Aristotle's arguments in the *Nicomachean Ethics* about the role of habituation in character development.

The poets: the first quote is from the elegies of the sixth-century BCE poet Theognis of Megara (35–6), also cited by Xenophon at *Smp*. 3.4, and Plato at *Meno* 95de, although both alter the wording. Theognis' poetry, with its emphasis on the 'good' (*esthla*), reflects the political context of his times, with archaic aristocratic values under pressure from social changes in the polis. The second quote is from an archaic poem by an unknown author, and is also cited by Plato's Socrates (*Protagoras* 344d). This pair of quotations may show contact between Plato and Xenophon, their reliance on a common anthology, or report a favourite quotation of the historical Socrates.

1.2.24 *Thessaly*: Critias was exiled from Athens (Xen. *Hell*. 2.3.25) and went to Thessaly, a tribal region north of Athens where many elite Athenians had family connections. After the restoration of democracy in 410 BCE Xenophon reports him provoking unrest to establish a democracy there, although he does not specify details (*Hell*. 2.3.36). In Plato's *Crito*, Crito suggests that Socrates should evade his execution by fleeing to Thessaly (*Crito* 45c).

grand ladies: the mutual attraction between Alcibiades and a wide array of Greek women is a notable feature of his biographical tradition (Plutarch *Life of Alcibiades*); his lovers were said to have included Timaea, queen of Sparta, an unnamed woman captured and enslaved in the Athenian conquest of Melos and, in later tradition, Theodote (see 3.11). His Athenian wife, however, sought to divorce him (Plutarch *Alcibiades* 8).

1.2.27 *deteriorate after moving on*: a related point about teachers' waning influence after students leave them is raised in Plato's *Gorgias* 514bc.

1.2.29 *in love with Euthydemus*: Xenophon shows Socrates criticizing Critias' intemperate desire, which fell outside the accepted form of the Athenian practice of pederasty, in which older men engaged in the erotic pursuit of youths. Critias' desires ran counter to Socratic ideas of self-control. The youthful Euthydemus and his education are the focus of Book 4, with his introduction in 4.2 mirroring this passage. This Euthydemus is not the same as the sophist from Chios (Plato *Euthydemus*) or the son of Cephalus (Pl. *Rep.* 1.328b), but is probably the same person whom Alcibiades describes as rejected by Socrates as a lover (Pl. *Smp.* 222b).

1.2.31 *Charicles*: Athenian politician and general, who was one of the Four Hundred oligarchs (411 BCE) and then one of the Thirty who governed the city as an oligarchy or, in the view of many, a collective tyranny (404 BCE, listed by Xenophon, *Hell.* 2.3.2); Aristotle represents him as an extremist. Socrates' discussion with Charicles here parodies the Socratic form of discussion by question and answer familiar from Plato's dialogues (see the Introduction).

the art of argument: this is one way to describe the teaching of sophists, who taught their students how to argue both sides of the same case (parodied in Aristophanes' *Clouds*) but also evident in rhetorical works such as Antiphon's *Tetralogies*, which showed both sides of legal arguments, and philosophical works such as the *Dissoi Logoi* or 'double arguments' which did the same thing for philosophical problems. Socrates' elenctic method of question and answer was different from these approaches but easily grouped with them for argumentative purposes.

1.2.32 *the Thirty*: the 404/3 BCE oligarchy, at the end of the Peloponnesian War, resulted in a violent civil war (*stasis*) in which many citizens were killed, but which resulted in the restoration of democracy (Xen. *Hell.* 1–2).

herd of cattle: the first appearance in this text of the 'shepherd of the people' motif which Xenophon associates with Socrates and with Cyrus (*Cyr.* 8.2.14); at 3.2 Socrates discusses how Homer applies it to Agamemnon. Plato uses the motif, traditional in both Greek and Near Eastern epic sources, to explore the motivation of rulers (Pl. *Rep.* 1.343a–345e), and criticizes it as an analogy for political rule (Pl. *Statesman* 274e–275a).

1.2.35 *maturity of judgement*: although young men undertook many civic and military roles before the age of 30, that was the age qualification for eligibility for the Council (see 1.1.18). After this age, Charicles implies, young men's education was considered complete (it was also the age at which they might marry), and they would no longer be liable to 'corruption' by Socrates' teaching.

1.2.37 *cobblers, carpenters, and smiths*: Socrates conducted philosophical discussions with craftspeople in Athens, as Xenophon depicts him doing in 3.10. Other sources connect Socrates with Simon the Shoemaker, who was said to have written Socratic dialogues himself (DL 2.122–3).

1.2.40 *Alcibiades had a discussion about law with Pericles*: here, Alcibiades personifies the influence of sophistic teaching and its conflict with the more traditional respect for convention voiced by his guardian, Pericles, the Athenian statesman and general who led the city during the mid-fifth century, and oversaw the growth of the Athenian empire and the rebuilding of Athens' acropolis temples, before leading the city into war with Sparta, and dying of the plague which befell Athens during the early years of the war.

1.2.41 *what law is*: the conversation is presented as a Socratic search for a definition. Socrates will argue for the identity of law and justice in Book 4, offering a view which strongly opposes the conventionalism offered by Pericles here.

1.2.43 *oligarchy*: literally 'rule of the few', used by Xenophon and others to describe a regime in which a small group of citizens, usually distinguished by wealth (as Xenophon notes below, 1.2.45), were the only ones qualified to participate in political activities, and so ruled over the other citizens.

tyrant: fourth-century Greeks distinguished tyranny from kingship, the legitimate form of rule by a single person, by its reliance on force rather than the consent of the governed; the most developed form of the typology of regimes is found in Aristotle's *Politics*; Plato presents tyranny as emerging from the corruption of democracy (*Rep.* books 8–9) and the tyrant as subject to uncontrolled physical appetites.

1.2.44 *the stronger*: Alcibiades' view echoes that expressed by the Athenians to the defeated people of Melos in Thucydides' Melian dialogue, 'the dominant exact what they can and the weak concede what they must' (Thuc. 5.89).

1.2.48 *Crito*: depicted by Plato as one of Socrates' oldest friends, and a reliable supporter; Plato's *Crito* shows him trying to help Socrates evade his death sentence, and he is present at Socrates' death in the *Phaedo*.

Chaerephon: another long-term friend of Socrates; he fought for the democrats during the 404/3 civil war, but died before Socrates' trial in 399. Plato and Xenophon both show him consulting the Delphic oracle, which insists that no one was wiser than Socrates (Pl. *Ap.* 20e–21c; Xen. *Ap.* 14). Aristophanes, in his *Clouds*, depicted him as a manager of the philosophical school run by Socrates.

Chaerecrates: the younger brother of Chaerephon; the difficulties of their experience of brotherhood are the topic of 2.3.

Hermogenes: appears in several works by Xenophon and Plato, although rather differently in each. Xenophon represents him as poor and in need of employment (*Mem.* 2.10), and as religious (*Smp.* 4.48). However, this depiction is at odds with Plato's version. Plato presents him as a lively interlocutor (*Cratylus*), who was present at Socrates' death (*Phd.* 59c). As an illegitimate member of a wealthy family (he was the half-brother of the wealthy Callias), Hermogenes' status was ambiguous, perhaps permitting such varied depictions, although none of the characterization is necessarily historical. Hermogenes is presented as an important source for Xenophon's account of Socrates' final years, when Xenophon himself was away from Athens; Xenophon attributes the account he gives of Socrates' death to him (see 4.8.4–11; *Ap.* 2).

Simmias and Cebes: students from Thebes, who are among Socrates' interlocutors in Plato's *Phaedo*, where they present Pythagorean arguments about the harmony of the soul. The biographical tradition attributes various dialogues to them, but none survive. They appear again at 3.11.17.

Phaedondas: another friend of Socrates present at his death (Pl. *Phd.* 59c).

1.2.49 *treat their fathers with contempt*: the Greek word used means 'hurl mud at'; Socrates' disruption of unearned parental authority is explored by both Plato and Xenophon, and appears to underlie the charge of 'corrupting the young'. Xenophon goes on to give examples of this alleged disruption.

insanity: madness (*mania*) is a recurring topic in the *Memorabilia*, as a state of mind entirely distinct from the reasoned self-control Socrates advocates and encourages. Later (3.9.6–7), Xenophon will clarify that by madness he means an extreme state of delusion, and he lists madness (3.12.6) as a possible consequence of neglect of physical fitness. Madness also provides the basis for counter-examples in argument; in the opening arguments of Plato's *Republic*, for example, the thought that you would not return a weapon to someone who is mad provides a counter-example to the prevailing definition of justice as ensuring that people have access to their own property (*Rep.* 1.331cd). Xenophon presents a similar argument at 4.2.17.

1.2.51 *doctors...trained advocates*: the question of professional skill demonstrated by doctors, compared with that of public speakers, is explored by Plato in many dialogues, notably the *Gorgias*.

1.2.56 *perverse passages*: Xenophon evokes Socrates' criticisms of poetry, and of poets' representations of god and myth, expressed in Plato's *Republic* books 2–3 and 10.

Hesiod's line: a line (311) from the didactic epic poem *Works and Days* by Hesiod, who lived and wrote in Boeotia in the early seventh century BCE; in Plato's *Charmides* (163b), Critias cites the first part of this line, and his discussion with Socrates on the subjects of worthwhile labour matches that given here.

1.2.58 *Homer about Odysseus*: *Iliad* 2.188–91, 198–202; the two passages come from the main debate of the Greek forces at Troy, and contrast Odysseus' encouragement of the elite to participate in decision-making, and physical prevention of the poor. While Xenophon argues that Socrates used the passage to distinguish between useful and useless contributions to society, Odysseus' violent rebuke to the common soldier Thersites offers some insight into aristocratic values of the archaic era.

1.2.60 *a man of the people and a friend of humanity*: unlike Odysseus, Socrates cares both for the common people of his own city and for humanity more broadly, and so can be described as *dēmotikos* and *philanthrōpos*.

1.2.61 *Lichas*: an elite Spartan involved in a controversial episode at the Olympic Games of 420 BCE. He crowned the victorious charioteer, making it clear that the team was not the Boeotian team it had been entered as, but his own (Thuc. 5.50.4); as Sparta had been excluded from the games, he was punished with a flogging. Xenophon describes the Spartan revenge in a war twenty years later (*Hell.* 3.2.21–3).

Gymnopaidiai festival: this Spartan festival in honour of Apollo was known as the 'festival of naked boys' because of the athletic competition it featured, probably originating in competitive dances of groups of unarmed boys and men (Hdt. 6.67).

1.2.62 *death is the penalty*: there was no fixed tariff of crimes and punishments in Athens. Prosecutors might seek the death penalty in cases where the crime was conceptualized as an affront to shared values rather than purely an affair of personal loss or injury. Both Demosthenes and Isocrates represent speakers seeking the death penalty for relatively minor assaults (Isocrates *Against Lochites* 5–8; Demosthenes *Against Timocrates* 113–14), arguing that the threat to the community warranted the greater punishment.

Chapter 1.3

This chapter presents Socrates in his most characteristic activity, conversation with his followers. The topics of discussion—the dangers of erotic love and the importance of controlling physical appetites—represent religious and ethical themes which will recur throughout the work.

1.3.1 *I shall now record*: Xenophon shifts to narrating examples of Socratic conversation, grouped thematically and starting with his religious practice.

Delphic priestess: while Chaerephon's query to the Delphic oracle about Socrates was unusual (see note on 1.2.48), Socrates' own religious observance was scrupulously in line with the practices laid out by the priestess.

1.3.3 *small sacrifices from small resources*: Xenophon applies the concept of proportionate equality to religious practice. Gifts to the gods should be valued proportionately in respect of the donor's resources rather than in accordance with their absolute value. Proportionate or geometric equality, assessed in terms of ratio rather than number, was key to fourth-century political thought, as a means of expressing and bridging the differing worth of rich and poor citizens. Aristotle develops it in detail (*NE* book 5) while Xenophon considers its role in rewarding and motivating troops through the distribution of the spoils of war (*Cyr.* 2.2.17–28).

To the best of your ability: Hesiod, *Works and Days* 336, offers some support for the view that effort rather than absolute cost is what counts in offerings to the gods.

1.3.4 *some signal*: again Xenophon emphasizes Socrates' extreme piety through the priority he gives to acting on the gods' wishes as signalled through oracles and portents, and his own *daimonion*.

1.3.5 *so frugal*: Socrates' self-discipline enabled him to exist with minimal resources and expense, leading to an ascetic lifestyle that was criticized and caricatured (for example by Antiphon, 1.6).

the only sauce: delaying the satisfaction of bodily desires meant that when food and drink were taken, the plainest options would provide pleasure; with food, no *opson* (prepared fish, meat, or sauce to accompany bread) would be needed. Xenophon criticizes gourmands with a taste for *opson* in 3.14. Xenophon's depiction of Socrates shows how he inspired traditions that would be developed by later ascetic schools, such as the Cynics.

1.3.7 *Circe*: Odysseus encounters the sorceress Circe on his travels, when she transforms his men into pigs (Homer *Odyssey* 10.274–400). Odysseus himself is helped by the god Hermes, who gives him advice and a magic herb to ward off Circe's magic, avoid transformation himself (although he does not resist her sexual allure), and rescue his crew. Socratic education in self-restraint, Xenophon suggests, can replace such divine and magical supports.

1.3.8 *matters of sex*: sex (*aphrodisia*) is another appetite which should, in Socrates' model, be controlled by self-restraint. Encountering beautiful youths such as Alcibiades' son would challenge that self-control; Xenophon does not distinguish here between heterosexual and homosexual desire, and in the Athens of Socratic dialogue expressing desire for a beautiful youth was more acceptable than expressing desire for a citizen woman. Xenophon reworks this theme at *Smp.* 4.6.

<......>: Dorion suggests that this sentence is incomplete, and points to papyrus evidence that Xenophon might have gone on to develop a comparison between the effects of uncontrolled erotic passion and fire. See Notes on the Greek Texts.

Critobulus: Critobulus, son of Socrates' friend Crito, features in several dialogues by Plato and Xenophon (as well as fragments by Aeschines), often in the context of his education being planned and discussed (Pl. *Euthydemus*, *Crito*), or his youthful foolishness serving to introduce a theme, such as desire. Socrates even proposes to Crito that his sons might act as 'bait' for sophists (*Euthydemus* 272d). Critobulus is depicted as present at Socrates' trial (Pl. *Ap.* 33a) and at his death (*Phd.* 59b). He is Socrates' interlocutor in the *Oeconomicus*, as a young man seeking advice on marriage and running a household, and in the dialogue on friendship (*Mem.* 2.6); he is both an *erastēs* (older lover) and an *erōmenos* (young beloved) in Xenophon's *Symposium* (8.2), and also described there as newly-wed (*Smp.* 4.8). The presentation of Critobulus is typical of the blurred dramatic time of Xenophon's dialogues.

Xenophon: this, the first reported conversation between Socrates and his companions in the *Memorabilia*, marks Xenophon's presence among that group, as does 1.4.2 and a similar comment much later (4.3.2). Several commentators suggest that Xenophon intends to assert the authenticity of this conversation and those he goes on to report.

1.3.9 *turn somersaults*: the actions to which the love-struck Critobulus might be driven are reminiscent of one of the displays performed by the erotic dancers of the *Symposium* (*Smp.* 2.11).

1.3.12 *widow spiders*: Plato likens the bite of these spiders (*phalangia*) and other venomous creatures to the charms of Athenian democracy (*Euthydemus* 290a). Xenophon will also describe the courtesan Theodote as hunting like a spider (3.11.6–7).

Chapter 1.4

This chapter provides further evidence of Socrates' impact on his associates, as counter-examples to the cases of Critias and Alcibiades, through a conversation with a less well-known follower, Aristodemus. Socrates engages with topics central to philosophical enquiry about the natural world—the origins of the universe, the design of life forms and the possibility of an intelligent divine force as their creator, and the workings of human intelligence—which are found in the fragments of Presocratic thinkers, and also seen in Plato's dialogues. Although Xenophon presents Socrates as an advocate of a theory of intelligent design, it is unclear whether the views expressed are those of Socrates himself or of Xenophon.

1.4.1 *a few written or oral accounts*: Xenophon notes the existence of other writings on Socrates: Socratic dialogues were written by many of Socrates' followers, including Antisthenes and Antiphon as well as Plato and Xenophon.

1.4.2 *Aristodemus*: appears in Plato's *Symposium* as the narrator of the dialogue's main events, as retold by Apollodorus, who describes him as obsessed with Socrates, going barefoot in imitation of Socrates' style, and accompanying him to Agathon's dinner party (the scene of the *Symposium*) uninvited. Here his atheism, coupled with his refusal to conform to normal religious practice, provides a counterpart to Xenophon's depiction of a pious Socrates.

1.4.3 *Homer*: the greatest epic poet introduces a group of leading practitioners of a range of arts. Whether or not the works of Homer represent the output of a poet or the gathering of a collective tradition, Homer is a paradigm of artistic production and poetic practice for both Plato and Xenophon.

Melanippides for dithyramb: a celebrated fifth-century BCE composer and poet famed for his use of the 'new style'. Dithyrambs were a traditional form of choral ode to Dionysus, performed at festivals by citizen choruses; Melanippides introduced new structures and harmonic patterns. Comic poets and Plato (in the *Laws*) criticized these developments.

Sophocles for tragedy: Xenophon's choice of Sophocles, one of the three great tragedians of fifth-century Athens, is interesting: Plato tends to treat Aeschylus as the prime example of a tragedian.

Polyclitus for sculpture: Polyclitus of Argos, active 460–410 BCE, produced sculptures in bronze; his most famous work was a Doryphorus, a statue of a youth with a spear, believed to be the prototype for many Roman sculptures on that theme. He also wrote a *Canon* or manual of sculpture and proportion.

Zeuxis for painting: Zeuxis of Heraclea (Zeuxippus in some sources), late fifth century BCE, was a painter resident in Athens, although he also worked at Archelaus' court in Macedon. He appears as a youth in Plato *Protagoras* (318bc) and is alluded to at Xenophon *Symposium* 4.63 and *Oeconomicus* 10.1. He was famous for painting mythical subjects such as centaurs, and for innovations in shading.

1.4.4 *images that cannot think or move*: Socrates distinguishes between the living creations of the gods and the lifeless creations of human art. There are obvious echoes of Plato's arguments about art as imitation in *Republic* 10; for Plato, an image cannot incorporate the qualities of the original. Xenophon has a more positive account of the ability of art to communicate values; see the discussion with the painter Parrhasius at 3.10.

conscious design...random chance: this passage parallels elements in Plato's *Timaeus* with its account of a rational divine craftsman (*dēmiourgos*, *Mem.* 1.4.7; Pl. *Timaeus* 28a) creating the universe and supervising the creation of the creatures within it. 'Design' translates *gnōmē*; the features are the result of a rational thought process. Xenophon shows Socrates mediating between conventional piety and philosophical enquiry, in exploring the possibility of a divine providence. See the Introduction on the radical nature of the Socratic ideas on intelligent design, expressed in this chapter and in 4.3.

useful purpose: that actions should have a practical benefit (*ōpheleia*) is a continuing concern of Xenophon's. It introduces a Xenophontic twist to his survey of Socrates' engagement with philosophical enquiry into nature.

1.4.5 *means of perception*: perception and its relationship with thought were of great interest to early philosophers: the following sections show that Xenophon was aware of a wide range of thinking on this topic, while having a distinctive viewpoint which emphasized the intelligent design of the natural world, and the similarity of humans to and their special treatment by that divine intelligence. A similar point is made at 4.3.11.

1.4.6 *eyelids*: a similar discussion appears in Plato *Timaeus* (45d). The attribution of specific tasks to parts of the body also resembles analogies used by the Presocratic philosopher Diogenes of Apollonia (fl. 460–430 BCE), whose ideas on physics and the natural world are represented as those of Socrates in Aristophanes' *Clouds*.

eyebrows: Aristotle in *De Partibus Animalium* (2.15.658b14–18) uses the same metaphor of the cornice.

1.4.7 *urge to live*: the idea that there was a natural instinct for self-preservation evident in animals, including humans, from birth would later become a foundation of the Stoic doctrine of *oikeiōsis*, in which humans come to recognize their shared predicament.

1.4.8 *intelligence*: with this question, Xenophon engages with discussions of philosophy of mind, and the possibility that each human soul (*psychē*) contains an element of the divine intelligence of the universe (*nous*), in parallel with the physical materiality of the body. Plato *Philebus* 29a–30a offers a parallel; both Plato and Xenophon draw on the same Presocratic source, possibly the philosopher Diogenes of Apollonia (see 1.4.6), or possibly Socrates himself.

important elements: that the body and other material entities are ultimately composed from the same basic matter as other physical objects in the world was a view explored by several Presocratic thinkers, although the identification of this matter and the number of basic substances were disputed.

1.4.10 *too exalted*: the idea that the gods needed resources from human offerings was familiar from archaic texts such as Hesiod *Theogony*; Aristophanes in Plato's *Symposium* (189–93) depicts Zeus responding to humans expressing this view. Xenophon here gives Socrates views similar to those expressed by Euthydemus (4.3) and criticized by Socrates in Plato's *Euthyphro* (14e–15a).

1.4.11 *any concern for human beings*: Aristodemus expresses another atheist position, that the gods exist but have no concern for humans, one of the three forms of atheism identified by Plato's character the Athenian Stranger in *Laws* 10 (885b), a detailed set of arguments against atheism.

more fortunate: achieving happiness (*eudaimonia*) is an important goal; Socrates here argues that the gods have made it easier for humans to do so than for other animals. Socrates' insistence on the pursuit of *eudaimonia* recurs throughout the work.

1.4.12 *the pleasure of sexual intercourse*: Xenophon implicitly contrasts heterosexual and homosexual pleasure in his *Symposium* (as a critique of Plato's homoerotics), here emphasizing the practical purpose of reproduction.

1.4.13 *rational soul*: that humans had a distinctive mental capacity for thought and understanding which differentiated them from other living creatures was a fundamental of ancient thought. See 4.3.11 for a similar passage.

1.4.14 *men live like gods*: the similarity between men and gods is a double one: both have bodies equipped with hands, and souls with the capacity for rational thought. The Presocratic philosopher Anaxagoras also suggested that humans were the creatures most like gods, because they had hands (Fr. 102); Aristotle regarded human hands as a consequence of the possession of the rational soul, given by an intelligent nature to a creature with the capacity to use them (*Parts of Animals* 4.10.687a2–20).

1.4.15 *divination*: Xenophon connects this philosophical discussion with the earlier discussion of more ordinary attempts to understand the gods, and perhaps hints at the special status of Socrates with his *daimonion*.

1.4.16 *most enduring*: placing particular value on the most ancient things was a conventional thought. Dorion suggests that this argument prefigures

Aristotle's use of established opinion (*endoxa*) as the starting point for philosophical enquiry.

1.4.17 *thought which is active in the universe*: Xenophon uses two technical words here, but emphasizes the earlier suggestion that part of the universal mind (*nous*) is found in individuals, and that that mind is characterized by the practical wisdom (*phronēsis*) which humans should aim to achieve.

god's eye: the idea that Zeus saw all was well established (for example, in Hesiod *Works and Days* 267–9); Xenophon would show powerful kings echoing that capability, with Cyrus as a 'seeing law' (*Cyr.* 8.1.22).

1.4.18 *a service or a favour*: the idea of generous acts (*charis*) beginning a cycle of reciprocal and beneficial favours which connect people in friendship is central to Xenophon's ethical thought; see 2.6, and the Introduction).

Chapter 1.5

This short chapter presents Socrates engaging in exhortation rather than argument, and introduces the key Xenophontic virtue of bodily self-control (*enkrateia*), presented as the foundation of virtue.

1.5.1 *self-control*: bodily self-control (*enkrateia*) is a key quality of the *kalos kagathos*; Xenophon shows Socrates arguing that it is a necessary quality for both the good general and the good slave; and if Socrates encouraged such self-control, he cannot be guilty of corrupting the young.

1.5.2 *entrust*: the guardianship of subadult males and female members of the household, and stewardship of property, were a major concern of Greek legal codes, reflected in disputes about inheritance which came before the Athenian courts.

slave: in allowing that the enslaved can demonstrate the rational capacity of self-control, Xenophon shows a different view from that expressed in Aristotle's account of 'natural' slavery (*Pol.* 1.5.1254a17–1255a3), in which the enslaved are said to lack the capacity of rational thought and hence would be less able to develop or actualize the capacity to control physical appetites.

1.5.3 *Profiteers*: these are people exhibiting the vice of *pleonexia*, the desire to acquire a greater share of resources than a fair distribution would permit. The lack of self-control is a parallel vice; both vices lead individuals to harm others while seeking advantage for themselves.

1.5.4 *call-girls*: the man who lacks self-control fails to control a range of appetites (see 1.2.1). The symposium featured food, drink, and sex workers (those invited to symposia were usually referred to as *hetairai*, companions, rather than *pornai*, prostitutes), and provides an opportunity for displaying restraint in physical and sexual appetite.

1.5.5 *By Hera*: the oath, to Hera, wife of Zeus, perhaps follows the mention of sex; Socrates swears by Hera to mark a particularly strong point, or opposition to another character. He (and other characters) more normally swear by Zeus, an oath so commonplace that we have left it unmarked in the translation.

Chapter 1.6

Two reported conversations with the sophist Antiphon show criticisms of Socrates and his method of teaching, and his refusal to charge fees to his followers. Antiphon's description of Socrates' shabby clothing and ascetic lifestyle prefigures later descriptions of the Cynics.

1.6.1 *Antiphon*: Antiphon 'the sophist' was an Athenian teacher of rhetoric and author of the *Tetralogies*, sets of example arguments for both sides of contentious cases. Another Antiphon, who may or may not have been the same person, was politically active in Athens at the same time; this Antiphon was a leader of the Four Hundred, the Athenian oligarchy of 411/10 BCE during the Peloponnesian War, for which he was tried and executed (Thuc. 8.68.1–2).

1.6.2 *happier*: while Xenophon represents the pursuit of happiness (*eudaimonia*) as a major concern of Socrates', characters such as Antiphon show that Socrates' was not the only form of hedonism (treating pleasure as a good) in circulation.

coat: Antiphon uses Socrates' indifference to his appearance and ascetic practices to position him as an anti-hedonist. Socrates will respond that his asceticism makes it easier for his desire for pleasure to be satisfied with less, thus increasing his happiness. Wearing a battered cloak (and nothing else) would later become a symbol of the Cynics.

1.6.3 *money*: both Plato and Xenophon emphasize that Socrates took no fees for his teaching; Antiphon turns that claim against him.

a freer…life: the adjective *eleutherios* describes qualities and behaviours seen as appropriate to a free citizen, transforming freedom from a political and social status into a character virtue (see the Introduction).

1.6.9 *bettering yourself*: control of physical desires is now shown to be the first step in achieving other, less physical, forms of virtue, as well as a social asset in gaining and interacting with friends, and the ability to serve the city better.

1.6.13 *prostitute*: returning to the topic of charging fees for teaching, Socrates draws a parallel between sophistry and prostitution (here, male prostitution), and by implication between his own practice and the exemplary practice of pederasty between the virtuous. He claims that the problem is not just that sophists charge fees, but that they are willing to take anyone's money. The topic recurs at Xenophon *Symposium* 8.21–2.

1.6.14 *the books*: the delight Socrates expresses in reading books and learning from them runs contrary to views Plato gives Socrates on the utility of the written word, but is suggestive of the circulation of written texts at the time when Xenophon was writing.

1.6.15 *politicians*: Antiphon seizes on another apparent paradox in Socratic practice, that he prepares students for political life while abstaining from seeking office himself. Plato presents Socrates as avoiding political activity (Pl. *Ap.* 31cd, 32e; *Gorgias* 473e–474a); Xenophon presents him fulfilling his duties when selected by lot (4.2.2). But Xenophon's Socrates is much more aware of and accepting of the likely career path of his young followers, providing them with practical advice for achieving their goals.

Chapter 1.7

Socrates encourages his followers to avoid flattery and to seek out accurate assessments of their own skills, as a means of ensuring that they and others are not given military or political positions beyond their competence.

1.7.1 *empty pretence*: Socrates' warnings against *alazoneia* (pretence or boasting) provide a mirror for his encouragement towards *aretē* (virtue or excellence).

1.7.2 *pipe-player*: Xenophon along with Plato and Aristotle often uses the pipe-player as an example of a skill, even though such musicians were of low and possibly even slave status. Yet even this example opens up the question of what one would copy to copy their skill. Xenophon here uses the language of refutation—elenchus—suggesting a nod to a more Platonic Socrates.

fans: in a political culture which lacked party structures, it was thought that some politicians would create an atmosphere positive towards them by packing meetings with their own supporters.

1.7.3 *general... helmsman*: two further roles also much deployed in discussions of the acquisition and use of technical expertise; the general will reappear as an important role for leading citizens in Book 3.

BOOK 2

Chapter 2.1

This chapter is about self-discipline and the 'choice of lives' at different levels. Firstly the young Aristippus must choose the kind of life he wants to lead—and, as Socrates argues, not evade either the duties or benefits of participating in the public life of the city. Secondly, in the story Socrates retells to persuade Aristippus, the young Heracles must choose between two paths, of Virtue and hard work, or Vice and easy pleasure. In this story, attributed to the sophist Prodicus, these qualities are represented by two women.

2.1.1 *control over their desires*: the bodily self-control (*enkrateia*) which Xenophon has already (1.5) shown to be the hallmark of the virtuous man is the ostensible theme of this programmatic dialogue, although it encompasses a much broader exploration of the choices and responsibilities of individuals and citizens.

Aristippus: the Aristippus of Cyrene who appears in this dialogue was either the founder of the Cyrenaic school of hedonistic philosophy, or the grandfather of that founder, an associate of Socrates. Aristippus appears

often in Socratic dialogues by different authors, mentioned (as absent
from Socrates' deathbed) in Plato's *Phaedo*, and appearing in a fragment
of Aeschines, as well as *Memorabilia* 3.8; later sources suggest further
travels to the court of Dionysius at Syracuse, where he served as court
philosopher (DL 2.66–9, 73). Here, Aristippus represents the 'choice of
life' taken to extremes: the choice usually lies between participating in
politics or withdrawing from public life for a life of philosophical contem-
plation. Aristippus, in refusing to participate in civic life, claims to avoid
the slavery of social and political obligation; if he did end up subject to the
whims of a Sicilian tyrant, Xenophon's point is made.

capable of governing: the assumption was that young Athenian men would
want to participate in the life of the city, and seek an elected office such as
the generalship or, in the fourth century when Xenophon was writing,
a growing range of financial and administrative roles.

2.1.2 *educated for government*: the education of elite young men by sophists was
supposed to prepare them for speech-making and to win arguments in the
assembly and other civic bodies, although as Socrates' conversations will
show, they did not necessarily gain the practical skills Xenophon thought
necessary for success.

2.1.4 *Quails and partridges*: quails were often kept as fighting birds, but were
also notorious for their sexual appetites (and thus lack of *enkrateia*), as
implied here. Plutarch tells a story about Alcibiades speaking in the assembly and a quail he was carrying being startled by the noise of the crowd,
and flying out of his cloak (Plutarch *Life of Alcibiades* 10.1).

2.1.5 *adulterers… private quarters*: adultery between men and married women
of citizen status was treated severely in Athenian law. In these circumstances, consensual extramarital sex was seen as a worse crime than non-
consensual rape and assault, because it involved the alienation of a wife's
affection from her husband. Athenians still knew of an ancient law according to which a husband could kill an adulterer found in flagrante in his
house; it is claimed as a defence by Euphiletus, the speaker of Lysias 1, *On
the Murder of Eratosthenes*. It was considered improper for a man to enter
the private interior spaces of another citizen's home, where the women
lived and worked, in the absence of the male head of household (e.g. Lysias
3.29–30); symposia attended by male guests usually took place in dining
rooms near the entrance to the property.

2.1.6 *the open air*: in the *Oeconomicus*, Xenophon divides the world into the
masculine space of the open air and the feminine space of the domestic
interior; this extends the contrast with the interior world of the home.

2.1.8 *open himself to prosecution*: that the work of the elite in leading the city
and its military forces brought no positive reward but only the risk of
prosecution and punishment is a major theme of Xenophon's work.
During his lifetime many prominent generals were prosecuted for military
failures in the field; the case of the Arginusae generals (see notes on 1.1.18
and 4.4.2) is a significant instance of the phenomenon, partly because of

Socrates' claimed presence at the trial (*Hell*. 1.7.15), but during the early fourth century the prosecution of generals through *eisangelia* (impeachment) proceedings was common, and many of the city's leading generals were prosecuted for their (later) efforts. These included generals whose actions are reported and appraised by Xenophon in his *Hellenica*: Timotheus (*Hell*. 4.4.63–6) and Iphicrates, appointed to take his place (*Hell*. 6.2.12–14; cf. 6.4.49–52, where Xenophon criticizes his tactics). Thucydides' Diodotus, analysing the weaknesses of Athenian democratic procedure in the Mytilene debate, also argues that politicians are subject to unfair risk (Thuc. 3.42–3).

2.1.9 *Cities expect to treat their rulers as I do my household slaves*: the enslaved had no choice in following their masters' orders and no legal capacity to make decisions. Aristippus introduces an inversion of the usual understanding of ruling, one in which leaders who are subjected to the control and scrutiny of a democracy are enslaved rather than empowered by ruling. Plato attributes the view that political freedom could only be found in ruling to sophists such as Gorgias (*Gorgias* 452d; cf. *Meno* 73cd). By extension, being ruled was necessarily an intolerable infringement of freedom for the free citizen and placed him in the position of an enslaved person. Socrates will go on to explore the consequences of the parallel Aristippus draws.

as easy and enjoyable life: Aristippus suggests that there is an enjoyable life available by forgoing the competition required to participate in political life, and that the costs of political participation outweigh any possible benefit to the individual politician.

2.1.10 *that lived by the rulers or by the ruled*: Socrates responds by reframing Aristippus' claim in the usual opposition made in Greek political thinking, that between the ruler and the ruled, rather than Aristippus' opposition of the ruler and the non-ruler. Some political commentators (notably those in the Straussian tradition; see the Introduction) suggest that the arguments Xenophon gives to Socrates in this discussion mark him as a political realist who conceptualizes politics as a zero-sum competition for power, with no excluded middle ground between ruling and being ruled. Socrates uses a conventional principle of *polis* politics, as developed in Athenian democracy; that equal citizens should take turns in ruling—that is, holding political office—and being ruled—that is, following the instruction of those in office. This principle is elaborated by Aristotle in *Politics* book 3, chapters 1–5, a focused discussion on what it means to be a citizen of a polis.

the nations known to us: Socrates makes another move in framing the analysis of the differing pleasure of rulers and ruled by considering it at the level of the community rather than the individual. Again, this was a conventional analysis in late fifth-century Athens, as the city was recognized as a ruler of subject cities across the Greek world. That this was an uncomfortable position for the ruler is acknowledged by Thucydides' Pericles

(Thuc. 2.63). Socrates begins by looking at nations (*ethnē*) rather than cities (*poleis*)—enabling him to incorporate Persia into his framework.

Asia: by bringing in examples from outside the world of the Greek polis, Socrates is able to make a sharp distinction between rulers and ruled. The Persian Empire was the archetype of despotism in Greek thought, and the status of subject peoples such as the Syrians and Lydians was viewed as a form of slavery.

Europe: Xenophon means places north of the Greek world. The Scythians, who lived in what is now the Russian steppes and around the Black Sea, were in the Greek view notoriously brutal warriors (Herodotus' ethnography at 4.59–77 is a good example); subjection to them could not be considered a pleasant life.

Africa: Carthage held an unusual position in Greek political thought as a non-Greek polis with political arrangements which could be analysed in the same way as those of Greek cities (e.g. Ar. *Pol.* 2.11, 1272b24–1273b24). But the western Greeks of Sicily were engaged in a continuing war against Carthaginian settlements on the island, conflicts which would continue for centuries as the Romans' Punic Wars.

those who dominate or those who are dominated: based on the examples he has deployed, Socrates is able to reformulate his opposition between ruling and being ruled in terms of the exercise of power. Aristippus will find it hard to argue that being defeated can be a pleasant life.

2.1.11 *in the position of a slave*: Aristippus shows that he has recognized Socrates' reframing of the argument, but rejects the idea that not ruling necessitates being enslaved.

a middle road: Aristippus asserts that there is a further option and that ruling and being ruled do not exhaust the options for living the good life. By using the image of a 'path' (*hodos*) and walking down it (*badizein*), Aristippus appears to suggest that this is a life lived outside the polis. The language also introduces both Socrates' counter-argument—the danger of life outside the protection of a community—and the myth of Heracles at a crossroad in his life journey.

2.1.12 *stronger...slaves*: Socrates' response here draws together the implications of his previous statement and suggests that only ruling offers freedom from political slavery.

2.1.13 *cut the corn*: invading armies either took crops for their own use (as Xenophon often does during the *Anabasis*, foraging for supplies), or destroyed them to reduce the resources available to their enemy.

remain a foreigner: Socrates has suggested a brutal state of nature operating within political entities. Aristippus' response is to suggest that he can exist outside the framework of the polis and its political obligations by declaring that he is a *xenos* or guest/foreigner. He is setting aside the complex reciprocal obligations between guests and hosts associated with *xenia* (hospitality) in Greek culture, which would be familiar to Xenophon's contemporaries from works such as Homer's *Odyssey*, in which Odysseus' status as a guest was a major theme.

2.1.14 *Sinis and Sciron and Procrustes*: Socrates can counter Aristippus' claim using the stories of these three notorious brigands, who attacked travellers on the road from Megara to Athens, until the hero Theseus killed them on his own journey to the city. Sinis tied travellers to two bent pine trees; when the trees were released, the victims were torn apart. Sciron would accost travellers on the narrow clifftop path at Megara to stop and wash his feet, then kick them off the cliff into the sea, where they were devoured by a monster. Procrustes offered travellers a bed, but made them fit it by stretching them or chopping off their extremities. These stories were much retold and illustrated for Athenian audiences (Bacchylides 18.16–30; Euripides *Hippolytus* 976–80; Isocrates *Helen* 29–30) They were further developed by later writers (Plutarch *Life of Theseus* 8–11). Athenians liked to balance stories and images of Theseus and Heracles, sometimes implying that Theseus' deeds were 'more useful' (Isocrates *Helen* 23–4), so this mention of Theseus' labours points to the story of Heracles which will conclude the chapter. Dorion suggests that Socrates makes an ironic point that the Athenians and their hero had not in fact ensured the safety of travellers.

2.1.15 *no use as a slave*: Socrates moves ground and suggests that Aristippus is protected from harm by his uselessness; no one would want to enslave him because there would be no benefit in doing so.

2.1.17 *"the royal art of government"*: this is the first mention in the *Memorabilia* of an important Socratic concept, that of the master or ruling art (*basilikē technē*). It is both a skill which controls other skills and a skill in some way peculiar to those with high authority. The concept appears in one form or another across the philosophical sources for Socrates, from Antisthenes' fragments, in which kingship is a recurrent concern, to the dialogues of Xenophon and Plato. Plato treats *basilikē technē* as an elusive concept; the *Euthydemus* turns on its identification. Arguably Plato develops it into his broader concept of rule by philosophers, introduced in the *Republic*. But the concept is most fully worked out in a slightly different form, as the political knowledge (*politikē epistēmē*) which enables the skilled political leader to weave a stable body politic from his disparate citizens (Plato *Statesman*).

happiness: happiness (*eudaimonia*) was identified by Aristotle as the goal of human community, and not just as a personal emotion; Xenophon likewise shows it as an aim of those ruling as a benefit for their communities. It will recur as a goal and benefit of friendship throughout this book. In the story of Heracles at the crossroads, Vice will claim it as her own name (2.1.26).

compelled to hardship: Aristippus reprises his initial point that there is no difference between the hardships voluntarily undergone by those being educated in the royal art (*basilikē technē*) and the involuntary hardships of those who are enslaved and subject to their masters' will.

2.1.18 *voluntary and involuntary*: Socrates makes the important point that individuals can choose hardship now in favour of greater pleasure later, a point that will be debated in the story of Heracles which follows.

2.1.20 *Hesiod*: *Works and Days* 287–92. Plato cited versions of this passage repeatedly (*Rep.* 2.364cd; *Laws* 4.718e–719a; *Protagoras* 340d); for Plato's Socrates the image of the longer and more difficult path was an analogy for education and intellectual enquiry. The contrasting images of virtue and vice are developed in the myth of the Choice of Heracles, which follows.

Epicharmus: Epicharmus of Cos, who lived and worked in Syracuse in the first half of the fifth century BCE, was primarily known as one of the first comic playwrights; he is identified as the foremost comic poet by Socrates (Pl. *Theaetetus* 152e). He was also known for his philosophical writings. Diogenes Laertius cites a Sicilian historian Alcimus who claimed that Plato took many of his metaphysical ideas on being and becoming and his Theory of Forms from him (DL 3.9.17), part of a broader tradition linking Plato to the Pythagoreans of Italy and Sicily. Only fragments of his work survive. The two lines quoted here are Epicharmus fragments 271 and 236 in R. Kassel and C. Austin, *Poetae Comici Graeci* (Berlin: Du Gruyter, 1983–).

2.1.21 *lecture*: Prodicus of Ceos (see note below) was known for his versions of myths, including a book in praise of Heracles (Pl. *Smp.* 177b), and for his expensive set-piece lectures (Ar. *Rhetoric* 1515b). Whether this story about Heracles sticks closely to an original work by Prodicus, contains contributions from Socrates himself, or is developed or embellished by Xenophon, is unknown. But the presence of Xenophontic themes and Socrates' closing remarks suggest that any material from Prodicus has been transformed in the retelling.

Heracles: the hero Heracles is a significant exemplar of idealized masculinity in Greek myth, despite or perhaps because of the complications of his life story. As an adult Heracles faced many challenges, including his twelve labours; here he is depicted at the age when a youth was no longer accompanied by a tutor but had discretion over his own actions (the Greek word for 'independent', *autokratores*, also has a political sense of not being subject to oversight in decision-making and action). Heracles' life of toil and travel made him a favourite figure of the Cynics. Plato's Socrates presents himself as a less-successful Heracles fighting the hydra (*Euthydemus* 297bd).

Prodicus: Prodicus of Ceos was probably a contemporary of Socrates, and a much-respected teacher in Athens as well as an ambassador for his home city. Aristophanes associates him with Socrates (*Clouds* 358–63). Plato shows Socrates sending potential students to him and treating him as an expert on the meaning of words (*Protagoras* 337ac), although he also suggests that Prodicus was rather self-important, and mocks his booming voice and conscious self-presentation (*Protagoras* 315c–316a).

2.1.22 *fine-looking*: Xenophon's presentation of Virtue and Vice combines the aesthetic and the ethical, in his usual way, although here extended through the use of Athenian ideas about women's appearance. Virtue exemplifies the presentation of femininity expected of a good Athenian citizen wife, and Vice that associated with bad behaviour and non-citizen prostitution.

fleshiness: visible evidence of failure to control appetite, and thus of lack of the qualities exemplified by Virtue.

cosmetic enhancement: Vice's physicality matches the practices—wearing make-up—which Ischomachus warned his wife against, arguing that an artificial appearance compromised the open and honest connection between husband and wife (Xen. *Oec.* 10). While Athenian citizen women did wear make-up, the practice was associated with sexual appetite; Euphiletus, the speaker of Lysias' *On the Murder of Eratosthenes*, notes that in retrospect his wife's use of make-up was a sign of her infidelity (Lysias 1.14).

2.1.23 *pleasantest and easiest path*: a contrast with Hesiod's path of virtue, cited above.

2.1.27 *your parents*: Heracles' situation is like that of an elite youth in Athens, where parents were responsible for arranging education, unlike the Spartan polis-organized training regime. But Virtue is also hinting that she knows Heracles' divine father Zeus.

2.1.28 *all Greece*: truly great reputations extend beyond the circle of friends and one's own city to the entire Greek world; Virtue offers another route to the universal status Aristippus sought.

2.1.30 *professional chefs*: expertise in cookery has an ambivalent status for Xenophon, implying luxuriousness and lack of control of the appetite. While he deprecates pleasure in gourmet food, the Socratic principle of specialization in labour requires him to acknowledge that there is an expertise in preparing food. Xenophon depicts Cyrus employing specialist chefs when he sets up his palace system after conquering Babylon (*Cyr.* 8.2.5–6), while warning his subordinates against pleasure in food (*Cyr.* 7.5.80–2).

using men like women: while same-sex erotic attachments between men were institutionalized in the Athenian practice of pederasty, such relationships took place within a strict set of limits of acceptable behaviour, in which the older party was expected to control physical desire. More usually, citizen men who allowed other men to penetrate them were subject to criticism and indeed to political penalties; Aeschines' speech *Against Timarchus* accuses that politician of having prostituted himself in his youth, and thus made himself ineligible for political office. Xenophon reframes the pederastic relationship as an opportunity for the *erastēs* to demonstrate self-control and moderation in not engaging in socially unacceptable sexual activity with the *erōmenos*.

2.1.32 *craftsmen…slaves*: virtue and happiness are not the exclusive prerogative of the elite.

2.1.34 *more elevated language*: although Xenophon presents this story as a plain retelling of Prodicus' work, it contains many typical Xenophontic touches, such as the use of superlatives.

Chapter 2.2

This chapter introduces a series of discussions on friendship (*philia*), which start with the closest familial relations. Socrates admonishes his son Lamprocles for his sulky disrespect towards his mother, and explains the work that parents, especially mothers, put into raising children, and the concern they show for them. The work parents perform for their children provides the first opportunity for showing gratitude for benefits received, fundamental to all kinds of friendship.

2.2.1 *Lamprocles*: Socrates' eldest son is still a boy in this short dialogue, our best source for his name; although Plato does not name him, he reports that an elder son and two younger ones are present at Socrates' trial (*meirakion*, Pl. *Ap.* 34d) and subsequently visit him in prison (*Phd.* 116b).

mother: Xenophon presents Socrates' wife as difficult and argumentative (*Smp.* 2.10), a portrait supported by Lamprocles' account here, although not perhaps by Socrates' response. Plato names her as Xanthippe and depicts her displaying appropriate emotion while visiting Socrates before his death (*Phd.* 60a, 116b), and makes no mention of any negative character attributes. There are suggestions that Xanthippe was from an aristocratic background, based on the *-hippe* ('horse') element in her name.

ungrateful: gratitude (*charis*) is important as both an emotion and a social practice in Xenophon's thought. The expression of gratitude is fundamental to building and maintaining interpersonal relationships.

2.2.2 *unjust to enslave*: Xenophon hints at the injustice of slavery; in traditional Greek morality, to which Xenophon frequently refers, it counts as harming enemies rather than helping friends (see 2.3.14, 4.5.10).

2.2.4 *a desire for sex*: Xenophon acknowledges that marriage is not the only outlet for sexual desire for men (see also *Oec.* 7.11), although the end of his *Symposium* suggests that he believes it to be the best one (*Smp.* 9.5–7).

the best children: Xenophon here acknowledges eugenicist currents in Greek thought, also seen in Spartan approaches to the reproduction of its elite citizen class (*Lac. Pol.* 1–3). Eugenicism was a major feature of Plato's ideal city Kallipolis (*Rep.* 5.458e–461b), where the philosopher rulers control citizens' sexual relationships to produce children of desired qualities, in the same way that an elite Athenian might breed hounds or fighting birds.

2.2.5 *this burden*: the contribution of women to conception and gestation was not well understood by the ancient Greeks. Xenophon's awareness of the physical burden of pregnancy and child-rearing, and of maternal emotions, is unusual compared with other ancient authorities such as Aristotle.

2.2.7 *an animal's or a mother's*: comparing women to animals came very easily to Greek writers, most notoriously in the vicious iambic poem by the seventh-century poet Semonides of Amorgos (Fragment 7), in which women are criticized through comparisons to animals possessing a range of negative characteristics.

2.2.11 *not following anyone's instructions*: Xenophon hints that Lamprocles' attitude, disdaining reciprocal social bonds, parallels that of Aristippus in the previous chapter.

2.2.12 *your neighbour ... will bring you light for your fire*: this was an essential act of neighbourliness symbolic of functioning community, mentioned at *Odyssey* 5.488–90 and Lysias 1.14.

2.2.13 *failing to look after his parents*: failure to care for parents could disqualify a candidate from office; see note below.

vetting candidates: candidates for political offices were vetted to check their eligibility and good standing, a process called *dokimasia*. Candidates had to show that they had treated their parents properly among other social obligations such as participating in the cult of the city's patron gods, and demonstrate that they held full Athenian citizenship and so were qualified for office ([Ar.], *Ath. Pol.* 55.3).

Chapter 2.3

Chaerecrates, the younger brother of Socrates' friend Chaerephon, feels that his brother is failing to show him enough respect. Socrates encourages Chaerecrates to rebuild his relationship with his brother.

2.3.1 *Chaerephon and Chaerecrates*: the older brother Chaerephon appears to have been the closer friend of Socrates (Pl. *Ap.* 20e–21a) although both are listed as companions of Socrates at 1.2.48. Here the younger brother Chaerecrates is the focus, and the complex balance of sibling relations within the context of agonistic city life the topic.

brother: the relationships and rivalries of brothers are a stock theme of Greek literature, from Agamemnon and Menelaus, and Hector and Paris, in Homer's *Iliad*, to the warring Eteocles and Polyneices in the Theban myth cycle featured in many tragedies.

2.3.3 *buy slaves ... acquire friends*: the comparison of the acquisition of friends and slaves is a recurrent theme of this book. A brother should be a friend with little or no cost of acquisition.

2.3.9 *a dog that was good with sheep*: working dogs, especially those used by shepherds to control their flocks, and the hounds trained for hunting, are favourite examples for both Plato and Xenophon. Both authors use them as examples familiar to their elite students; Plato notably turns to the breeding of hunting dogs to explain his eugenic ideas for the imagined ideal city of Kallipolis (see note on 2.2.4; *Rep.* 5.458e–459a). Here the dog is one specialized in another canine task, assisting the shepherd, pointing back to the image of the shepherd king.

2.3.11 *an invitation to the dinner*: an invitation to dinner at a house which had just held a private sacrifice would be likely to include red meat, which was only eaten by the Greeks on such festive occasions.

2.3.13 *hospitality*: hospitality (*xenia*) was a revered Greek tradition, associated with Zeus Xenios as its god. It was also an important way of managing political and commercial relationships between the citizens of different poleis, as Socrates and Chaerecrates note here. It is as a guest (*xenos*) that Aristippus hopes to evade the obligations of citizenship (see 2.1.13–14).

2.3.14 *do harm to his enemies*: a traditional Greek view of justice; see 4.5.10.

2.3.18 *a pair of hands*: the idea that brothers should work together naturally is emphasized by this comparison with body parts which come in pairs, and are typically expressed in Greek using the dual form, a plural only used for natural pairs of things, such as body parts or siblings.

Chapter 2.4

This short conversation, not addressed to any specific individual, compares the treatment of friends with the treatment of slaves and other property. Socrates argues that people consistently fail to place a calculated value on their friendships in the way that they value slaves and other property, causing them to underinvest in maintaining relationships and ensuring the well-being of their friends.

2.4.1 *I once heard*: this chapter, unlike the others in this section, does not describe a conversation with a named individual. Instead, Xenophon emphasizes that he heard the conversation and approved of its content.

   possessions: a corollary of treating friendship as a material good is that it enables it to be analogized to slavery, another way in which Greeks treated human relationships in property terms. Aristotle's *Politics* contains the most detailed exploration of slavery as the use by one human of another human as an 'ensouled tool' (*Pol.* 1.5), but the views Xenophon attributes to Socrates here clearly follows similar lines.

2.4.2 *slaves*: emphasizing that slaves are property, Xenophon lists them here as *andrapoda*, literally 'man-footed things', perhaps the harshest of the many Greek terms for the enslaved.

2.4.3 *household slaves*: here the word for slaves is *oiketai*, slaves who worked within the house or *oikos* (as opposed to doing agricultural work on the farm, or being hired out for wage labour within the city). The distinction between indoor and outdoor work echoes the gendered division of labour Xenophon explores in the *Oeconomicus*. It also implies a hierarchy among the enslaved, seen in other slave societies such as the early colonial American states.

2.4.5 *superior worth*: the conceptualization of friendship as an economic good enables it to be used for establishing and comparing economic values. Constructing mechanisms for comparing and ranking values, even apparently disparate ones, was central to Greek thought on administering justice; see Aristotle *NE* 5.5 for a detailed account of mechanisms of arithmetic and geometric equality to use for this purpose.

   possession...service: the long list of tasks for which a friend can be useful suggests that Xenophon is conceptualizing the friend as a tool, in a manner similar to the Aristotelian conception of the enslaved person as an 'ensouled tool' (see note on 2.4.1).

Chapter 2.5

Socrates uses a conversation with Antisthenes about the wealthy Nicias to encourage another associate to be more supportive of a friend in need, extending the comparison between the value of friends and the value of slaves.

2.5.1 *stimulate...to self-examination*: throughout the *Memorabilia* Xenophon emphasizes the way in which Socrates encouraged his followers to take up philosophical practice; he emphasizes the protreptic ('turning towards') mode of Socrates' engagement with followers like Antisthenes.

Antisthenes: a close companion of Socrates (3.11.17), Antisthenes makes a memorable speech on the subject of poverty and fulfilment in Xenophon's *Symposium* (*Smp.* 4.34–44), a speech which represents the ascetic views associated with his later followers. The historical Antisthenes lived *c*.446–366, and in his earlier years was associated with Gorgias as well as Socrates. After Socrates' death he became one of the leading proponents of Socratic thought, and his views on ethical topics as well as philosophical method, extensively documented across multiple works of which only small fragments survive, were of great influence on two key groups of post-Socratic thinkers, the Cynics and the Stoics (DL 6.15).

2.5.2 *two minas*: 1 mina was 100 drachmas; the drachma was itself the largest unit of currency for everyday transactions. An inscription containing surviving fragments of the accounts for the building of the Erechtheion, the temple on Athens' Acropolis which featured the caryatids, give us some insight into Athenian wage rates during the late fifth century (full text at https://www.atticinscriptions.com/inscription/IGI3/474 and see R. Osborne and P. J. Rhodes, *Greek Historical Inscriptions: 478–404 BC* (Oxford: Oxford University Press, 2017), No. 181). Skilled craftsmen, free and enslaved, were paid roughly 1 drachma a day for working on architectural details such as carving the fluting on columns; some less skilled workers received a little less. Athenians could also be paid 3 obols (1/2 drachma) a day for performing public roles such as jury duty, and poverty relief was set at 2 obols a day (1/3 drachma).

Nicias the son of Niceratus: Athenian businessman and general, whose public career began as a supporter of Pericles and who followed him as a political leader. Nicias was not from an aristocratic background but from a family which had made its fortune from hiring slaves to the Athenian silver mines (see note below); he earned a reputation as a lavish sponsor of Athenian culture, often winning prizes for his productions. His political rivalry with the populist Cleon was parodied by Aristophanes in the *Knights*. After Cleon's death on campaign, Nicias negotiated a treaty that paused the Peloponnesian War until Alcibiades persuaded the Athenians to invade Sicily (415 BCE); Nicias died on that expedition as the Athenians were defeated. Nicias appears as one of the experienced generals in Plato's

Laches, where he offers advice on education for public life and military service.

a whole talent: a talent was 60 minas or 6,000 drachmas, although it was an amount more usually expressed in metal ingots rather than coins. The calculable economic value of a slave enables a value to be set on the support received from a friend. Such a calculation of economic benefit from friendship is taken up by Aristotle (*NE* books 8–9); there, he identifies three types of friendships, one based on the mutual recognition of benefit from transactions, one on pleasure in company, and the best on the mutual recognition of virtue.

silver mines: Nicias' father had made his fortune by hiring out slaves to the leaseholders of silver mines at Laurium in Attica, a trade which Nicias continued, at one point controlling 1,000 slaves in this work (Xen. *Poroi* 4.14). In the *Poroi*, his pamphlet on the Athenian economy, Xenophon suggests that the city should emulate this business and lease slaves bought from public funds to mining enterprises, to improve the city's finances. The discovery of silver on Athenian soil in the early fifth century powered Athenian defence during the Persian Wars; the conditions for slaves working in the mines were brutal and unhealthy (see 3.6.12).

Chapter 2.6

This long conversation with Critobulus, son of Crito, explores what kinds of friends are useful, and how best to go about acquiring useful friends. Since Critobulus has already been introduced as an eager lover, the dialogue explores the parallels between and intersections with friendship and erotic love, across erotic and educational contexts.

2.6.1 *how to test*: Xenophon uses the verb *dokimazein* which described the formal test and interview which candidates for a range of political office had to undergo before their candidacy was confirmed (see note on 2.2.13).

Critobulus: the son of Crito, already featured in 1.3.8–13. With this eager lover as the interlocutor, the dialogue draws together erotic and educational contexts, explored through literary allusion.

2.6.3 *businessman*: the businessman who values money is regularly cited as a negative exemplar in Plato's dialogues. Despite the pragmatic interest in worth and value which Xenophon ascribes to Socrates, seen in the previous discussion, he shares the view that the pursuit of money can be damaging to the collective well-being of the city, also seen for example in Aristotle's *Politics* (1.10–11).

2.6.4 *political agitator*: another negative exemplar is the political agitator (*stasiōdēs*) who exploits political faction (*stasis*) and dissent within the city.

with no thought of reciprocating: another instance of the fundamental role of reciprocal support as a way of maintaining social bonds between citizens. A friend who did not provide help in return was useless as a political ally.

2.6.6 *sculptors*: see 3.10 for more on the role of sculpture.

2.6.8 *divine guidance*: whether this is a reference to Socrates' divine sign or other forms of receiving divine advice, finding a new friend is treated as a serious endeavour (akin to finding a bride, 1.1.8), the success of which cannot be known in advance.

2.6.9 *hare...bird*: although this is explicitly an allusion to hunting, birds and hares were also courtship gifts offered in pederastic relationships; hunting and pederasty were regularly compared, for example in Plato's *Sophist* (221d–222c), where the sophist is likened to someone hunting for young men in a rich meadow.

2.6.10 *enchantments*: Socrates uses magical terms as an analogy for persuasive speech, an analogy which will recur in the discussion with Theodote, at 3.11.

2.6.11 *Sirens...Odysseus*: the Sirens were birdlike female figures who sang to lure sailors' ships on to the rocks. Alcibiades compares Socrates' words to their song (Pl. *Smp.* 216a). Odysseus describes his encounter with them during his travels after the fall of Troy (Homer *Odyssey* 12.8–54, 153–200). Following the instructions given to him by Circe, Odysseus blocked his crew's ears with wax so that they could not be tempted, but listened to the song himself while tied to his ship's mast so that he could not respond. The Sirens flatter him by acknowledging his fame (Xenophon quotes *Odyssey* 12.184), and attempt to persuade him to leave the ship and come closer to listen to their beautiful song, but his sailors cannot hear his pleas to be released and so the ship continues on its journey.

2.6.13 *Pericles*: see note on 1.2.40. Here, Socrates presents Pericles as capable of charming the people through the magical power of his words. Pericles' rhetoric and actions are subject to extended criticism in Plato's *Gorgias*.

Themistocles: Athens' leader during the Persian Wars of 480/79 BCE, who fortified the city and built up its navy, using revenue from the then newly discovered Laurium silver deposit.

amulet: an allusion to the fortifications around Athens built at Themistocles' suggestion, including the Long Walls, which protected Athens and connected it to its port at the Piraeus (Thuc. 1.89–93).

2.6.14 *say and do*: Critobulus summarizes the examples of Pericles' speech and Themistocles' actions.

2.6.18 *Cities*: Parallels are again drawn between the actions of individuals and political entities.

2.6.22 *moderate substance*: Socrates suggests that there is a mean amount of property appropriate to the *kalos kagathos*, and contrasts the untroubled enjoyment of moderate property with the unrestrained and competitive pursuit of acquisition, as another example of the proper control of appetite.

2.6.26 *athletic games*: major religious festivals across the Greek world often included an athletic competition; there was a regular circuit of such competitions, which typically involved separate individual events in athletics, including track and field events, wrestling, and chariot racing. Winning a prize at a major festival, such as the Olympic festival or Athens' own Panathenaea, brought honour to both the individual athlete (or the team sponsor, in the case of chariot racing) and to that individual's city.

2.6.28 *my expertise in matters of love*: both Plato and Xenophon present Socrates as an expert on erotic interactions, with hints of humour. In Plato's *Symposium*, Socrates asserts that love is the only thing of which he has positive knowledge (Pl. *Smp*. 177de); he goes on to describe how the priestess Diotima of Mantinea (probably an imagined character) taught him erotics, while Alcibiades describes Socrates' almost magical charm in attracting those around him (*Smp*. 215a–216a). Xenophon returns to this theme in Socrates' encounter with the *hetaira* Theodote at 3.11; the next few paragraphs contain many ideas reworked in that later discussion.

2.6.31 *Scylla*: another danger encountered by Odysseus in the same part of his journey, the monstrous Scylla held one side of a narrow strait; at the other was the whirlpool Charybdis. However, Circe advised Odysseus to sail closer to Scylla than to Charybdis, as it was more likely that his ship would survive that encounter even if all his crew did not (Homer *Odyssey* 12.80–126). Scylla was imagined as a multi-bodied female figure, part dog, part sea monster, part woman, who would snatch sailors from ships and eat them (*Odyssey* 12.222–58).

Sirens: see note on 2.6.11.

2.6.36 *Aspasia*: Aspasia of Miletus was the partner of Pericles although not his legal wife. There is little firm evidence about her life, although she is thought to have been a member of a high-status family in her home polis, before moving to Athens where she did not have citizen status. Her relationship with Pericles began after his divorce from his Athenian wife, but her status as a resident alien (metic) meant that they could not have a legal marriage. The couple were the frequent target of comedy; Aspasia's non-citizen status meant that she could easily be portrayed as a *hetaira*, as sex work was permitted for metic women, and in a culture of arranged marriages their affectionate relationship was unusual and noteworthy. Aspasia was the mother of Pericles Jr (Socrates' interlocutor in 3.5); after the death of Pericles' two sons from his marriage, the city granted citizenship to this young man so that Pericles could have a legitimate heir. Plato presents Aspasia as Socrates' teacher of rhetoric and author of a funeral speech (*Menexenus* 235e–236e), while Xenophon presents her as an expert in household management (*Oec.* 3.14).

2.6.39 *study and practice*: the importance of persistent hard work in developing skills and understanding is a key theme of the *Memorabilia*, first introduced in the opening chapters (see 1.2.23) and further developed in Books 3 and 4.

Chapter 2.7

Socrates gives practical advice to Aristarchus on how to live in straitened financial circumstances. If he puts the women of his household to work making clothes, the business will provide for the household, and everyone will be happier.

2.7.1 *Aristarchus*: the precise identification of this character remains difficult; the name is quite common in late fifth-century sources. The most prominent bearer of the name was strongly opposed to the democracy when he became involved in the 411/10 oligarchy (Thuc. 8.90.1) and was probably executed before 406 (Xen. *Hell.* 1.7.28),

2.7.2 *civil war*: Xenophon's description of events gives an unusually precise dramatic date, during the 404/3 BCE oligarchy when many (but by no means all) of the citizens who favoured democracy withdrew from the city to its nearby port, the Piraeus; other Athenians were confined to the city as its surrounding farmland was occupied by the Spartans.

Piraeus: Athens' port, a few miles south of the city itself, had a distinctive political culture. It was home to many metics and traders, as both renting property and gaining access to the courts were easier for non-citizens there than in the main city centre. It played a vital role in the democratic resistance to the 404/3 BCE oligarchy. Athenians sympathetic to democracy flocked there and mounted their resistance to the oligarchs from the well-defended port.

womenfolk: in classical Athens it was difficult for citizen women, especially those of the propertied classes, to live independently of men; usually, the nearest male relative held the family property and acted as *kurios* or guardian for daughters, sisters, and nieces. It was thought improper for such women to engage in paid work—lower-status women might make goods and sell them in the marketplace, but Aristarchus' reputation would suffer if his women were seen to work outside the home.

2.7.3 *Ceramon*: nothing is known of this individual, who again represents a typical situation for a wealthy Athenian, earning from enslaved labour; Dorion suggests that the name might be intended to describe someone who ran a pottery.

2.7.6 *Nausicydes*: a miller with a large workforce of the enslaved; Aristophanes implies that he charged a high price for his barley meal (*Ecclesiazusae* 424–6).

sponsor public services: one way in which wealthy Athenians were taxed was by the imposition of liturgies, which required them to pay for a public good, such as sponsoring the production of a play for one of the city's festivals, or outfitting a warship for its navy. See note on 3.4.3.

Cyrebus: nothing more is known of this wealthy baker.

Demeas of Collytus: nothing more is known of this maker of cloaks; Collytus was one of the wealthiest central demes or districts of the city of Athens, and the home of Plato's family.

Menon: nothing more is known of this maker of blankets; not the same person as the Meno of Thessaly, who appears in Plato's dialogue *Meno* and Xenophon's *Anabasis*.

Megarians: the city of Megara, just to the west of Athens, was renowned for its production of woollen cloaks, mentioned by Aristophanes (*Acharnians* 519; *Peace* 1000–2) and Thucydides (1.139).

2.7.10 *anything shameful*: the implication is that the women might be forced into sex work, a common although not the only form of paid work open to (non-citizen) women in Athens. Prostitution was not compatible with citizen status for men or women, and most women engaged in sex work would have been either enslaved, the property of their brothel-keeper, or of non-citizen metic status.

2.7.11 *take out a loan*: a sophisticated range of financial services was available in the Athenian *agora*, including credit for business and trading ventures, and bureaux de change for converting between the many different coinages of the Greek world. Xenophon's interest in business differentiates him from Plato, who proposes the abolition of such services in the imagined city of Magnesia (*Laws* 5.542cd).

2.7.13 *the fable of the dog*: Xenophon's love for dogs may contribute to this story, which resembles the fables of Aesop although does not match the detail of any specific fable. Gigon suggested a parallel between the sheep of the fable and the wool-working women of the dialogue.

Chapter 2.8

Eutherus has been impoverished by the war and lost his estates. Socrates advises him not to scrape a living by manual labour but to seek a managerial position on a large estate, a job he would be able to do even when old and less strong.

2.8.1 *Eutherus*: nothing is known of this Athenian beyond the information Xenophon gives here.

our foreign property: Eutherus appears to have held a cleruchy, an allotment of land in overseas territory conquered by Athens, taken from the defeated inhabitants and redistributed to Athenians. Athens used this process for distributing the spoils of war throughout the fifth century BCE, starting with Chalcis in 506 BCE. During the Peloponnesian War the city repopulated Lesbos (427) and Melos (416) by this route, after the original inhabitants had been killed or sold into slavery. Athenian citizens could take up a cleruchy without losing their rights as Athenian citizens. However, Athens lost control of these territories at the end of the Peloponnesian War in 404 BCE, depriving the cleruchs of their land, which gives a fairly precise dramatic date for this dialogue. Like Eutherus, the cleruchs could return to Athens, but were now without property or income.

manual labour: while cleruchs were not necessarily of high social status, Xenophon implies that Eutherus is unused to manual labour. Although many poor Athenians without their own land (such as the lowest property census class, the *thētes*) earned their living by hiring out their labour for building or agricultural work, political commentators saw such work as a low-status activity, and a key political tenet of oligarchy at Athens and elsewhere was that those without property should not be allowed full participation in the political life of the city.

2.8.3 *assistant manager*: such a role might be undertaken by a trusted and well-trained slave. Xenophon depicts Ischomachus training and relying on enslaved managers in the *Oeconomicus*, and earlier in this book (2.5.2) describes Nicias paying a substantial sum for a skilled slave to manage his mining interests.

2.8.5 *someone holding me to account*: Eutherus compares the possible evaluation of his work performance with the scrutiny and audit to which Athenian office-holders were subjected after the end of their period in office. By collapsing the distinction between public and private employment, Socrates makes the case that working for an employer does not transform a free citizen into an enslaved person.

Chapter 2.9

The wealthy Crito finds himself to be a target for vexatious litigation; his opponents hope that he will settle rather than defend cases. Socrates suggests that he hires Archedemus to act as a sort of legal sheepdog, to protect Crito's assets and reputation, and to deter frivolous complaints. Archedemus does this so well that he becomes a personal friend to Crito and is valued by Crito's wider circle.

2.9.1 *Crito*: Socrates' friend; see note on 1.2.48. Crito's difficulties are those which a prominent and wealthy citizen would be likely to face.

his own business: this phrase (*ta heautou prattein*, literally 'to do his own things') was often invoked in Greek political thought, to indicate what citizens would do in a flourishing and stable society. Plato associates it with moderation (*Charmides* 162d), albeit as part of a definition which is discarded, and with the parts of the city (and by analogy the soul) undertaking the work that is proper to them (*Rep.* 9.586e); by implication, Athenian democracy disturbed such arrangements, and prevented individuals from pursuing their own business or the activities suitable and proper to their character and station.

legal actions: because prosecutions in Athens were brought by individual citizens, it was possible to launch vexatious lawsuits against the wealthy or prominent. Those doing this were known as sycophants—the term may have originally referred to those denouncing crimes against public fig-trees (*suka*)—and are criticized in many surviving law-court speeches.

2.9.4 *Archedemus*: an Archedemus of Pelekes, a northern deme of Athens, was an active litigant in Athens during the period of the Peloponnesian War. He was notorious enough to be mentioned in comedies (such as Aristophanes *Frogs* 416); Xenophon elsewhere describes him as a prominent speaker and overseer; he shows him bringing charges against Erasinides, one of the Arginusae generals, for embezzlement of a poverty relief fund (*Hell.* 1.7.2), in addition to the charges related to the battle. Lysias presents him as the lover of Alcibiades' son and himself an embezzler (Lysias 14.25). It is not clear whether Xenophon intended a specific reference to this historical person, or simply to conjure up the figure of a legal activist who would suit Crito's needs.

Chapter 2.10

This chapter returns to the comparison of the value of slaves and friendship through a conversation with Diodorus, who is willing to spend money to recover runaway slaves but has not thought to give paid employment to a needy friend, Hermogenes.

2.10.1 *Diodorus*: nothing is known about this individual, depicted by Xenophon as a wealthy Athenian.

2.10.2 *If one of your household slaves falls ill*: a similar point to 2.4.3; slaves are treated as an asset to protect, while friends are not.

2.10.3 *Hermogenes*: see note on 1.2.48. A son of Hipponicus and brother of Callias, and a character in many works of Xenophon and other Socratics, Hermogenes is a speaker in Plato's *Cratylus*, and was present at Socrates' death (Pl. *Phd.* 59b). However, there is little consistency in his various appearances in dialogues, and here Xenophon may simply be seeking to represent a type. While Hipponicus and his heir Callias were among Athens' wealthy elite, Hermogenes as an illegitimate child did not enjoy the same status or rights, although he was acknowledged and referred to by his father's name. Xenophon may simply intend to show the situation of someone with a precarious connection to elite status.

BOOK 3

Chapter 3.1

This chapter introduces the theme of how Socrates helped those who aimed for high office in the city, by reporting how Socrates showed a young hopeful that Dionysodorus' teaching on generalship was inadequate.

3.1.1 *aspired to high office*: Xenophon's phrase can be read more broadly as 'aspiring to fine things', but the focus of this section are the specific goods of personal and political success within the context of Athenian democracy.

Dionysodorus: it is probable that this teacher is the same person as Dionysodorus, one of the pair of sophists from Plato's *Euthydemus*; they had begun their careers teaching subjects similar to Dionysodorus' offering here (Pl. *Euthydemus* 273c). An Athenian of the same name was a general supporting the democrats in 399 BCE (Lysias 13.13).

generalship: the most prestigious of Athenian offices and also one of the few elected rather than selected by lot; each year ten generals were elected, one for each citizen 'tribe'. Many famous generals such as Pericles held the position repeatedly.

3.1.2 *more punitively*: Athenian punishment of generals for military failure and mishap is a recurring theme of the *Memorabilia*; see 3.5, and note on 2.1.8.

3.1.4 *Agamemnon*: as leader of the Greek forces against Troy, Agamemnon, king of Mycenae, is the prime example of leadership and authority in Homer's *Iliad*. Socrates notes how Agamemnon is given a special status through Homer's descriptive epithets; this is expanded in the next chapter, 3.2.

lyre-player... doctor: Socrates frequently uses different technical and professional skills, which require study and practice to develop, as analogies for more abstract knowledge. The benefit of constant practice, for example, is readily apparent from the example of the musician.

3.1.5 *troop formations*: the Greek word is *taktika*, meaning 'matters of arrangement'; the primary sense of its root verb was to array troops on the battlefield (so as best to meet the immediate threat of the opposing forces). 'Tactics' were a primary function of the general on campaign. The opposition between longer-term strategy and immediate tactics continues to be a key theme of business and leadership education.

3.1.6 *arrange for the provisioning*: supplying an army in the field was a constant challenge, as Xenophon reports in the *Anabasis*, usually resolved by raiding local farms, and liable to generate further conflict, as Xenophon notes from the perspective of an occupied land, 3.6.13.

watchman and thief: a good leader possesses skills that are double-edged; Odysseus, for example, is a trickster figure, associated with theft through his grandfather Autolycus and his possession of double-edged character traits such as cunning (*mētis*), yet himself also associated with the prosecution of theft (Palamedes) and its consequences (the loss of his men after their theft of the cattle of the Sun). Whether Xenophon's depictions of leaders such as Cyrus are intended to display similarly contradictory qualities is a matter of scholarly dispute.

lavish and grasping: Xenophon illustrates how these qualities work together in his portrait of Cyrus, who continually grasps for more resources in part so that he can subject his subordinates to him through excessive gifts which leave them permanently in his debt (*Cyr.* 8.2.21–4).

3.1.7 *building materials*: the construction of a house, a process which required the arrangement of varied materials and the use of several skills, was often invoked by philosophers as an example of craft; Aristotle uses it frequently in his *Physics*, *Metaphysics*, and even his political and ethical writings. Xenophon expands this image at 3.8.8–9.

3.1.9 *true coin*: the integrity of coinage provides a metaphor for personal integrity; see Euripides' *Hippolytus* 615–17, where the character of women is compared to counterfeit coin, for another example. While the image of the contrast between good and bad coins does not need to be tied to specific events in order to work, Athens did have recent experience of debased coinage, which adds some further bite to Xenophon's comments here. Higher-value Athenian coins, such as the famed tetradrachms or 'Athenian owls', were usually minted from solid silver, but during the crisis of 406/5 towards the end of the Peloponnesian War, with access to the Laurium silver mines (see 3.6.12 and note on 2.5.2) prevented by the Spartan occupation of Attica, silver-plated bronze was used.

Chapter 3.2

Socrates offers Homer's Agamemnon as an exemplar to a newly elected general, exploring the traditional comparison between shepherd and leader and beginning a conversation on the qualities of the good leader.

3.2.1 *"shepherd of the people"*: this traditional characterization of leadership is exemplified by the Homeric epithet for Agamemnon, king of Mycenae and leader of the Greek forces at Troy; it is used, for example, at *Iliad* 2.243, although the epithet occurs frequently across the epic. The image of the leader as shepherd has been introduced earlier (1.2.32), but plays a more significant role here in the chapters analysing leadership qualities.

3.2.3 *A king is elected*: in many ancient monarchies kingship was not solely or straightforwardly hereditary, but required the formal or informal assent of a council or assembly, typically to select a successor from candidates within an extended royal family. New monarchies could also be created by election, as when Deioces is elected king of the Medes (Hdt. 1.97–101).

3.2.4 *particular virtue*: virtue or excellence (*aretē*) was conceptualized as taking different forms (see the Introduction), but here Xenophon asserts the importance of the application of virtue to the delivery of specific social goals, and that the excellence of a leader lies in delivering the happiness (*eudaimonia*) of those led. That happiness was the goal of human social activity is underscored by Aristotle in the opening sections of the *Politics*, in which the polis is identified as the form of social organization most capable of delivering the conditions for good living (*Pol.* 1.2.1252b27–30), and in the *Nicomachean Ethics* where good living is identified with happiness as the overall human good (*NE* 1.4.1095a14–22).

Chapter 3.3

Socrates emphasizes the importance of training both horses and riders to a newly elected cavalry commander, and the role of speaking skills in securing troops' obedience.

3.3.1 *cavalry commanders*: drawn from Athens' wealthy elite, these would need expertise in the deployment and arrangement of cavalry forces on the battlefield. A short treatise on the role and skills of the cavalry commander, the *Hipparchicus*, is attributed to Xenophon.

mounted archers: mounted archery was more often associated with non-Greek forces, but the Athenians made use of them during the Peloponnesian War. Pericles lists mounted archers in the Athenian cavalry at the start of the war (Thuc. 2.13.8), and twenty mounted archers were in the Athenian forces at Melos (Thuc. 5.84.1). A fifth-century vase painting in the Ashmolean depicts archers on horseback in Greek costume, and Plato suggests that such forces are used by Cretan cities (*Laws* 8.834d). But Xenophon's *Hipparchicus* does not discuss their training or use.

3.3.3 *look after his own horse*: in practice, citizen hoplites (infantry) and cavalry brought slaves with them on campaign to look after equipment, so while the responsibility for maintaining a horse rested with individual cavalry members, the actual work was not necessarily performed by them.

3.3.6 *practice manoeuvres*: both mounted and foot soldiers needed to know how to practise battlefield manoeuvres so that, for example, a line of hoplites or other unit where safety depended on staying in formation could change direction without breaking ranks. Failure to execute battlefield man-oeuvres was dangerous; Xenophon describes the forces of the Spartan general Mnasippus failing to complete such a manoeuvre as the Athenians attacked them at Corcyra (373 BCE), leading to a rout in which Mnasippus himself was killed (*Hell.* 6.2.20–3).

3.3.8 *obey your orders*: the capacity to inspire obedience is a key attribute of leaders on and off the battlefield; one of the most notable qualities of Xenophon's Cyrus is the obedience he inspires, which makes his story a worthwhile case study (*Cyr.* 1.1.2–3).

3.3.9 *the most expert doctor…farmer*: Xenophon uses a string of superlative adjectives here, all based on the *-ikos* suffix which implies expertise.

3.9.10 *bad is better than good*: making a paradoxical case that the bad was better than the good was the signature skill of the sophist. Aristotle attributes the practice to Protagoras (*Rhetoric* 2.24.1402a23–5), while Plato suggests that suspicion of this type of argument motivated the charges against Socrates, with which he was erroneously associated (Pl. *Ap.* 19bc).

3.3.11 *a good speaker*: while rhetoric is often treated as a dangerous and decep-tive art in Socratic dialogues, Xenophon here offers a reason why it has a claim to being a useful art for leaders who need to persuade others to follow their instructions.

3.3.12 *a chorus, like the one which is sent to Delos*: Delos was a Panhellenic sanc-tuary, revered as the birthplace of the god Apollo. Athens sent a chorus there every year as part of a festival in honour of the Athenian king and hero Theseus. Socrates' execution in 399 BCE was delayed because such acts caused religious pollution and so could not be carried out while a reli-gious mission was underway, and the returning delegation from Delos was delayed by adverse winds (see 4.8.2; Pl. *Phd.* 59de).

3.3.13 *collective sense of pride*: desire for honours, *philotimia*, is normally a qual-ity of individuals, but here Xenophon attributes it to the Athenians en masse. Elsewhere Xenophon identifies *philotimia* as a specifically human trait (*Hiero* 7.3); possessing it to a greater degree than others is a marker of Athenian exceptionalism.

Chapter 3.4

When Nicomachides is disappointed not to have been elected as a general, Socrates assesses the strengths of the successful candidate Antisthenes, and points to similarities between running an army and managing a large estate.

3.4.1 *Nicomachides*: nothing else is known about this Athenian commander, other than that he rose through the ranks as is stated here. Scars from battle wounds were treated as a sign of a courageous character.

Antisthenes: not the Socratic philosopher (featured in 2.5, and mentioned as a close friend of Socrates in 3.11.17) but a wealthy Athenian of the same name; multiple bearers of the name are known from inscriptions, but none can be firmly identified with the Antisthenes named here.

3.4.3 *sponsor a chorus*: paying the production costs of a play at Athens' dramatic festivals was a liturgy, a form of taxation levied on the wealthy along with paying to outfit warships. The competitive nature of the festivals meant that it was an opportunity for glory; sponsors commemorated their victories with monuments erected between the Theatre of Dionysus and the agora; see also 2.7.6.

3.4.5 *his own tribe*: Athenians had been divided into ten tribes, based on the neighbourhood (deme) in which they were registered as a citizen, since the democratic reforms of Cleisthenes in 509/8 BCE. Each tribe was named after one of Athens' heroes. Civic activities, from military service to dramatic festivals, were organized by tribe, and usually one of the city's ten elected generals came from each tribe.

3.4.6 *chorus... army*: this continues Socrates' statement of the identity of a range of management and leadership roles, occupying the rest of this chapter. The question of whether managing a household or estate required the same skills as ruling a city was one of the major debates in Greek political thought of Xenophon's time; see Pl. *Statesman* 258e; Ar. *Pol.* 1.1.1252a7–18.

3.4.12 *differs only in scale*: the equation between estate-manager and political leader only worked if one accepted that the sole difference between household and city was one of size, rather than one of quality, and therefore that the relationship between the leader and led in each was the same.

Chapter 3.5

Pericles Junior is keen to become a general, but Socrates shows him that he needs to ensure that he is well informed about Athens' strengths and weaknesses, and understands the skills needed to take up the role.

3.5.1 *Pericles, the son of the great Pericles*: Xenophon's choice of interlocutor here is particularly pointed, as part of a sustained critique of the failure of Athenian democracy to value its leaders. This Pericles was the son of Pericles and Aspasia (see note on 2.6.36); because his mother was not Athenian, he did not have citizen status until it was granted by special decree after Pericles' other sons, who held citizenship from his legal marriage, died of the plague. Pericles Jr followed his father into political and military leadership; he was an elected treasurer of Athens in 410/9, and was elected as a general in 406. As Xenophon recounts in the *Hellenica*, Pericles was a commander at the Battle of Arginusae in 406 (see notes on 1.1.18 and 4.4.2). He was executed along with several colleagues after an illegal trial.

3.5.2 *Boeotians*: Boeotia, the region which bordered Attica to the north, was the principal rival of Athens in the 370s, when its major city Thebes enjoyed a period of military success and brief hegemony of the Greek world under the leadership of Epaminondas, rather than at the dramatic date before 406 when Athens' enemies were the Spartans and Persians.

3.5.4 *Tolmides and his thousand men at Lebadea*: this Athenian defeat came towards the end of an Athenian intervention in Boeotia in 447, responding to several cities across the region which came under the control of returned exiles seeking to liberate the region from Athenian control. Tolmides led an Athenian force to stabilize the region, capturing the city of Chaeronea as a base but failing to win the larger city of Orchomenos. Boeotian forces attacked them at Coronea (referred to as Lebadea by Xenophon) as they withdrew from the region in the following year. The general Tolmides was killed, along with Cleinias, father of Alcibiades; many other Athenians were killed or captured (Thuc. 1.113).

Hippocrates at Delium: Hippocrates was an Athenian general during the Peloponnesian War; he was killed in 424 during the battle and siege of the temple complex at Delium in Boeotia, in which the Athenians suffered heavy casualties (Thuc. 4.90–101). Socrates fought courageously at Delium as a hoplite (heavy-armed infantry) in the battle (Pl. *Laches* 181b; *Smp.* 221a).

3.5.7 *courage . . . of the old days*: the idea that the Athenians had declined in virtue and happiness from some point in the glorious past was a commonplace of Athenian conservative thought of the fourth century BCE, best represented by Isocrates in works such as the *Areopagiticus*.

3.5.9 *the earliest of their ancestors*: this introduces a short series of examples of excellence from Athens' mythical past. These stories were often invoked in Athenian funeral speeches for the war dead, and used to compare the achievements of those being commemorated (Lysias 2 is a good example of the genre, although it might not be a speech actually delivered at a state funeral). A notable exception is the speech given by Pericles' father, in Thucydides' *History of the Peloponnesian War*. The older Pericles uses the rhetorical device of *praeteritio* or omission to pass over the usual recounting of mythical deeds (Thuc. 2.36.4); Xenophon may be responding to the Thucydidean speech, just as Plato does in his *Menexenus*, in which Socrates recites a funeral speech attributed to Pericles' partner Aspasia.

3.5.10 *the judgement between the gods*: a key moment in the story of Athens' foundation. The gods Athena and Poseidon demonstrated the benefits they could offer the city, Athena by making an olive tree grow on the rock of the Acropolis, Poseidon by making a spring emerge. The Athenians led by their first king, Cecrops (see note below), voted for Athena as provider of the greatest benefit, although both gods had special roles within Athenian cult and received cult worship and offerings on the Acropolis.

Cecrops: one of the first kings of Athens (Thuc. 2.15.1), according to the versions of Athenian myth in circulation at Xenophon's time. He was sometimes depicted with the lower body of a snake. Cecrops was credited with forming the twelve villages which would later be united as Athens. His name was given to one of the ten tribes formed by Cleisthenes' democratic reforms.

Erechtheus: the Athenians believed that one of their first kings, Erechtheus (or Erichthonius in some versions) was born from the earth, from the semen of Hephaestus, god of craftsmen, after his attempted assault on the goddess Athena. This foundation myth was often conflated with Athenian claims to autochthony, that they were the indigenous people of Attica. Erechtheus was renowned for his defence of the city against invading forces of the Thracians (in some versions, the Eleusinians) led by Molpus. He saved the city by sacrificing his daughters, ensuring the gods' favour in battle. That battle was one of the 'great deeds' often recounted in Athenian funeral speeches and also explored in tragedies (see Pl. *Menexenus* 239b; Lycurgus *Against Leocrates* 98–101). Another of the Athenian tribes was named after Erechtheus.

Heraclids: a reference to the Athenian support given to the descendants of Heracles, the Dorian Greeks, as they attempted to return to the Peloponnese after the Trojan War. The Athenians (in some versions, Theseus himself) offered the Heraclids sanctuary and then fought their enemy Eurystheus, who was blocking their return home (Lysias 2.11–16; Pl. *Menexenus* 239b; Euripides *Children of Heracles*).

Theseus' time: although the many myths of Theseus' labours and heroic exploits overshadow the political achievements which Athenians attributed to him, both sets of activities were celebrated by the Athenians, including his defence of Athens from the Amazons, his killing of the Minotaur, and his unification of the villages of Attica into the single city of Athens (synoecism); see Isocrates *Helen* 23–31. Festivals celebrating these events were fixtures on the Athenian religious calendar. Fitting stories of Theseus into other mythical chronologies, particularly stories of Heracles and of the Trojan War, challenged Athenian mythographers and later writers such as Plutarch (*Life of Theseus*); one solution, adopted by Euripides in his *Children of Heracles*, was to make a son of Theseus rather than Theseus himself responsible for supporting Heracles' descendants on their return to the Peloponnese.

3.5.11 *entirely on their own*: by Xenophon's time the achievements of the Athenians at the Battle of Marathon in 490 BCE had taken on a legendary force, and those who had fought were held up as exemplars of good citizenship and courage (Lysias 2.20–6; Pl. *Menexenus* 240ce). Unlike the later battles of the war against the Persians in 480/79, the Athenians had fought at Marathon on their own.

masters of all Asia and Europe...Macedonia: the Persian Empire under Darius and Xerxes, which mounted invasions of Greece in 490 and 480, extended to the edges of the Greek world in Macedonia.

shared the honours: discussing the relative contributions of Athens and Sparta to the Greek defeat of the Persian invasion of 480/79, and also the distinctive contributions made by land and sea forces in important battles such as the sea battle at Salamis and the land battle at Plataea, was a familiar topic in the literature of Xenophon's time, seen for example in Isocrates' *Areopagiticus*.

3.5.12 *migrations*: that the Athenians had always lived in Attica and were therefore autochthonous, unlike the Spartans who had long ago migrated to the Peloponnese, was a key element of Athenian political identity (Lysias 2.17–19; Pl. *Menexenus* 237ac). Even Pericles Sr, represented by Thucydides as resistant to myth, includes this point in his Funeral Speech (Thuc. 2.36.1).

found refuge: that Athens offered safety to other Greeks was another component of Athenian ideology, evident in the mythical aid granted to the children of Heracles and in taking in the refugees from Plataea after it was first besieged by the Thebans and then destroyed by the Spartans in 427. On that occasion the Athenians welcomed the Plataeans and granted them citizenship, although they did not do the same when the Thebans sacked the city a second time in 373.

3.5.14 *ancestors*: suggestions that the decline in Athens' status could be fixed by returning to the values and customs of earlier generations were a commonplace of fourth-century Athenian political rhetoric, expressed most fully by Isocrates in his *Areopagiticus*, which seeks to roll back democratic reforms to return to a more aristocratic form of governance.

3.5.15 *like the Spartans*: the superiority of Spartan practice in education and training the young was another claim made by some Athenian conservatives; Xenophon's *Constitution of the Spartans* sets out the features Athenians admired, such as the commitment to the communal good and civic unity shared by the Spartan elite.

3.5.18 *the navy*: Socrates offers a more democratic perspective in offering the navy, the part of the Athenian forces in which the poorer citizens served, as an example of Athenian training and discipline; this turn in the discussion might support the view that Xenophon has Athenian democratic rhetoric in mind in this chapter.

members of a chorus: ordinary Athenian citizens might perform in the chorus of tragedies and comedies, as well as in other forms of choral performance in festivals, such as the dithyrambs dedicated to Dionysus. Only the main speaking parts in plays were performed by professional actors.

3.5.20 *Council of the Areopagus*: this council, comprised of former archons, had become less politically significant as Athenian democracy developed during the fifth century, and at one point its main role was as a court for serious trials. During the fourth century it regained some political functions; it was also idealized, for example by Isocrates in his *Areopagiticus*, as a repository of the good qualities of the 'ancestral constitution'.

formal scrutiny: see notes on 2.2.13 and 2.6.1 for more on Athenian processes of scrutiny (*dokimasia*) for candidates for official roles in the city.

3.5.26 *Mysians and Pisidians*: these peoples lived at the edges of the Persian Empire, and were engaged in conflict with the Persians. Xenophon mentions them in the *Anabasis* along with a third people, the Lycaonians, in the key speech he gives to the Greek forces as they decide to cross Persia and return home (*Anab.* 3.2.26). So Xenophon is here giving Socrates a point based on his own experiences.

3.5.27 *lightly armed*: the type of activity suggested here, as well as its location in the border regions, is one that might have been undertaken by young citizen soldiers in training (ephebes) rather than established forces in full battlefield armour, and so is appropriate to Pericles' youth.

Chapter 3.6

The young Glaucon's first attempts at speaking in the assembly have been ridiculed; Socrates encourages him to gain a better practical understanding of the city's needs so that he can make more compelling proposals.

3.6.1 *Glaucon*: Plato's elder brother. He is one of Socrates' main interlocutors in Plato's *Republic*, along with another brother Adeimantus. In the *Republic*, Glaucon has recently fought sufficiently bravely for Athens that his lover (*erastēs*) has composed a poem in his honour (*Rep.* 2.368a), suggesting a youth of around 20 years, similar to the age presented here. Although no specific date is suggested, the situations Socrates outlines are consistent with the late stages of the Peloponnesian War, the final decade of the fifth century BCE.

Charmides: Plato represents his uncle Charmides as a particularly beautiful young man who enchants Socrates and shows some philosophical promise in his discussion of *sōphrosunē* (Pl. *Charmides*). Charmides was convicted along with Alcibiades and others for the profanation of the Eleusinian mysteries in 415; his property was confiscated and he was sent into exile. Hence, perhaps, the Charmides of Xenophon's *Symposium* is represented as a poor man. However, the historical Charmides did return to Athens and regain his citizen status (probably at the same time that Alcibiades was allowed to return); he then supported the oligarchy of the Thirty in 404/3 as one of the Ten appointed to oversee the Piraeus. He was killed in 403 at the Battle of Munychia between the oligarchs and Athenian democrats (Xen. *Hell.* 2.4.19).

Plato: this is Xenophon's only mention of Plato in his extant corpus. Plato never mentions Xenophon, although there is convincing evidence that he read Xenophon's work (see the Introduction). Ancient biographers imagined a rivalry between them (for example, DL 3.4) but there is no further contemporary textual evidence for this.

3.6.2 *Themistocles*: the Athenian general of the Persian Wars and architect of Athens' naval power, who was forced from the city a few years after the victories for which he was responsible. After staying at Argos he was forced out by the Spartans, and ended up in the Persian Empire, first at the court of the Persian king Artaxerxes and then as governor of the Asian city of

Magnesia (Plutarch *Themistocles*). Themistocles is often used as an example of a politician by Plato, for example in the *Gorgias*, because of his connection with the rise of the navy which in turn empowered the city's poor citizens (who were paid to row the city's warships) to participate in the democracy more fully.

3.6.5 *sources of revenue*: Athens' main source of revenue in the fifth century, until the end of the Peloponnesian War and the collapse of its empire, was tribute paid by other members of the Delian League (up to 600 talents a year at its peak). Wealthy Athenians could expect to pay liturgies, funding a trireme or sponsoring a religious activity, on a regular basis. One-off taxes (*eisphorai*) were levied on both citizens and metics (resident aliens of free status) at moments of particular need. Liturgies and taxes weighed heavily in the fourth century, and from 378/7 and the formation of the second Athenian League hard-pressed citizens were organized into syndicates (*symmoriai*) to pay taxes, and later trierarchies too. Xenophon explores ways of improving Athens' cashflow in his pamphlet *Poroi* (often translated *Ways and Means*), which expands several points raised in this chapter.

3.6.6 *the city's expenditure*: equipping the navy was a major expense for Athens; it cost around 1 talent a month to keep a fully crewed trireme at sea. The city also paid citizens for serving as jurors, and from the fourth century onwards for attending the assembly. Civic funds enabled poor citizens to attend the dramatic festivals.

3.6.10 *frontier-posts*: this is a further pointer to the youth of Glaucon; Athens' border-posts were typically protected by young citizens (ephebes) in military training before their deployment in the city's forces. By the time Xenophon was writing, this was a formalized system of training, although whether it was so at the dramatic date of the dialogue is uncertain.

3.6.11 *theft of our crops*: a continuing feature of the Peloponnesian War was the theft or destruction of crops in Attica by invading forces; Spartan forces occupied much of Attica from 413 onwards. Armies on campaign needed to forage for food in the territory they were occupying; foraging is a major activity of the Greek forces in Xenophon's *Anabasis*. As 2.7 showed, the food supply from Athenian farms was insecure as farmers stayed in the city and invaders occupied the land.

3.6.12 *silver mines*: the mines at Laurium in Attica; see note on 2.5.2.

3.6.13 *home-produced grain*: Athens was not self-sufficient in basic foods such as the grains barley and wheat, and war conditions made food production in Attica much more uncertain.

a shortage of food: because Athens imported much of its food, especially wheat, disruptions to shipping caused by war could create food shortages in the city. As the final stages of the Peloponnesian War disrupted trade through the Bosporus and across the Aegean, it became difficult to import wheat from the fertile agricultural lands around the Black Sea.

3.6.14 *ten thousand houses*: Xenophon may be using the number 10,000, as many Greeks did, to suggest an uncountably large number, rather than a demographic statistic. There is little certainty about the population of Athens; Herodotus, writing several decades before Xenophon, suggests about 30,000 citizens (Hdt. 5.97.2), while a census in the late fourth century suggests 21,000 citizens (Athenaeus 272c).

your uncle's: as this is most likely to be a reference to Glaucon's maternal uncle Charmides, already mentioned, it adds further irony to the dialogue if it is read alongside the following chapter. Charmides there demonstrates many skills in his private life which Socrates thinks should be used for the public good; Glaucon may have nothing more to add to the running of Charmides' family estate than he does to the city.

Chapter 3.7

Socrates also tried to persuade older citizens to play a greater part in civic life, especially those like Charmides whose success in managing their own affairs suggested a talent for leadership. Charmides' response reflects Xenophon's views about the Athenian democracy's mistreatment of its leaders.

3.7.1 *Charmides*: the references to Charmides in the previous dialogue (3.6.1, 14) make no suggestion about his age, but he was of the previous generation to his nephews Plato and Glaucon. This dialogue suggests a man of age to participate in politics, but who has not taken an active part in it, lending the dialogue an ironic tone in view of the historical Charmides' turbulent political career. The dialogue presumably is set before Charmides became involved in politics, but all readers would have been aware of his subsequent actions. Perhaps Xenophon wanted to illustrate how Socrates would have addressed a successful older citizen who had stood back from active political involvement, as one might imagine a follower of Socrates would have chosen to do. Charmides would have been in his forties if this dialogue is set in the last decade of the fifth century.

major athletic contests: the circuit of Panhellenic games which crowned their victors, and conferred status on both themselves and their cities, included those held at Delphi, Nemea, Olympia, and Corinth. Events such as the chariot race, which required substantial wealth to fund the costs of training and maintaining horses, equipment, and charioteer, were favoured by the wealthy from across the Greek world; Alcibiades boasts to the Athenians of his chariot teams' victories at the Olympic Games as he seeks support for his policies (Thuc. 6.16.2).

3.7.4 *in private . . . assembly*: this dramatizes the distinction between Charmides' willingness to act on private business but not to participate in civic business; in stepping back from public life he exemplifies a quality of detachment from politics, *apragmosunē*, which would be associated with the philosophical life by later philosophers, and contrasted with *polypragmosunē*, over-involvement with the political life of the city, which was seen as a defect encouraged by democracy. For Xenophon, detachment from the political life offered some protection against the risks of prosecution (*eisangelia*) and exile faced by those who held official roles in the city.

3.7.5 *face crowds rather than a private meeting*: Charmides extends his contrast to the democratic mob (*ochlos*) and a private group of people of similar status to himself (*homilia*). He claims that his reluctance to participate is for a personal reason, shyness, rather than any ideological reason, although the career of the historical Charmides makes this doubtful.

Chapter 3.8

This chapter turns from questions of political leadership to philosophical practice and skill in argument. Socrates humours Aristippus by participating in a discussion which sets out the importance of qualification within definitions, but anticipates Aristippus' argumentative move by providing qualifications to qualities, which prevent him from deploying the sophistic move exploiting the ambiguity of unqualified qualities such as 'good'.

3.8.1 *Aristippus*: the same Aristippus as in the dialogue in 2.1; see note on 2.1.1. The choice of Aristippus, who rejects participation in civic life, as an interlocutor marks a change of subject following the tight focus on civic life in 3.1–7. Commentators have suggested that Socrates is still discussing the good, albeit in a more philosophical sense, that Aristippus is striving for philosophical excellence, and that this chapter therefore enables Xenophon to introduce some core philosophical arguments and themes familiar from Plato's Socratic dialogues. Xenophon may echo the philosophical digression of the central books of the *Republic*.

3.8.2 *anything that was good*: Aristippus hopes to trap Socrates into giving an example of a good thing which can be shown to be good in some circumstances and not in others, a favourite move in sophistic argumentation that philosophers took up. Socrates will use a similar argument in discussion with the young student Euthydemus at 4.2.31–5; perhaps the most thorough display of the use of fallacies of scope is found in the argumentative sections of Plato's *Euthydemus*.

3.8.3 *good for a fever*: Socrates heads off Aristippus' argument by insisting that anything identified as 'good' should be qualified with details of what it is 'good for', a move which prevents him from deploying any fallacy of scope.

3.8.4 *like ... unlike*: Socrates' argument here turns on the specificity of beauty in different contexts; a beautiful shield is not beautiful in exactly the same respects as a beautiful javelin. Xenophon points here towards Plato's Theory of Forms, attributed in his dialogues to Socrates, in which real-world objects share in abstract and ideal qualities through resemblance (see the Introduction).

runner ... wrestler: Socrates uses the same examples to demonstrate how 'the beautiful' is evidenced in different instances in Plato's *Hippias Major* (295cd). That the beautiful is specified relative to a function means that the same quality can be apparent in quite different people or objects; Xenophon uses precise technical language to express this.

3.8.5 *"beautiful and good"*: Aristippus recognizes that Socrates has made the same move in both arguments, and Socrates uses this to shift to argue for the identity of the beautiful (*kalon*) and the good (*agathon*), on the basis that the same criteria are used when determining whether any specific thing is beautiful and good. The identity of the beautiful and the good is central to the Platonic Socrates' thought (*Protagoras* 360b; *Charmides* 160e; *Gorgias* 474cd; *Lysis* 216d; *Meno* 77b; *Smp.* 204e among others). See the Introduction on the connection between virtue and the aesthetic in Socrates' thought.

3.8.6 *dung-bucket*: Aristippus counters with an example of a mundane object with a lowly function; again, this resembles the discussion of pots and spoons in Plato's *Hippias Major*. Socrates' response, that beauty is associated with function, foreshadows the principle of modern art movements that 'form follows function'. Xenophon may also be responding to Plato's *Parmenides*, in which the philosopher Parmenides criticizes the Theory of Forms attributed in the dialogue to Socrates (Pl. *Parmenides* 130c). The emphasis on the aesthetic sense of goodness makes it difficult to see how there can be Forms of mundane and unattractive things; Parmenides asks if there is a Form of mud.

3.8.8 *house*: Socrates has already used house-building as an example craft (3.1.7). Here it offers a complex example in which different criteria need to be satisfied at different times of the year.

3.8.10 *temples and altars*: temples were often placed in visible but secure hilltop positions, in cities or the countryside; Greeks might turn towards a visible temple to pray.

Chapter 3.9

This chapter continues the display of Socrates' philosophical practice, running through Socratic definitions of key virtues such as courage, character traits and emotions such as envy, as well as the importance of expertise.

3.9.1 *he was asked*: the lack of a named interlocutor in this chapter further interrupts the sequence of discussions with named speakers; Dorion and others suggest that this chapter would be better placed at the end of 3.1. The range of abstract ideas and concepts defined in this chapter echoes themes explored by Plato, and at points tracks closely the discussion of Plato's *Protagoras*.

could be taught or was a natural gift: the question of whether virtue in general, or any specific virtue such as courage, could be taught was explored in Plato's *Meno* (70a); the question is discussed in relation to courage in his *Laches*, and also explored in the *Protagoras*.

3.9.2 *learning and practice*: Xenophon frequently links these (among many examples 2.1.28, 2.6.39, 3.9.14; *Cyr.* 3.3.57). The possibility that virtue develops through practice complicates the stark alternative set by the unnamed interlocutor, but also positions Xenophon's Socrates against Plato's as less of a pure intellectualist; while Plato's Socrates appears to think that knowledge alone is sufficient for virtue, Xenophon's envisages practice as completing the process of learning (see the Introduction).

Scythians and Thracians...Spartans: while all these peoples were renowned for their courage and ferocity in battle, they used very different weapons and tactics on the battlefield. Thus they provide an example which demonstrates that courage depends on training and practice.

3.9.4 *wisdom and self-control*: the claim that these two qualities cannot be separated is later subsumed within the claim for the unity of the virtues (see 3.9.5 and note). The linkage Socrates claims between wisdom (*sophia*) and self-control (*sōphrosunē*) is a stronger claim in which Xenophon departs from Plato's view that self-control is associated with all the virtues (*Rep.* 4.431e–432a). This and the following section also respond to Plato's *Protagoras* (332a–333b and 358cd); there the unity of wisdom and self-control is demonstrated through their shared opposite, folly (*aphrosunē*).

those who act wrongly: Xenophon here alludes to one of the Socratic paradoxes, the claim that 'no one does wrong willingly' (Plato *Protagoras* 345de; *Gorgias* 509e5–7; *Ap.* 25e–26a). Xenophon presents Socrates developing an argument for the identity of wisdom and justice, which defuses the paradox: the possession of wisdom or knowledge removes the likelihood of wrongdoing, because no one will act unjustly when they are in possession of knowledge.

3.9.5 *justice...is wisdom*: the unity of the virtues, and their association or even identity with wisdom, is a central topic of Socratic enquiry evident in Plato's work. However, as discussions such as that in Plato's *Protagoras* (329b–331a) show, the claim is a far from simple one, and the way in which the virtues are interrelated is not straightforward.

3.9.6 *madness*: Xenophon opposes wisdom to madness (*mania*), in the sense of failure of self-recognition, but goes on to tighten the definition to include failure of perception. This may be a response to the discussion in Plato's *Protagoras* (above), or to the role of madness in Plato's *Phaedrus*; but madness is a frequent topic for Xenophon (for example, at 1.2.49 and 3.12.6).

3.9.8 *envy*: Xenophon introduces this topic as a search for a Socratic definition. Envy (*phthonos*) could be seen as both a positive and negative emotion in different contexts, and was a topic of great interest to many Greek writers and thinkers. The kind of envy under consideration here, that aroused by the success of a friend, is also described by Cyrus (*Cyr.* 2.4.10). Xenophon may well be responding to a discussion of envy by Plato (*Philebus* 48b–50a), which makes the different claim that envy is a mixture of pleasure and pain at the misfortunes of friends.

3.9.9 *leisure*: a concept central to the ideal of the aristocratic citizen, for whom leisure is the freedom to choose what to do, opposed to the constraints imposed by the need to work for a living. Critics of Athenian democracy often argued that participation in politics should be restricted to those with leisure to attend meetings, to contemplate important issues, and to devote their energies to self-improvement rather than paying work or craft production (e.g. Ar. *Pol.* 7.9.1328b33–1329a2).

3.9.10 *Kings and rulers*: the claim that rulers are distinguished by knowledge rather than by traditional trappings of power such as the sceptre was much developed by Plato, but knowledge that enables them to administer justice is attributed to rulers in the wisdom literature of the ancient Near East. Herodotus' story of the rise to power of Deioces, said to be the first king of the Medes (Hdt. 1.95–101), is a non-Greek example of a ruler gaining authority through such knowledge.

3.9.11 *wool-spinning*: spinning and weaving were the traditional work of women, a way to demonstrate womanly virtue (as Penelope in Homer's *Odyssey*) and yet also a metaphor for the construction of a unified political community (Aristophanes *Lysistrata* 572–86; Plato *Statesman* 279b–283b, 309b). That women had areas of specialist knowledge such as weaving and baking was granted by Plato (*Rep.* 5.455cd).

3.9.12 *tyrant*: Xenophon explores the relationship between tyrant and adviser in his *Hiero*, a dialogue between the Sicilian tyrant and the poet and wise man Simonides. But there is also an element of defence; Socrates' relationship with the tyrannical Critias (see 1.2.12–18) arguably contributed to his prosecution by the Athenians, and ultimately to his death.

3.9.14 *'Successful action'*: this final definition again channels Xenophontic ideas. Xenophon is aware throughout his works that successful action is dependent on fortune and circumstance (*kairos*); a skilled commander can turn a wider range of circumstances to his advantage than an unskilled one, as Cyrus showed through his actions as he rises to power in the *Cyropaedia*, and as Xenophon himself showed in confronting adverse circumstances in the *Anabasis*.

Chapter 3.10

Returning to his conversations with Athenians, Socrates uses visits to three craftsmen in Athens—a painter, a sculptor, and an armourer—to explore questions about the artistic representation of ethical qualities, and the importance of an appropriate fit.

3.10.1 *artistic skill . . . professionally*: this chapter explores the craft analogy (see the Introduction) through conversations with craftsmen, conversations which Plato never depicts in his dialogues, although he does allude to Socrates' conversations with Athenian craftsmen in the *Apology* (Pl. *Ap.* 22d1–e5). Socrates was himself reputed to have trained and worked as a stonemason (DL 2.19).

Parrhasius: unlike the other two craftsmen featured in this chapter, Parrhasius of Ephesus is a known historical person, active in Athens between 440 and 390. His paintings decorated civic buildings. He was famed for his technique, which included extraordinary skills in *trompe l'œil* representation of objects; while his rival Zeuxis painted grapes which attracted birds, Zeuxis himself was deceived by Parrhasius' painting, and attempted to pull back a curtain which turned out to be painted (Pliny *Natural History* 35.64–7).

representation...imitate: Plato argued at length that painting created a defective copy of that which is represented. The impossibility of representation through art and craft is central to his Theory of Forms, in which he postulates that entities are imperfect instantiations of ideal originals, which can only be understood through extended study of philosophy. In depicting Socrates discussing the possibility of representing emotions in painting, Xenophon is offering a veiled critique of Plato's claims about the limitations of art.

3.10.2 *combine the best features*: the idea of a composite figure using the best features of many separate individuals hints at Plato's Theory of Forms (see note above). Creating an ideal example was also recognized as a skill possessed by artists (e.g. Zeuxis, in Ar. *Poetics* 1461b11–14).

3.10.3 *character of a soul*: Aristotle attributes the ability to depict character to another painter, Polygnotus (*Pol.* 8.5.1340a37–8), while Pliny attributes this skill to Parrhasius (*Natural History* 35.69). Whether character traits and virtues could be depicted was a continuing debate in antiquity; at 1.4.9 Socrates relies on the invisibility of the soul.

3.10.6 *Clito the sculptor*: although there are records attesting to this personal name, there are no known sculptures attributed to anyone bearing it.

pancratiasts: the *pankration* was a notoriously brutal form of no-holds-barred wrestling, and a prize event at major Greek games. Athletes were common subjects for sculpture, often shown in action.

3.10.8 *figures...soul*: Xenophon extends the argument made in Socrates' discussion with Parrhasius into three-dimensional art, in which different poses of the body can convey the emotional state and character of the individual.

3.10.9 *Pistias the armourer*: no other details are known of this craftsman, although a reference in the much later *Deipnosophistae* by Athenaeus may be to the same person.

3.10.10 *fit*: the production of customized armour turns out to be an excellent example of the good relative to something; armour can be excellent because it fits well (and so works properly to protect the body) even if the body it is fitted to is ill proportioned and unattractive.

Chapter 3.11

Socrates' visit to see the glamorous courtesan Theodote at her home inspires two conversations, about the benefits of being admired and about ways to attract and keep friends, in which parallels emerge between Socrates' and Theodote's professional relationships.

3.11.1 *Theodote*: the historicity of Theodote is uncertain, although late sources link her, as they do many other women, to Alcibiades. She has also been seen as a cipher for Aspasia, the companion of Pericles, another high-status woman of non-citizen status, and may in turn, like Aspasia, be linked to the elite male non-citizen figure of the sophist.

to keep a man company: a *hetaira* was more literally a 'companion' than other forms of sex worker; a man might retain a *hetaira*, paying her living expenses in return for exclusive or near-exclusive access to her as a social companion and sexual partner. The word is a feminine form of *hetairos*; this masculine form denoted friendship and occasionally also fellow membership of a dining club or even conspiracy, rather than sex work. However, the figure of the *hetaira* is very much a literary confection, and Xenophon's depiction of Theodote illustrates many characteristics attributed to *hetairai* in later accounts such as Athenaeus' *Deipnosophistae*: wealth, luxury, wit, and the ability to hold intellectual conversation with men.

3.11.2 *spectators*: the centrality of viewing and judging to Athenian civic life is explored and perhaps parodied in this episode, as the beautiful Theodote turns out to be far from a passive object to be looked at.

3.11.4 *mother... maids*: the presence of an older woman and other well-dressed women has led some commentators to suggest that Theodote's home is a brothel.

friends: Theodote's assertion that she is supported by generous friends opens up a parallel between her and Socrates, who is also dependent on the generosity of friends for his living expenses; it also links this dialogue to the previous discussion of friendship in 2.6.

3.11.7 *hares*: the typical prey of Athenian hunters and also represented as a gift between male lovers (see note on 2.6.9); Xenophon manages to incorporate the erotic context and his own enthusiasm for hunting in Socrates' monologue.

3.11.9 *someone who can track down*: Plato's Socrates often uses hunting as a metaphor for the search for knowledge, most notably at *Rep.* 4.432be.

3.11.10 *nets*: hares were caught by being chased into nets (Xen. *Cyn.* 2, 6). There may be some innuendo in the analogy between funnel-shaped nets and Theodote's body, which suggests the two levels of the conversation between the bodily, represented by Theodote, and the intellectual, represented by Socrates.

3.11.16 *girlfriends*: Socrates casts his associates as lovers, perhaps with a nod to his claim to expertise in love, outlined at 2.6.28 (cf. Pl. *Smp.* 177de), and deepening the parallel between him and Theodote.

love potions and spells: using love potions and magical incantations to attract friends has already been considered in the context of love (2.6.10); persuasive argument is also an incantation (see note on 2.6.13). It is unclear whether Theodote understands these phrases as analogies or not, but Xenophon hints that the conversation is being carried on at two different levels.

3.11.17 *Apollodorus...Antisthenes*: introduced here as Socrates' most devoted Athenian followers; Apollodorus was present at Socrates' death (Pl. *Phd.* 59a; Xen. *Ap.* 28), while the Antisthenes here is the philosopher who appeared in 2.5 and Xenophon's *Symposium*.

Cebes and Simmias: representing Socrates' non-Athenian followers (see 1.2.48 and note).

Chapter 3.12

Socrates encourages the unfit Epigenes to pay more attention to his bodily health and to undertake physical training.

3.12.1 *Epigenes*: an associate of Socrates present at his trial (Pl. *Ap.* 33e) and death (*Phd.* 59b). Beyond Plato introducing him as the son of Antiphon of Cephisia (not the sophist or writer), nothing is known about him.

poor physical shape: Socrates voices Xenophon's concerns about physical fitness, which recur throughout his work, and in which lack of fitness is often associated with non-Greeks, seen when they are captured and sold as slaves (as at *Hell.* 3.4.19).

sooner or later: although Xenophon does not suggest any specific military campaign here, the conversation is perhaps set, like others in this book, during the final years of the Peloponnesian War when Athens faced the greatest danger, although the sentiment is equally applicable to the period in the fourth century in which Xenophon may have written the work.

3.12.4 *good condition*: the benefits of good physical condition (*euexia*) to the individual and the community here match those of physical self-mastery (*enkrateia*) listed in earlier conversations (1.2, 1.5).

3.12.5 *military training at public expense*: public training for military service features in Xenophon's ideal societies, both Sparta (*Lac. Pol.*, especially 11–12) and Persia (*Cyr.* 1.2). Athens did institute public training for young men at some point during the fourth century, although the date is not clear.

Chapter 3.13

This chapter rounds up anecdotes about Socrates' witty and biting responses to various social situations.

3.13.2 *Acumenus*: the views of this doctor, father to the doctor Eryximachus (who gives a speech in Plato's *Symposium*), are also reported in Plato's dialogues. Plato's *Phaedrus* reports his advice that country walks outside the city walls are better for you than walks inside the city (*Phaedrus* 227a).

3.13.3 *temple of Asclepius*: while a new sanctuary was dedicated to Asclepius, the healing god and son of Apollo, on the slopes of Athens' acropolis, this is more likely a reference to the larger and older sanctuary at Epidaurus. Sanctuaries dedicated to Asclepius provided healing through incubation; visitors slept in the temple, and their treatment was based on interpretation of the dreams they had there. Xenophon uses these religious destinations as examples of places to which Athenians might travel.

shrine of Amphiaraus: this site, at Oropus on the disputed border between Attica and Boeotia, was an oracular site dedicated to the hero and seer of that name, one of the Seven who fought against Thebes (despite his foreknowledge that the expedition was doomed). The shrine became popular with Athenians during the Peloponnesian War; it too offered healing through incubation.

3.13.5 *journey to Olympia*: from Athens south-west to the sanctuary of Zeus at Olympia is roughly 250 kilometres, although most road routes are longer as they skirt the northern edge of the Saronic gulf to the west of Athens.

Chapter 3.14

Socrates' strong views on the moderation of appetite introduce a discussion of the etiquette of taking more than your share of delicacies at communal meals.

3.14.1 *dining club*: Xenophon here refers to an informal social arrangement rather than any formal society.

pooled food: similar 'potluck' dinners to which all attendees contributed were part of more formal religious events, and are used by Aristotle as a metaphor for the epistemic diversity produced by democratic deliberation (*Pol.* 3.11.1280a40–b7).

3.14.2 *cooked dishes*: *opson* or prepared food could be either savoury or sweet delicacies, and in this scenario a selection of both.

"guzzler": Xenophon's term *opsophagos*, literally 'eater of prepared delicacies' is difficult to translate, although the connotation of greed in taking more than one's share of the expensive delicacies is clear.

3.14.5 *several of the prepared dishes*: the variety of foods that counted as *opson* meant that it would be possible to make complex combinations, but such gastronomic adventurousness is firmly ruled out by Socrates' austere preference for simplicity.

BOOK 4

Chapter 4.1

The final book of the *Memorabilia* focuses on Socrates as a teacher; this introductory chapter restates his manner of engaging with those who chose to spend time with him, and sets out the outlines of his ethical teaching.

4.1.1 *The very memory of him*: this chapter returns to the defence of Socrates from the opening chapters of Book 1. Remembering Socrates, as this text does, is a way of continuing to benefit from his presence.

playful talk: earlier Xenophon connected the serious and playful sides of Socrates; here he affirms the usefulness of his playfulness, also emphasized at *Symposium* 1.1.

4.1.2 *in love*: Xenophon sets up the main theme of the following chapters, the Socratic intellectual seduction of the young and handsome Euthydemus. See also 2.6, in which the erotic permeates the discussion with Critobulus, and 3.11, where Socrates discusses methods of pursuing friends and lovers with the courtesan Theodote.

natural quality: emphasizing the Xenophontic point that any innate qualities in an individual must be improved through hard work and practice.

4.1.3 *thoroughbred horses... pedigree dogs*: Xenophon turns to a familiar analogy with animals (dogs were invoked at 2.3.9 and 2.9.2–7) to emphasize the role of training in the achievement of excellence.

4.1.4 *best breed of men*: an uncomfortable eugenicist parallel with breeding horses and dogs, but one familiar to Xenophon's readers; the idea of marriage and breeding for human excellence was introduced at 2.2.4.

Chapter 4.2

The young Athenian Euthydemus has many books but lacks an instructor; Socrates entices him into conversation, demonstrates his need for teaching across a range of ethical and political topics by engaging him in philosophical discussion, and sets out the case for the importance of self-knowledge as the foundation of all good decision-making.

4.2.1 *Euthydemus (the handsome one)*: described as 'the handsome one' to distinguish him from others of the same name: see note on 1.2.29, where he is introduced as the object of Critias' pederastic affections. Here he provides an example of a Socratic intellectual seduction, although when Euthydemus is mentioned in Plato's *Symposium* (by Alcibiades, *Smp.* 222b) he is said to have been, like Alcibiades, rejected and not pursued by Socrates. Dorion suggests that Xenophon's account of Euthydemus is a positive version of Alcibiades, used by Xenophon here as an example of successful Socratic education; he lists the many parallels between this dialogue and the Platonic *Alcibiades I*, although that dialogue's authorship by Plato is contested. The Straussian view (expressed by both Strauss and Pangle; see the Introduction) is that Euthydemus is a weak student, but the description of him as handsome (*kalos*) goes beyond the aesthetic to imply his potential to become a *kalos kagathos*.

writings: Euthydemus' collection of texts (also referenced at 4.2.8) represents another way of accumulating knowledge, through the written word. Socrates treats reading the written word as a deficient means of acquiring knowledge (a topic explored at length in Plato's *Phaedrus*), although here it may be his choice of authors (professors and poets) rather than any limitation of the written word which is the problem.

marketplace: the Athenian agora was not a respectable place for a youth to socialize (Isocrates *Areopagiticus* 48). Euthydemus' positioning of himself at its edge suggests both his eagerness to participate in civic life and his marginal social position as a youth.

a saddler's shop: Xenophon once again places Socrates in an artisan's work-shop, but this time his conversation is with an elite youth of the type Plato places in more elite settings such as gymnasia and private homes. The Athenian cobbler Simon was said to have been an author of Socratic dia-logues, which he based on conversations of Socrates he had heard in his shop (DL 2.122).

4.2.2 *Themistocles*: see note on 2.6.13, where the Athenian general of the Persian Wars also serves as a positive exemplar.

4.2.3 *preamble*: Greek rhetoric favoured the construction of speeches in parts; the preamble (*prooimion*) established the character and credentials of the speaker, and demonstrated their connection to their audience.

4.2.5 *public physicians*: that Greek cities appointed doctors is widely attested (Hdt. 3.131), but the point here is to connect the knowledge Euthydemus claims with accounts of teaching, such as Plato's *Gorgias*, in which the sophist claims that his possession of the skill of rhetoric enables him to replace or outdo those skilled in other branches of knowledge such as medicine (*Gorgias* 455b).

4.2.6 *practise...instruction*: Xenophon links the themes of study and practice to the craft analogy. This will do much work in the following sections, which draw heavily on related discussions in Plato (see the Introduction).

4.2.9 *by Hera*: an oath used here for emphasis and to mark the opposition between Socrates and Euthydemus, who had sworn by Zeus.

4.2.10 *geometry*: identified as an important subject for developing reason, and so a key stage in the education of philosophers, but also a subject which can be put to practical uses (Pl. *Rep.* 7.626c–527c).

Theodorus: Theodorus of Cyrene was a mathematician who taught both in his North African home and in Athens during the late fifth century; he was associated with Protagoras. Theodorus appears in several of Plato's later dialogues, notably the *Theaetetus*, although his main contribution to those discussions is to introduce other characters and vouch for their intellec-tual capability and achievement. The historicity of Theodorus' contribu-tion to mathematics has been doubted, but Xenophon follows Plato in using him to represent geometry as a discipline. Socrates asserts the lim-ited practical value of advanced geometry at 4.7.2.

astronomer: astronomy was often linked with geometry as a higher-level study in discussions of education (Pl. *Rep.* 7.527d–530c; *Hippias Minor* 366c–368a); it was treated by Isocrates as non-practical knowledge and linked to the study of disputation, a disparaging term for philosophical enquiry (*Antidosis* 261; *Panathenaicus* 26).

rhapsode: rhapsodes were professional performers of Homeric epic, who sang the poetry while accompanying it on the lyre. They were known for their flamboyant presentation. Plato criticizes the reverence for Homeric epic as an educational text, a discussion to which Xenophon appears to allude here, in the *Ion*, a short dialogue in which Socrates demonstrates to a rather pompous performer of that name that his knowledge of Homer does not translate to knowledge of generalship or other skills possessed by Agamemnon.

4.2.11 *"the royal art"*: already discussed at 2.1.17, where Aristippus suggests that Socrates identifies it with happiness. Here, the royal art (*basilikē technē*) is identified as the outcome of a good (Socratic) education which will equip a young man to take a leading role in civic life (see the Introduction).

4.2.12 *do just people produce things*: the analogy between crafts and virtues has a weak point; while the material products of craft workers, such as carpenters, are easily identified, the immaterial products of virtuous people are less concrete and less easily recognized, a preoccupation which Plato explores across many dialogues, notably the *Gorgias* (see the Introduction). Xenophon elsewhere explores (and rejects) the possibility that beautiful people necessarily produce beautiful things (*Oec.* 6.13–14).

4.2.13 *list*: the two letters in the Greek text are delta (Δ, for *dikaiosunē*, 'justice') and alpha (Α, for *adikia*, 'injustice'). Socrates sets out a relativistic conception of justice, in which the justice or injustice of a particular action depends on the context in which it occurs. This sophistic argumentative move destabilizes Euthydemus' sense of his own existing knowledge, making him more keen to learn from Socrates; see the Introduction on sophistic education.

4.2.15 *deception*: Xenophon's Cyrus is encouraged by his father to use deception as a weapon against the enemy, though not against his own troops (*Cyr.* 1.6.26).

4.2.17 *refuses to take the medicine*: the reluctance of patients to take foul-tasting medicine is a useful analogy for the competing skills of rhetoric and philosophy; see Pl. *Gorgias* 467c, 521e–522a; Lucretius *On the Nature of Things* 1.935–50.

steals or removes any sword or other lethal weapon: the justice of taking a weapon away from a distressed person who might harm himself or others is a favourite counter-example in discussions of justice; see Pl. *Rep.* 1.331e–332c.

4.2.20 *justice can be taught*: the question of the teachability of virtue is a constant topic of Socratic dialogue, central to Plato's *Meno*.

deliberately...unintentionally: the question of the intention behind just and unjust actions gives rise to the 'Socratic paradox' that no one does wrong intentionally (see 3.9.4).

4.2.22 *slavish*: Xenophon maps the distinction between productive crafts and higher-order skills on to a status distinction, that between the leisured and those who must work in a productive trade to earn a living, a status analogized to the distinction between free citizen and enslaved non-citizen. While knowledge of some kinds is associated with freedom, the type of knowledge involved in knowing a craft or trade condemns its knower to a lower condition and status. This is an anti-democratic and elitist perspective, with parallels in Aristotle's arguments in the *Politics* that labourers should not have full political rights (*Pol.* 7.9.1328b23–1329a2).

4.2.24 *"Know yourself"*: one of the maxims inscribed on the temple of Apollo at Delphi. Plato's Socrates identifies self-knowledge with moderation (*sōphrosunē*) (Pl. *Charmides* 164d–165c); Xenophon's treatment offers a subtle exploration of what might be involved in knowing oneself, that it takes the form of recognizing one's capacities in relation to planned actions. Socrates' conversation with Euthydemus initiates him into the process of self-examination, central to the Socratic educational project.

4.2.25 *people who buy horses*: appraising a horse for both its physical qualities and its temperament provides an analogy for the thorough self-appraisal which Xenophon has Socrates present as the route to achieving self-knowledge, contrasted with the limited knowledge of simply knowing your own name. Such an analogy is most appropriately addressed to a wealthy citizen who might buy horses to train for chariot races or as a mount for service in the cavalry, and provides further evidence of the elite audience Xenophon is addressing. The treatise *On Horsemanship* attributed to Xenophon contains a chapter on buying horses.

function: one might question whether the function or use (*chreia*) of a horse is a suitable comparator for the function of a human, although Xenophon appears to have both physical and mental characteristics in mind, and to suggest that self-knowledge involved understanding what one might contribute to a collaborative activity in which others depended on one's skills. Xenophon does not offer any examples, but the assessment of military capabilities and logistics would be a good option.

4.2.26 *self-deception*: the opposite of self-knowledge is not simply ignorance, but the introduction of error through inaccurate assessment of capabilities. Just as self-knowledge enables the knower to assess others, self-deception is matched by a dangerous inability to evaluate the capabilities of others. Thucydides represents Athens' doomed invasion of Sicily in 415 BCE as an action arising from a collective failure of knowledge (Thuc. 6.1.1).

4.2.29 *without knowing its own capability*: self-knowledge also operates at the level of the city; as became clear in the conversation between Socrates and Glaucon (3.6, especially 3.6.7–8), understanding the capabilities and resources of the city is fundamental to being able to act on its behalf as a politician or general.

4.2.33 *Daedalus*: the mythical inventor and fabricator of sculptures, automata, and buildings, who here serves as an example of cleverness without wisdom. Daedalus was said to have been exiled from Athens after killing his nephew, student and rival Talos, and ended up serving Minos of Crete, for whom he built the labyrinth.

Minos: a son of Zeus who was the legendary ruler of Crete, who used Daedalus' skill to construct the labyrinth and imprison the Minotaur. In other stories, such as the myth which Socrates tells at the end of Plato's

Gorgias (523a–527a), Minos and his brothers Rhadamanthys and Aeacus appear as judges in the afterlife.

Palamedes... Odysseus: Palamedes offers a second mythical exemplar of cleverness which rebounded fatally on its possessor; he was executed after his long-term rival Odysseus successfully framed him for attempting to betray the Greek forces to Priam during the Trojan War. Palamedes was also credited with the invention of some of the letters of the alphabet and with originating aspects of the art of rhetoric. Plato's Socrates hopes to meet Palamedes, unjustly executed, in the afterlife (Pl. *Ap.* 41ab; echoed in Xen. *Ap.* 26). Plato's version of Socrates' defence speech contains many echoes of the sophist Gorgias' paradoxical defence speech written for the character Palamedes.

Great King's court: the King of Persia; this may be an allusion to Themistocles, but the idea that demonstrating wisdom could be disadvantageous to the individual appears elsewhere (Xen. *Smp.* 3.4).

4.2.34 *happiness*: there could be no question of happiness being classified as anything other than a benefit, so it cannot be disputed.

ambiguous goods: this refers back to the classification of actions and qualities in the exploration of justice, above. Plato's Socrates classifies goods in a hierarchy (goods of the soul, goods of the body, and exterior goods), but that does not seem to be Xenophon's point here, although the goods listed would occupy different places in that hierarchy.

4.2.35 *pretty boys*: Socrates uses the adjective *hōraios* which suggests a seasonal and transient blooming, appropriate to the youths; Xenophon continues to use Athenian pederasty as an analogy for education while offering a firm criticism of the practice itself as potentially destructive to the individuals involved.

4.2.37 *what is meant by "the people"*: the ambiguity between two senses of *dēmos* (people) is often exploited by Greek political writers. *Dēmos* can mean the entire citizen body of a polis, or it can mean the lower property class of a polis, conceived of as outnumbering and opposing the wealthy elite; see Ar. *Pol.* 4.4, especially 1291b14–38.

poor... rich: another relativizing move; Socrates defines poverty as having insufficient resources to meet needs, whatever they are, and wealth as having sufficient. So the individual with restrained appetites will be more likely to be wealthy.

4.2.38 *tyrants*: because their appetites are unlimited and uncontrolled, tyrants will always have insufficient resources and thus be 'poor' on this account. Xenophon depicts Hiero, tyrant of Syracuse, complaining about such poverty (*Hiero* 4.6–11).

4.2.39 *slave*: Euthydemus here identifies himself as *andrapodon*, a dehumanized 'man-footed beast', because Socrates has undermined his confidence that he possesses any knowledge, and being without knowledge, it has been agreed, is associated with the status of being enslaved.

4.2.40 *reducing him to confusion*: Xenophon suggests that Socrates uses the question-and-answer method (the elenchus) as an introduction to his teaching, but that his usual mode of teaching established students did not rely on it, and was perhaps as a result more constructive.

Chapter 4.3

Socrates and Euthydemus discuss the relationship between gods and humans; how the gods' care can be discerned even when they are invisible, and how humans should show gratitude for this care. Socrates repeats his views on the role of divine intelligence in the cosmos.

4.3.1 *moderation*: like the following chapters, this dialogue makes its topic explicit. By presenting moderation (*sōphrosunē*) as the first lesson, Xenophon emphasizes its position as a foundational lesson of Socratic teaching; after mastering it, students can become better at a range of practical activities, such as those of speaking, acting, and organizing suggested by the previous sentence.

4.3.2 *gods*: Xenophon emphasizes Socrates' piety by showing the pre-eminence granted to the gods in the Socratic curriculum, but the account of the gods given here represents a radical departure in Greek thought, the idea that the cosmos is the product of their 'intelligent design' (see the Introduction). Socrates illustrates his argument by reframing themes from myths of early human life.

Others...own accounts: Xenophon shows awareness of the range of Socratic dialogues, perhaps pointing up his own literary artifice.

I myself was there: as with the previous instance (1.4.2), Xenophon's claim to have witnessed a conversation marks the importance of its topic, in both cases the relationship between humans and gods and the gods' provision of benefits to humans, as well as a way of distinguishing his contribution from the other Socratic writers just mentioned.

4.3.3 *care*: the gods' oversight of humans is described using the same language (*epimeleia*) of human management and oversight, the attention which Socrates encourages his followers to give to both their own self-management and their responsibilities to others (see note on 1.2.4).

our first need is for light: Socrates begins a description of the cosmos and nature focused on its provision for human needs. This vision of the cosmos contributes to his argument that it was so arranged deliberately to achieve this goal.

4.3.4 *moon*: although Socrates describes the usefulness of the moon's phases for the marking of time, he later (4.7.4–7) expresses reservations about the usefulness of astronomical research which has no clear practical purpose.

4.3.5 *food*: Socrates describes the production of food as if in a golden age of automatic harvest, not mentioning agriculture or human effort. In conventional myth, this only occurs in a distant past; see the great myth in Plato's *Statesman* (269a–274e), which draws on the tradition of the golden age represented as the 'Age of Gold' in Hesiod's myth of the ages, *Works and Days* 109–26.

kindness to humanity: this and the following sections develop the idea that the gods take care of humans and have arranged the cosmos for their benefit. This could rest on a conventional view of the gods returning the services men do for them (as expounded in Plato's *Euthyphro*), as well as reflecting Xenophon's wider interest in reciprocal favours between those of different status, such as gods and men or rulers and ruled.

4.3.7 *gift of fire*: in the conventional version of the myth of Prometheus, Zeus does not give fire to humans but Prometheus steals it for them, and is punished (Hesiod *Theogony* 507–84). Dorion notes how Xenophon's version quietly sets this myth aside in favour of a philosophical vision of the gods as benevolent to humans.

4.3.9 *other living creatures*: the relative status of men and other animals is also discussed during the previous discussion of religious and cosmic matters between Socrates and Aristodemus at 1.4.11–14; there the physical and intellectual advantages humans have over animals are stressed, while this passage examines the other side of the argument and looks at the usefulness of animals for humans.

4.3.11 *senses*: Socrates returns to points similar to those raised in 1.4.11–14 about human capabilities.

4.3.12 *more friendly to you*: Socrates is favoured with special knowledge of the gods' plans through his *daimonion*, but Euthydemus' question hints at the difficult question of Socrates' unconventional piety.

Chapter 4.4

Although Socrates' attitude to justice is demonstrated by his honest behaviour, his conversation with the sophist Hippias of Elis gives him a platform to show the consistency of his views on justice, on the relationship between justice and law, and the place of written and unwritten law.

4.4.1 *justice*: this chapter offers an important account of the relationship between justice and law; its opening section offers a recap of the injustice which Socrates experienced, continuing the defence of Socrates.

discipline: Socrates' self-management is here expressed by *eutakton*; his good order is like that of a well-disciplined army arrayed on the battlefield.

4.4.3 *to arrest a man*: Leon of Salamis, a general eventually executed by the Thirty; see *Hell.* 2.3.39, Pl. *Ap.* 32cd.

4.4.4 *Meletus*: the previous discussion of Socrates' trial (1.1–2) did not mention his accusers by name; here Meletus, the main prosecutor for the charge that Socrates failed to honour the city's gods, is named and briefly discussed. Plato gives an unflattering description of his appearance (long hair and hooked nose, *Euthyphro* 2b10–11), and suggests that he was not well known or prominent in the city, unlike Anytus, the other prosecutor named by Plato and Xenophon, who had been a general and was well known. Little else is known about Meletus; later biographical sources embroider details and suggest that he was executed in turn by the regretful Athenians (DL 2.43). He also appears in Xenophon's *Apology* (19–21); as in Plato's *Apology*, Socrates questions him in court.

4.4.5 *Hippias of Elis*: a famous teacher, scholar, and diplomat of the fifth century BCE, known for his work on a wide range of topics and for works such as the list of Olympian victors, one of the first known Greek chronological works, which aided the development of historiography. Plato depicts his visit as a young man to Athens in the *Protagoras*; Hippias was a younger associate of Protagoras. Some of the discussion in this chapter echoes elements of the *Hippias Major*, a dialogue whose attribution to Plato is contested; in that work, Hippias and Socrates consider the reluctance of Sparta to change its laws, and the problems that poses for an innovative educator like Hippias (*Hippias Major* 284b–285c).

4.4.6 *the same old stuff*: the Platonic Hippias cannot teach new things to the Spartans, as they are forbidden to learn anything non-traditional, so has to tell them traditional stories (*Hippias Major* 285de).

something new: while Hippias' point is that he tries to entertain his audience with new material, Socrates' point is that he speaks about unchanging truths, and therefore must always say the same thing when he makes a positive statement.

4.4.9 *reveal your own thought*: in Plato's *Republic*, the sophist Thrasymachus joins the conversation with an angry outburst making this criticism of Socrates (*Rep.* 1.337a). Hippias himself does so in the *Hippias Major* (300de), in a fierce dispute about methodology. It seems less applicable to Xenophon's Socrates, who is more keen to voice his own ideas by encouraging rather than criticizing his students.

4.4.12 *"lawful" and "just" are the same*: this statement has given rise to much discussion as to whether it represents Xenophon's view, and would enable him to be identified as a legal positivist, emphasizing the priority of written and codified civic law. Xenophon often praises those who are obedient to the law (*Lac. Pol.* 1.2; *Ages.* 7.2).

4.4.14 *often repeal them*: the idea that law codes should be static was popular in ancient Greek thought. Critics felt that the ability of the Athenian assembly to issue decrees with the effect of changing the law was a defect of democracy akin to the overthrow of the rule of law (Ar. *Pol.* 4.41292a1–37), although Aristotle did criticize some cities for political arrangements which made it too hard to change the law (*Pol.* 2.8.1268b22–1269a28).

4.4.15 *the Spartan Lycurgus*: revered as the creator of the Spartan *politeia*, and described by Xenophon as 'extremely wise' (*Lac. Pol.* 1.2). Lycurgus was thought to have brought a pronouncement, the 'Great Rhetra', from the oracle at Delphi to Sparta, where it became the basis of the city's social and political institutions (Hdt. 1.65); Xenophon cites the oracle's greeting to Lycurgus, asking whether he was a man or a god (*Ap.* 15). The text of the Rhetra itself is not preserved. Other sources (notably Plato in the *Laws*, 3.691d–692a) point to revisions in the Spartan system and suggest that despite the powerful myth of the unchanging adherence to the Rhetra, Sparta did develop and change its political institutions over time.

4.4.16 *unity*: the ideas that the goal of political discussion was consensus, and that citizens whose interests were aligned might naturally reach the same view, underpin the concept of political unity or *homonoia*, literally 'thinking the same'. Unanimity was seen as a strength of Spartan political culture and a weakness of democracy.

oath: Athenian ephebes swore to obey the law when they swore to defend the country and uphold its traditional cults. A fourth-century inscription found in the outlying deme of Acharnae claims to present the 'ancestral oath' sworn on this occasion; in it the ephebes swear to protect their fatherland, obey the law, and honour the city's cults (P. J. Rhodes and R. Osborne, *Greek Historical Inscriptions: 404–323 BC* (Oxford: Oxford University Press, 2003), No. 88 = https://www.atticinscriptions.com/inscription/SEG/21519).

4.4.17 *individual*: Xenophon's claim that the benefits of civic unity played out within the household as well as the polis as a whole connects to his view that the leadership and management of household and polis are the same activity.

gratitude for a favour conferred: the expectation of reciprocity underlay a wide range of social transactions in the classical city. Xenophon views *charis*, the principle of reciprocity, as one of the most important social values, and makes frequent reference to reciprocity and reciprocal giving throughout his works: see 2.10.3, 4.4.24, and *Ap.* 17 for further examples.

4.4.19 *"unwritten laws"*: a central tenet of Greek political and ethical thinking was that there was a common set of laws observed by all humans (or sometimes, all Greeks), often revealed through divine command and addressing topics of personal propriety, such as religious observance and respect for elders. The conflict between political and unwritten law drives the debates of Sophocles' *Antigone*, in which the ruler Creon represents a warped politics and Antigone an illustration of the consequences of separating political and unwritten religious law. This discussion was further politicized in fourth-century Athens; Isocrates argues that good citizens of the past did not need to have precise and detailed law codes prescribing what they should and should not do (*Areopagiticus* 40–42). This strand of Greek thought is a precursor to the natural law tradition in later political thought.

worship of the gods: this first law, commanding piety, had its parallel in a written decree thought to have been in place at Athens, the decree of Diopeithes, in which impiety (*asebeia*) became an offence. According to Plutarch (*Life of Pericles* 32), the philosopher Anaxagoras was prosecuted for impiety under this decree (see note on 4.7.6).

4.4.20 *honouring one's parents*: while Socrates lists this as the second unwritten law, it was a positive law at Athens. Failure to treat their parents properly could disbar candidates from political office ([Ar.] *Ath. Pol.* 55.3); Socrates reminded his son Lamprocles of his obligations to his mother at 2.2.13.

parents having sex with their children: the third unwritten law, against incest between parents and children, exemplifies the way in which breaking an unwritten law results in an automatic punishment, in this case through the production of unhealthy children.

4.4.22 *production of poor specimens*: the poor health of babies born from inter-generational incest is attributed to the excessive age of one of the parents. The idea that there was a proper age for both fathering and bearing children also appears in Plato's *Laws* (4.721ad, 6.784e). In Athens, the father of a newborn infant determined whether it was healthy enough to rear; in Sparta, this decision was taken by public officials.

4.4.23 *sperm*: Xenophon shares his contemporaries' view that human repro-duction depended entirely on a 'seed' (*sperma*) from a man; women's con-tribution was seen as simply providing an environment in which the seed could germinate and develop, rather than providing any genetic material. The age of the father was thought to affect the quality of the seeds he produced.

4.4.24 *favours*: the recognition of favours is presented as a fourth unwritten law; Xenophon also makes this point in the story of Pheraulas, a com-moner enriched by Cyrus who in turn gives away his possessions (*Cyr.* 8.3.49). Dorion notes the relation between this law and the first two, which require the recognition of benefits received from gods and parents.

automatic punishments: the claim is that breaking the unwritten laws auto-matically incurs a punishment, whereas breaking positive human law requires a legal process to effect punishment and restitution.

lawgiver of more than human ability: while this refers directly to the gods, it may echo the claim reported by Herodotus that Sparta's Lycurgus was of more than human ability (Hdt. 1.65.2–4).

Chapter 4.5

A further conversation with the young Euthydemus explores self-control and its relationship to moderation, both central to Socrates' teaching on practical matters. Here, the experiences of the self-controlled and moderate are con-trasted with the experiences of those lacking control, the unfree and the enslaved.

4.5.1 *self-mastery*: this dialogue explores *enkrateia* as the self-mastery through which the individual can apply and demonstrate moderation (*sōphrosunē*) to their own life and actions; it also shows how Socratic thinkers envisaged self-mastery and moderation as a way of managing pleasure (see 4.5.9).

4.5.2 *moral virtue*: while the Greek noun *aretē* can denote personal excellence of many types, the focus in this chapter is on moral psychology.

freedom: Socrates' question conflates two senses of freedom, in a move typical of Greek political argumentation. For a city, freedom meant freedom from external domination, such as being ruled by or (sometimes) owing tribute to another power, an example being the domination of Persia over Greek cities in Asia Minor which Xenophon fought against. For the individual, freedom could mean freedom from domination in a political sense—being an equal citizen in a democratic regime such as Athens—or it could mean the distinction between life as an enslaved or free person. The conflation of the exertion of any external political authority with the personal experience of enslavement provided a powerful image; see the Introduction, and the discussion with Aristippus in 2.1.

individual ... city: the parallel between the individual and the city is familiar from Plato's *Republic* and its 'city-soul' analogy, in which the investigation of justice in the city is substituted for the more difficult investigation of justice within the individual.

4.5.3 *free*: a range of words for free and unfree is used here to cement the analogy between personal and political freedom; the questions become whether those driven by physical appetites can be of free status (*eleutheros*), and whether only those who take the best courses of action can be said to have the character appropriate to the free person (*eleutherios*).

masters who will prevent that: vices and passions are personified here as masters who place those they control in a state of unfreedom (*aneleutheros*).

4.5.4 *those who aren't masters of themselves*: from another perspective, those who cannot rule themselves and their passions lack self-control, and thus exhibit the opposite of *enkrateia*, *akrasia*, often translated as 'weakness of will'.

4.5.5 *The worst possible masters*: the idea that the experience of enslavement could be worsened by a brutal master, and ameliorated by a virtuous master, and even enable the enslaved to achieve a happier state than they might otherwise have done echoes views expressed in the conversation with Eutherus in 2.8. Aristotle's model of 'natural slavery' suggests that there are benefits to the enslaved in being controlled by a master and thus gaining a share in his virtuous qualities (*Pol.* 1.5.1254b2–16).

4.5.9 *pleasure*: the pursuit of pleasure presents a test of self-mastery, so Socrates asserts that pleasure can only be achieved through the self-controlled achievement of goals and desires, that the uncontrolled pursuit of apparent pleasure does not in fact result in happiness, and that the capacity to control the pursuit of pleasure differentiates rational humans from irrational animals (4.5.11).

4.5.11 *divide them into their categories*: the reference to discussion 'on the division of things' looks a little like the method of division and collection adopted by participants in Plato's later dialogues, in which a definition is reached by a repeated process of dividing according to key differences (division), until a unique descriptor is built up. But some commentators suggest that it is more likely to refer to the type of classification exercise undertaken by Socrates and Euthydemus in 4.2, a suggestion which would absolve Xenophon of a possible anachronism.

4.5.12 *facility for discussion*: Xenophon here plays on the different senses of the related but distinct verbs *dialegesthai* ('to discuss') and *dialegein* ('to pick out'), to establish an etymology for dialectic; Carlo Natali points out the distinctive claim Xenophon makes, which separates dialectic as a method from the negative and destructive question-and-answer method associated with Socrates (see the Introduction).

leadership and the greatest dialectical skill: the result of this intellectual activity is that those trained in this way are the best in both action and argument, embroidering the reference to thought and action in the previous paragraph and also asserting Xenophon's view that the outcome of Socratic education was excellence in skills of practical benefit.

Chapter 4.6

Another conversation with Euthydemus illuminates the way in which Socrates' teaching developed skills in argument; Xenophon cites a series of conversations which aim to find definitions for qualities such as piety, the just, wisdom, and the good.

4.6.1 *dialectical argument*: picking up the closing word of the previous discussion, Xenophon appears set to launch an exploration of dialectic, but delivers a set of definitions of key Socratic terms and concepts related to the capacity of the man who has mastered himself, illustrating his own description of dialectic in 4.5.12.

definitions: Xenophon here points to one of the methods most closely associated with Socrates, the asking of questions in the form of 'what is [*ti esti*] x?', a phrase which appears in the previous sentence.

4.6.2 *piety*: in this and the following sections, the key word being defined appears at the beginning. Socrates will lead Euthydemus through a condensed version of the discussion of 4.4, in which the relationship between piety and law was explored.

laws: the previous discussion of law considered both unwritten/divine and written/positive law, but here the latter is the focus.

4.6.4 *what is lawful*: there is a slight shift in language here; the Greek word *nomimos* means not only lawful in a legal sense but also customary, hinting at the importance of unwritten custom and practice.

4.6.5 *people*: in showing Socrates talking about 'human beings' (*anthrōpoi*) Xenophon is more inclusive, suggesting that ethical responsibilities attach to dealings with humans beyond those with whom one has a civic and political relationship.

4.6.7 *wisdom . . . knowledge*: here Xenophon offers an abbreviated glimpse into a complex debate on the nature of knowledge; the identity of wisdom (*sophia*) and knowledge (*epistēmē*) is the starting point for the exploration of what knowledge is in Plato's *Theaetetus* (145de). Unlike Plato, Xenophon rarely explores epistemology.

wise in respect of all things: by this conclusion, Socrates' knowledge is limited to knowledge of those things for which he can provide a definition, although there are many such things.

4.6.8 *"the good"*: the Good is the highest object of knowledge in the epistemology which underpins Plato's Theory of Forms, as set out in the central books of the *Republic*. Here Xenophon appears to acknowledge Plato, while also offering a more conventional assessment of the good as the useful (see the Introduction).

beneficial to everyone: another relativistic argument from Socrates; see 3.8.7.

4.6.9 *"the beautiful"*: again Xenophon shifts an abstract discussion into a practical consideration of usefulness.

4.6.10 *courage*: one of the cardinal virtues (see the Introduction), explored by Plato most closely in the *Laches*, and also in the *Protagoras*. The discussion here echoes the conversation of Nicias and Socrates at *Laches* 194c–197c.

madmen: discussed at *Laches* 197ac, where it is argued that being said to be courageous requires knowledge of a dangerous situation, and so the mad and those without knowledge of their situation cannot be courageous, only rash.

4.6.12 *kingship and tyranny*: the two forms of single-person rule understood within the Greek framework of types of constitution; kingship differs from tyranny in the subjection of the monarch to the law and in the willing assent of the subjects to being ruled.

constitution: Xenophon lists forms of *politeia*, following on from the discussion of single-person rule; aristocracy as the good form of rule by a few, plutocracy or rule according to financial worth taking the place of oligarchy (usually presented as the bad form of rule by a few), and democracy which can be both the good and bad form of rule by many (the entire citizen body, dominated by the more numerous poor and thus thought more likely to act in their class interests rather than those of the city as a whole)

4.6.14 *what the function of a good citizen is*: the final question in the series returns to the overall themes of the *Memorabilia*. The idea that everything has a function (*ergon*) specific and unique to it is also explored by Aristotle in the *Nicomachean Ethics* (1.7.1097b22–1098a18), where he argues that the function of humans must involve the unique capabilities of humans and so be related to the exercise of reason in their soul, in pursuit of happiness.

4.6.15 *a series of steps which met with general agreement*: a key part of the procedure of the Socratic elenchus is that the interlocutor must agree to each statement as the argument proceeds. That assent occasionally seems forced or reluctant in Platonic dialogue, where the careful reader can find objections or possible responses not given by Socrates' interlocutors.

a 'convincing speaker': that Odysseus was a convincing public speaker was a commonplace of ancient thought. The contrast between his physical appearance and speaking capability is noted at *Iliad* 3.216–24, and Odysseus himself describes the qualities of such a speaker (*Odyssey* 8.169–73). Odysseus was previously cited here as an example of self–control (1.3.7).

Chapter 4.7

Xenophon summarizes Socrates' educational practice. Socrates gave particular attention to the kind of education needed to become an exemplary person, the level of philosophical and scientific education that was appropriate, and the practical matters that should be of concern to such a person.

4.7.1 *declared his own opinion*: contrary to Hippias' earlier accusation that Socrates never gave his own views (see 4.4.9).

self-sufficient: self-sufficiency is closely associated with the human good by Aristotle for both the individual and the city as the means through which individuals might achieve the good (*NE* 1.7.1097b8–21; *Pol.* 1.2.1253b25–9), and this chapter offers a summary of the practical benefits of association with Socrates. Socrates' self-sufficiency was what attracted Critias and Alcibiades to spend time with him (1.2.14).

relevant experts: Socrates declared that he did this (1.6.14); an example might be his relaying the expertise of Ischomachus in estate management to Critobulus (Xen. *Oec.*), although no meeting is promised. Plato has the generals Nicias and Laches introduce Socrates to the conversation rather than the other way round (Pl. *Laches*).

4.7.2 *how far ... any given subject*: Xenophon reports Socrates' view that studying some subjects at an abstract rather than a practical level rendered an individual less happy and less competent in practical matters. He repeats the forms of study identified at 4.2.10, with further details of what constitutes appropriate and inappropriate levels of involvement with arithmetic, geometry, and astronomy. The idea that some subjects could be pursued in an impractical way, or one with no benefit to everyday life, is also noted by Isocrates, who defends their usefulness for educational professionals but warns against taking an undue interest in cosmological speculation (*Antidosis* 261–9).

geometry: the opposition to geometry Socrates expresses here would be alien to Plato's Socrates, for whom geometry was important in itself and as a step towards understanding the Forms. Socrates' lesson to the slave in Plato's *Meno* is a geometry lesson, which demonstrates the 'theory of recollection', that human souls have some innate knowledge of the abstract and immaterial which can be activated by education.

4.7.4 *night-hunters*: nocturnal hunting may have been an analogy for erotic pursuit previously (3.11.8) but here it straightforwardly notes the skill of hunters. Plato's Athenian Stranger explicitly discourages it along with other forms of practical subsistence hunting which relied on unattended traps (*Laws* 7.824a), and it is not mentioned in Xenophon's *Cynegeticus*, but here Xenophon suggests that some useful expertise is involved.

4.7.5 *planets and the variable stars*: understanding and modelling the movements of the planets and other celestial bodies was a central project of early Greek astronomy. Such endeavours did ultimately have a practical output in a more accurate annual calendar, a point noted earlier when Socrates outlined the usefulness of the changing phases of the moon (4.3.4).

4.7.6 *discouraged any speculation*: the language Xenophon uses here includes the noun *phrontistēs* (thinker) which was associated with the historical Socrates, notably in the name (*phrontistērion* or 'thinkery') given to Socrates' school in Aristophanes' *Clouds*. Xenophon here seems to be defending Socrates against what Plato's Socrates termed the 'old allegations', that his enquiry into astronomical phenomena was impious in itself, and perhaps also explaining Socrates' turn from natural philosophy to ethics (see the Introduction).

Anaxagoras: Anaxagoras of Clazomenae (*c.*500–428 BCE) was a philosopher who settled in Athens in the 450s and taught there until he was prosecuted for impiety and sent away. In the *Hippias Major* it is suggested that, unlike sophists such as Gorgias who were emerging as successful educators, he did not make any money from his teaching (Pl. *Hippias Major* 281c, 282e–283b). The prosecution was possibly under the Decree of Diopeithes of *c.*432 BCE, although the only source for this is the much later Plutarch's *Life of Pericles*. Anaxagoras is said to have written a single book; the surviving fragments show a systematic thinker attempting to establish a pluralist ontology in which all things contain 'a portion of everything', determined by the actions of a separate and unmixed Mind.

sun ... red-hot stone: this aspect of Anaxagoras' thought is also discussed in Plato's *Apology* (26d), where Socrates accuses Meletus of confusing his ideas with those of Anaxagoras.

4.7.10 *divination*: a further return to the themes of the opening chapters of Book 1.

Chapter 4.8

Xenophon returns to religious matters and Socrates' life for the closing chapter, showing how Socrates' behaviour once he was condemned to death illustrated his possession of many good qualities, and reporting a conversation between Hermogenes and Socrates during the latter's final days.

4.8.1 *'divine sign'*: see note on 1.1.4; this chapter returns to the themes of the opening chapter of Book 1, focusing on Socrates' response to being prosecuted.

4.8.2 *Delian festival*: as Xenophon explains, Athens did not permit any acts which might incur pollution while the sacred embassy to Delos was away from the city, so Socrates' execution was delayed until it had returned. See 3.3.12; Pl. *Phd.* 59de.

4.8.4 *Hermogenes*: described as one of Socrates' frequent associates (see 1.2.48 and note); this conversation (4.8.4–10) closely parallels sections 2–6 and 26 of Xenophon's *Apology*.

Meletus: see 4.4.4 and note; *Ap.* 19–21.

4.8.8 *life would not be worth living*: Plato's Socrates uses the same adjective (*abiōtos*) to describe the 'unexamined life' (Pl. *Ap.* 38a5–6), but Xenophon's Socrates emphasizes loss of pleasure as the factor which would make life unlivable.

4.8.11 *still…even now*: Xenophon marks the persistence of Socrates' influence with a favourite phrase (*eti kai nun*, 'even now') which he uses elsewhere (notably in the *Cyropaedia*) to mark the persistence of laws and social customs. While the *Cyropaedia* and the *Lacedaimonion Politeia* end with chapters noting the failure of customs to survive, the *Memorabilia* closes with a strong and personal assertion of the continuing influence of Socrates.

As for me: Xenophon asserts his own personal response to Socrates, echoing the opening remarks of Book 1.

so self-disciplined: this final remark confirms that Socrates is Xenophon's prime exemplar of self-discipline.

APOLOGY

1 *others too*: it is plausible that other Socratics beyond Plato and Xenophon wrote accounts of Socrates' trial; Diogenes Laertius and other later sources imply further versions, including a defence speech by Lysias (DL 2.38–9). But this may simply be a reference to Plato's *Apology*.

trial: like all trials held in Athens, this involved prosecutor and prosecuted making speeches setting out their case to a jury, which returned a verdict the same day. Before the trial, the prosecution and defence set out their case and counter-case to the *archon basileus*, the official (a citizen selected by lot) who was responsible for religious matters and serious crimes.

boastfulness: Xenophon's term *megalēgoria* suggests 'grandeur in public speaking', and was associated with arrogance; later it would be used to describe a high-flown literary style, but here it appears to mean the manifestation of magnificence (*megaloprepeia*) through speech in a public space. As Xenophon notes, Socrates' approach does not appeal to the Athenian jurors.

2 *Hermogenes*: Xenophon claims to rely on Hermogenes son of Hipponicus, a member of the Socratic circle, as a source for the events of Socrates' trial and death (24–6), as well as this conversation (2–9) taking place before the trial itself; see also *Mem.* 1.2.48 and 4.8.4–10 (which closely parallels the account in the *Apology*). Whether Hermogenes was Xenophon's informant, or this is a literary device for framing the story, is unclear.

4 *Athenian juries*: Xenophon continues to establish the difference between Socrates, steadfast in his assessment that he is acting correctly, and the jurors, whose opinion is easily swayed by powerful speech. Although the number of jurors in this case is not recorded, Plato's description of the votes suggests a panel of 501 jurors, which would be appropriate for a high-profile prosecution on a serious charge.

divine sign: Socrates' claims about his divine sign contribute to the jury's negative assessment of his character and actions; they combine with his manner of speaking to suggest that his enhanced connection to the gods results in arrogance (see 12–14, and *Mem.* 1.1.2–4).

5 *astonishing*: Hermogenes' response echoes that of Xenophon himself in the opening sentence of the *Memorabilia*.

6 *penalty of old age*: the idea that old age was marked by loss of physical strength and mental acuity was familiar in Greek literature; in Plato's *Republic*, the first conversation, between Socrates and Cephalus, is about Cephalus' experience of old age.

7 *looking after my interest*: Socrates suggests that the god is acting as a *proxenos*, a citizen who looked after the interests of those from another city.

9 *slavishly*: Xenophon implies that, if an individual's opportunity to stay alive is dependent on another's decision, that individual can no longer be considered free. Characterizing the *dēmos* as a tyrant was a familiar trope of Athenian political rhetoric.

10 *his opponents*: Plato lists three accusers, Lycon, Meletus, and Anytus (Pl. *Ap.* 23e4–24a1), of whom the last was the most prominent in Athenian life; Diogenes Laertius reports that Antisthenes (of Rhodes, not the Socratic) also named this trio (DL 2.39), and that Lycon prepared the case against Socrates. Xenophon only features Meletus and Anytus in his *Apology*, although Lycon is present at the party described in his *Symposium*, as the father of the Autolycus who is the object of the host Callias' erotic pursuit. On that occasion he observes that Socrates is 'truly a man of quality' (*kalos ge kagathos, Smp.* 2.5).

11 *Meletus*: the first of Socrates' prosecutors, who seems to have taken the greatest role in prosecuting the case, although he was younger and less well known than Anytus, the other prosecutor Xenophon names. See note on *Mem.* 4.4.4; for Socrates publicly seen sacrificing, see also *Mem.* 1.1.2.

12 *divination*: for Socrates' contention that his 'divine sign' was not different in kind from other commonly used forms of divination, see also *Mem.* 1.1.3.

Pytho: another name for Delphi, especially as the site of the oracle of Apollo; legend, and a fanciful etymology, attributed the name to Apollo's killing there of the monstrous snake Python (*Homeric Hymn to Apollo* 300–74). For the Pythia, the Delphic priestess, see also *Mem.* 1.3.1, 4.3.16.

13 *told many of my friends*: see *Mem.* 1.1.4, where Xenophon states that Socrates gave good advice based on the promptings of his divine sign.

14 *uproar*: uproar and disturbance were associated with democracy and the collective response of the crowd. Plato too describes the jury as responding noisily to Socrates' speech, because of Chaerephon's claims about the oracle's response about Socrates (Pl. *Ap.* 20e–21a), which Xenophon has Socrates mention here. The noise suggests the large number of jurors, 501 citizens, which in turn emphasizes the importance placed on the case.

Chaerephon: a friend of Socrates, named by both Plato and Xenophon as having obtained the oracle which pronounced Socrates' exceptionalism; see notes on *Mem.* 1.2.48, and the dialogue with his brother Chaerecrates (*Mem.* 2.3).

15 *Lycurgus the Spartan lawgiver*: Socrates is like the legendary Spartan, in that the Delphic oracle made a positive pronouncement about his abilities, although Socrates clearly distinguishes the oracle's claim that he was exceptional from the suggestion that Lycurgus was like a god. For Lycurgus, see *Mem.* 4.4.15 and note.

16 *slave to the bodily appetites*: Xenophon analogizes rational control of physical appetites to the control of a master over a slave, a point of view that aligns with Aristotle's account of 'natural slavery' (*Pol.* 1.5.1254a17–b16; see also *Mem.* 4.5) in which the rational master overcomes the deficiencies of the enslaved person by making rational decisions on their behalf and directing their action. See the closing section (30–1) for an exemplary narrative of failure to control the appetite.

17 *gift*: Xenophon recasts Socrates' famous refusal to accept payment for teaching within a framework of generosity and reciprocity (see the Introduction).

18 *blockade*: during the final stages of the Peloponnesian War (405–404 BCE), Athens was effectively besieged by Sparta, preventing both farming in Attica and the importation of food, and causing a famine which led the Athenians to surrender to the Spartans (*Hell.* 2.1.10–14; see also the discussion in *Mem.* 2.7). Xenophon suggests that control of his physical appetites made it easier for Socrates to endure the famine.

19 *do you still claim*: Xenophon's *Apology* follows Plato's in including a discussion between Socrates and Meletus (Pl. *Ap.* 24c–27d), although Xenophon's much briefer conversation only covers the charge of corrupting the young, and does not take the form of a philosophical refutation.

20 *parents*: the suggestion that Socrates alienated young men from their families is a convincing interpretation of the otherwise vague charge of 'corrupting the young'.

23 *alternative penalty*: there were no fixed penalties in the Athenian legal system; once a defendant had been found guilty, prosecutor and defendant made their own proposals, and the jury voted again on which it thought most appropriate. Plato's Socrates notoriously proposes that a fitting punishment for his activities would be free dining in the prytaneum, the hall in the agora where the current leaders of the council and honoured citizens dined at public expense (Pl. *Ap.* 36b–37c), while his friends offer to pay a large fine on his behalf (38b). Xenophon's Socrates more austerely refuses to name an alternative.

ready to spring him from prison: this alludes to Plato's dialogue *Crito*, in which Socrates' friend Crito visits him in prison and fails to persuade him to go into exile in Thessaly rather than remain in Athens to be executed (Pl. *Crito* 45bc). Socrates' argument in that dialogue, that he should obey the laws of Athens even against his own interest, is well aligned with the views about obedience to the law expressed by Xenophon's Socrates (*Mem.* 4.4, 4.6; see the Introduction).

26 *Palamedes*: according to myth, unjustly condemned by the Greeks at Troy for taking bribes from the Trojans, and used by both Plato and Xenophon as a parallel for Socrates in being unjustly accused and punished; see note on *Mem.* 4.2.33.

poets: Aeschylus, Sophocles, and Euripides all wrote tragedies about Palamedes, of which only small fragments survive.

28 *Apollodorus*: a devoted follower of Socrates; see *Mem.* 3.11.17. Before deciding to follow Socrates, Apollodorus had become wealthy; he was able to offer to pay a large fine on Socrates' behalf, along with Plato, Crito, and Critobulus (Pl. *Ap.* 38b).

stroked: Simmias describes a similar tender gesture from Socrates (Pl. *Phd.* 89b). Some commentators have suggested that this shared detail is a sign that Xenophon derived or even plagiarized his Socratic works from Plato.

29 *We are told*: historians such as Herodotus use the word with which Xenophon introduces this anecdote (*legetai*, 'it is said') to imply an element of doubt about the material being presented.

Anytus: the second of Socrates' accusers, Anytus was an established politician and general who, after initially supporting the Thirty as part of a moderate faction, had been exiled from Athens. His family's wealth came from operating a tannery; although much of this property was confiscated by the Thirty, Socrates' criticism of his background in a lowly trade suggests that he had regained control of it on his return. Anytus had then fought for the democrats; after the restoration of the democracy he remained highly involved in civic life, appearing as a witness for Andocides (*On the Mysteries* 1.150) in 399, and described by Isocrates as a man who did not bear grudges against other citizens despite the injustices he experienced under the Thirty (*Against Callimachus* 23–4). Plato depicts him warning Socrates about his behaviour (Pl. *Meno* 94e–95a), after Socrates has invited him to join a discussion about teachers of virtue. Later biographical traditions suggest that Anytus was punished in turn by the Athenians and banished from the city (DL 2.43), although Socrates' remarks about Anytus' family suggest that in fact they remained in Athens.

30 *Homer*: two key Homeric characters show foreknowledge (of the deaths of others) at the moment of their own deaths; Patroclus (*Iliad* 16.851–4) and Hector (*Iliad* 22.358–60).

Anytus' son... servile occupation: beyond this reference to a brief association with Socrates, nothing is known of Anytus' son. Like many Athenians, Anytus' wealth came from the profits from a manufacturing business (Plato also notes that the family's wealth was not long-standing, Pl. *Meno* 90a). In the aristocratic model of personal excellence which Xenophon ascribes to Socrates, such activities are deprecated compared with the traditional sources of aristocratic wealth, farming and estate management, as exemplified by Ischomachus in the *Oeconomicus*.

31 *hooked on wine*: this tale of the failure of a subsequent generation through drunkenness echoes similar accounts in other works by Xenophon, notably the *Cyropaedia*. There, Xenophon blames excessive drinking for the decline of the Persians after the death of Cyrus the Great (*Cyr.* 8.8.10–12); he describes them as 'weakened' or even 'defeated by wine'. For him, it is an exemplary case of the failure of the Socratic virtue of *enkrateia* or self-control over physical appetites (see the Introduction).

GLOSSARY OF GREEK TERMS

agora: public space at the centre of a polis, often containing or surrounded by key public buildings, in which citizens transacted personal and civic business.

aidōs: shame. If directed at or caused by actions to which shame is an appropriate response, *aidōs* can be a positive attribute as a regulator of behaviour.

aischros: shameful.

andrapodon: a slave: 'man-footed beast'. The harshest of the many Greek terms for the enslaved, making the dehumanization of enslavement explicit; see also *doulos*.

aphrodisia: sex: 'the things of Aphrodite' (the goddess of sexual love).

aretē: excellence or virtue. Excellence is achieved when a human or other creature fulfils its natural function, and *aretē* also comes to describe the qualities which would be demonstrated by that. While courage (*andreia*) was the form of excellence most recognized in Homeric epic, Xenophon and his contemporaries identified a range of qualities as forms of virtue, notably moderation (*sōphrosunē*). Plato depicts Socrates exploring arguments for the unity of the virtues, and the identity of virtue with wisdom.

basilikē technē: royal art/kingly craft. Xenophon uses this term both for a master craft which manages and oversees the work of other crafts, and for the skills taught by Socrates. Exploring the possibility of such a craft and what form it might take was a project shared by several Socratics, and may well originate with Socrates himself.

bia/biaios: physical violence; can cover a wide range of acts of interpersonal violence.

boulē: council. At Athens, this was a council of five hundred citizens selected by lot each year, fifty from each of the ten tribes into which the citizen body was divided. It met to discuss policy and to arrange the agenda for Assembly meetings.

charis: gratitude, favour. Social bonds constructed through reciprocal social obligations and the performance of favours connect citizens and help to ensure the stability and unity of the polis as a collective endeavour.

chorēgos: although the word means 'chorus-leader', in Athens it referred to the wealthy citizen who funded the production of a playwright's entry in one of the city's drama festivals.

daimonion: literally 'little spirit'. A *daimōn* was a lesser divine power; in Plato's myths of the distant past, *daimones* rule humans on behalf of the gods. Both Plato and Xenophon depict Socrates guiding his actions in response to communications from a personal *daimonion*, and acknowledge that this was unusual and unsettling for his fellow Athenians.

dēmiourgos: craftsman. Used of those producing goods but also in creationist thought to refer to the divine creator of the cosmos.

dēmos/dēmokratia: people/rule of the people. *Dēmos* can be used to refer to the entire citizen body of a polis, or the poor majority as a class. Translated as 'deme', it indicates one of the local administrative subdivisions of Athens and Attica established at the end of the sixth century BCE by Cleisthenes, which determined citizens' membership of the ten tribes through which almost all civic activity was organized.

dikē: law or justice as a positive process; in Athens, also the term used for some kinds of prosecution.

dikaiosunē: justice as an abstract principle.

dokimasia: the process of scrutinizing candidates for public duties and political office to check whether they were qualified for the role or suitable for holding office.

doulos/douleia: slave/slavery. Xenophon uses a range of words to describe the enslaved; some (*oiketēs*, *therapōn*) gloss over the enslaved status of the worker, but *doulos* is explicit. Chattel slavery was an essential part of the Athenian economy, permitting those of citizen status to spend time on politics and personal leisure pursuits.

eisangelia: denunciation or accusation. Used in Athenian law to refer to a prosecution of a state official for failure in the performance of his duties.

ekklēsia: assembly. The Athenian assembly was the citizen mass meeting, held on regular occasions throughout the year, at which policy was presented and voted on.

elenchus: argument, scrutiny. Used to refer to Socrates' method of investigation, notably his search for definitions of abstract terms and values, through asking questions of an interlocutor, who is eventually forced to concede the falsity of a definition offered at the start of the argument. The elenchus proceeds through formalized steps; the interlocutor should assent to each as the argument progresses.

eleutheria: freedom. This could be a personal status—free as opposed to enslaved—or the political status of a community—not subject to external rule by a foreign power.

eleutheros/eleutherios: free. The two Greek adjectives for 'free' emphasized different aspects of freedom. *Eleutheros* (the more common, and earlier word) describes the political status of a person or community; *eleutherios* is a normative term describing qualities and actions appropriate to a free person, the set of qualities which emerge as the product of a Socratic education.

enkrateia: self-control. Used especially in respect of bodily appetites and desires.

epimeleia: care or oversight. This can be exercised over others, in leadership roles such as that of a general commanding soldiers, or by the individual managing mind and body.

epistēmē: knowledge. Sometimes but not always suggesting a scientific, ordered form of knowledge gained using reasoning.

erastēs: 'lover', the older party in a pederastic relationship.

erōmenos: 'beloved', the younger party in a pederastic relationship; also on occasion referred to as *paidika*, 'child'.

erōs: erotic love.

eudaimonia: happiness. For Xenophon, this is a state of fulfilment, which can be achieved by all living creatures.

gnōmē: intelligence or judgement. In a legal sense, a verdict.

hetaira: female companion, retained sex worker. Greek had a wide range of terms for women who were sex workers, which could be used to imply different working arrangements. A *hetaira* was a sex worker, most likely of metic status, who might be engaged on a long-term or even exclusive basis, and was maintained in her own home, by a small number of clients, as depicted by Xenophon in Socrates' encounter with Theodote (*Mem.* 3.11). A *pornē* might sell sex on the street or work in a brothel under the control of a *pornoboskos*, and was more likely to be of enslaved status.

kalos kagathos/kalokagathia: 'fine and good' (*kalos kai agathos*). This pair of adjectives conveys a special evaluative force when applied to people. It has sometimes been translated 'gentleman', in the full sense of the holder of a specific social status who exemplifies a particular set of social and aesthetic values: in this translation it is rendered by 'man of quality'. When applied to objects a similar evaluative sense applies, with perhaps a greater emphasis on the aesthetic.

leitourgia: liturgy, public service. In Athens, a tax paid by the wealthy in the form of mandatory support for a community project; these included the production of plays for the dramatic festivals and fitting out warships for the city's fleet.

logos: speech or argument. Often opposed to *ergon*, deed.

mania: madness or inspiration. Can refer to both insanity and to being inspired by the gods.

megaloprepeia: magnificence; 'suited to great things'. Aristotle treated this quality as a character virtue only attainable by those of great wealth and social status.

metic: non-citizen worker, a person of free status who lives and works in a city in which they do not hold citizenship. In Athens, metics were subject to additional taxes and could not own property outside the port and trading centre of the Piraeus; many metics lived there, such as Cephalus, in whose home Plato's *Republic* is set.

nous: mind. Can refer to individual intellectual activity. However, central to the thought of Presocratic philosophers such as Anaxagoras was the idea that the cosmos as a whole was ordered by *nous*.

ochlos: mob, crowd. Xenophon uses a range of words to describe the mass of citizens, some descriptive and others (such as *ochlos*) pejorative.

oiketes: can mean any household member or relative, but most often used by Xenophon to refer to enslaved workers within the home.

oikos: the home, a household. *oikonomia*, the skill of managing a home or particularly an estate, is treated by Xenophon as equivalent to generalship and political leadership, albeit exercised on a smaller scale.

ophelos, ōpheleia: help, benefit, advantage. Xenophon is concerned with the calculation of benefit and worth, and the usefulness of goods (such as friendship) which do not have an obvious financial value.

opson: high-value prepared food, eaten with bread. *Opson* can refer to a wide range of savoury and sweet delicacies, including fish. Etiquette determined a polite ratio of *opson* to bread, and taking more than your share of expensive foods, or only eating the delicacies, as the *opsophagos* ('delicacy-eater') was criticized for doing, was seen as a demonstration of lack of self-control.

philia: friendship. The Greek word encompasses a much wider range of social relationships, from family to business connections, than the interpersonal emotional connection of modern usage.

philotimia: ambition. The 'love of honour' could be a virtue or a vice depending on the way in which it manifested in an individual.

phronēsis/phronimos: practical wisdom. The person displaying this quality in their actions is *phronimos*.

pleonexia/pleonektēs: greed/greedy: 'acquiring more'. A quality which may be evidence of a lack of moderation or self-control.

polis: city/city-state. The Greek polis is not quite a state in the sense of a modern nation-state. What qualified a settlement as a polis was a set of institutions governed by citizens, regardless of the nature of the *politeia* (a single citizen could rule in a tyranny), as well as other communal arrangements such as cults of patron gods.

politeia: political regime. Defined by Isocrates as 'the soul of the polis' (*Areopagiticus* 14), a *politeia* was not so much a political constitution as the encapsulation of a way of life, including both laws and customs. In written form, a *politeia* (such as Xenophon's *Constitution of the Spartans*, or *Lacedaimonion Politeia*) might focus on particular aspects of political culture and be framed as an argument rather than provide a thorough survey of institutions.

ponēros: worthless, oppressed by toil. Often used normatively in criticism of the lower classes, through its derivation from *ponos*, labour.

proxenos: a citizen who hosted official visitors from another polis and broadly represented its interests.

psuchē: soul. Believed in conventional Greek religion to survive death and less conventionally to be subject to reincarnation.

sōphrosunē/sōphrōn: self-control or moderation. The virtue of self-control, when exercised over higher-order rational desires, was often identified with moderation.

stasis: civil strife. Literally 'standing apart', denoting the splitting of the citizen body into rival factions, as well as any ensuing conflict.

sukophantēs: vexatious litigant, false accuser. 'Sycophants' launched opportunistic legal suits, usually without merit, against wealthy citizens or the political opponents of their friends.

technē: craft or skill. Originally applied to productive crafts such as carpentry (to which it is etymologically related), but used by Plato and Xenophon for a wider range of human activities with systematized bodies of knowledge; whether some activities, such as rhetoric, constituted such crafts was disputed by Plato, and all Socratics explored the question of whether there was a master craft or *basilikē technē*.

thētes: labourers. Members of the lowest of the four property classes of classical Athens. Thetes had citizen rights and could hold offices, but most would have been day labourers without the financial resources to attend the assembly. Because the crews of the Athenian fleet were largely drawn from this class, they were thought to play an important role in Athenian democratic politics, constituting the bulk of the *dēmos*.

NOTES ON THE GREEK TEXTS

FOR the translation of *Memorabilia* I have used the text established by Michele Bandini in the Budé edition edited by M. Bandini and L.-A. Dorion: *Xénophon, Mémorables*, 3 vols (Paris: Les Belles Lettres, 2000–11); and for the translation of *Apology* the text of François Ollier in the Budé edition: *Xénophon, Banquet, Apologie de Socrate* (Paris: Les Belles Lettres, 1961).

A text of both works in common use is that edited by E. C. Marchant in the Oxford Classical Texts (OCT) series: *Xenophontis Opera Omnia*, vol. ii (2nd edn, Oxford: Clarendon Press, 1921). This second edition reprints the text in the first (1901) edition, prefaced by a list of addenda and corrigenda.

I give below, with a few further textual notes, a list of those places where the texts of Bandini and Ollier differ in any significant way from that printed in the OCT, in each case giving first the reading in Bandini or Ollier. In *Apology* there is very little difference between the Budé and the OCT texts.

Memorabilia

1.1.5 ἀληθεύειν, not ἀληθεύσειν.

1.1.14 ἀπολέσθαι (and in the OCT corrigenda), not ἀπολεῖσθαι.

1.1.18 Retaining ἐννέα στρατηγοὺς, deleted in the OCT (Schenkl). Bandini obelizes †ἐννέα†, conjecturing ὀκτὼ or δέκα.

1.2.9 μηδέν᾽ ἂν θέλειν (Cobet), not μηδένα θέλειν.

1.2.12 Reading καὶ φονικώτατος after βιαιότατος, and καὶ βιαιότατος after ὑβριστότατος.

1.2.24 Retaining κολακεύειν after δυνατῶν, deleted in the OCT (Ernesti).

1.2.29 ἐπετιμᾶτο, not ἐπιτιμῷτο.

1.2.35 Retaining καὶ (Castiglioni for ὡς) ἄλλο τι ποιῶ ἢ τὰ προηγορευμένα, deleted in the OCT (Cobet).

1.2.58 ὅντινα δ᾽ αὖ δήμου τε [ἄνδρα] ἴδοι, not ὃν δ᾽ αὖ δήμου τ᾽ ἄνδρα ἴδοι.

1.2.64 μάλιστα πάντων ἀνθρώπων, not μάλιστα τῶν ἄλλων ἀνθρώπων.

1.3.1 οἷς δὲ δὴ (Hartman), not ὡς δὲ δὴ.

1.3.3 οὔτε γὰρ <ἂν> τοῖς θεοῖς (Heindorf).

1.3.6 τἀναπείθοντα (Schenkl), not τὰ πείθοντα.

1.3.7 τοιούτοις πολλοὺς, not τοιούτοις πολλοῖς.

1.3.8 On the evidence of a papyrus Bandini posits a lacuna between σωφρονεῖν and ἀλλὰ καὶ Κριτόβουλόν ποτε.

1.3.10 ὑποστῆναι, not ὑπομεῖναι.

1.3.11 οὐδεὶς οὐδ᾽ ἂν (Koraïs), not οὐδ᾽ ἂν.

1.3.12 ὅσον μόνον ἀψάμενα τῷ στόματι ὀδύναις τε, not προσαψάμενα μόνον τῷ στόματι ταῖς τε ὀδύναις.

1.3.13 ἀλλὰ κἄν τις (not ἐάν τις) αὐτὸ θεᾶται.

Retaining ἴσως δὲ καὶ οἱ ἔρωτες τοξόται διὰ τοῦτο καλοῦνται, ὅτι καὶ πρόσωθεν οἱ καλοὶ τιτρώσκουσιν, deleted in the OCT, after Dindorf.

Retaining τὸ δῆγμα, deleted in the OCT.

1.4.1 οἷς (Iacobs, not ὡς) ἔνιοι γράφουσι.

1.4.2 After οὔτε θύοντα τοῖς θεοῖς and before οὔτε μαντικῇ χρώμενον Bandini prints and obelizes the corrupt †μὴ μαχόμενον† of the two main MSS followed by a short lacuna, as indicated in a fragmentary papyrus. After θεοῖς the papyrus has [......]χομεν[..........]τα, validating F. Portus' felicitous conjecture οὔτ᾽ εὐχόμενον, which I translate. The OCT indicates no lacuna between θεοῖς and οὔτε μαντικῇ χρώμενον, but in the corrigenda to the second edition Marchant accepts οὔτ᾽ εὐχόμενον and fills the remaining lacuna with <δῆλον ὄν>τα.

1.4.5 οὔκουν (Bornemann), not οὐκοῦν.

1.4.8 Bandini deletes ἐρώτα γοῦν καὶ ἀποκρινοῦμαι, after Muretus. I retain in the translation this response of Aristodemus.

οὕτως οἴει (Löwenklau), not ὡς οἴει.

1.4.11 καὶ στόμα ἄνω ἐποίησαν (Heindorf), not καὶ στόμα ἐνεποίησαν.

1.4.15 ὥσπερ σοὶ φῂς (Cobet), not ὥσπερ σὺ φῂς.

1.5.2 ἡγησαίμεθ᾽ ἄν, not ἡγησόμεθα.

1.5.5 δουλεύοντι, not δουλεύοντα.

1.6.10 ἐγὼ δὲ νομίζω, not ἐγὼ δ᾽ ἐνόμιζον.

2.1.1 Something is wrong here. Either πρὸς ἐπιθυμίαν must be deleted (so Iacobs), or, if πρὸς ἐπιθυμίαν is retained, καὶ ῥίγους καὶ θάλπους καὶ πόνου must be deleted (so Bandini). The OCT retains both. I translate with πρὸς ἐπιθυμίαν deleted.

2.1.22 τὸ μὲν χρῶμα καθαρειότητι, not τὸ μὲν σῶμα καθαρότητι.

2.1.23 φίλην ποιησάμενος ἔπη (Radermacher), not φίλην ποιησάμενος, [ἐπὶ].

2.1.24 σκοπούμενος διαιτήσῃ (Valckenaer), not σκοπούμενος †διέσῃ† (in his corrigenda Marchant adopts Dindorf's διοίσῃ).

ἁπτόμενος ἡσθείης (and in Marchant's corrigenda), not ἁπτόμενος.

2.1.28 ὄντως ἀγαθῶν (Muretus), not ὄντων ἀγαθῶν.

2.1.30 Retaining τὰς κλίνας καὶ, deleted in the OCT.

2.1.32 οἷς προσήκει (with the MSS), not οἷς προσήκω (Schneider).

2.1.33 ἀπέχονται (Mücke), not ἀνέχονται.

2.1.34 διώκει, not διώκει.

2.2.8   Retaining δυσάνεκτα, deleted in the OCT.

2.3.9   μέγα ἀγαθὸν ἂν εἶναι, not μέγα ἀγαθὸν εἶναι.

2.3.16   λόγων ὑπεῖξαι (Valckenaer), not λόγῳ ὑπεῖξαι.

2.3.17   Bandini deletes ἐπιδεῖξαι, after Cobet. I translate with ἐπιδεῖξαι retained, as in the OCT.

2.4.1   κράτιστον εἴη (and in Marchant's corrigenda), not κράτιστον ἂν εἴη.

2.4.2   οἱ ὄντες ἑαυτοῖς (Bandini), not οἱ ὄντες αὐτοῖς.

2.5.3   τὸν δὲ [πρὸ] (Muretus) πάντων χρημάτων καὶ πόνων πριαίμην ἄν. The OCT retains πρὸ in the text (in his corrigenda Marchant agrees its deletion), and unnecessarily obelizes †πόνων†.

2.5.5   …εἶναι, <καὶ> τὰ τοιαῦτα πάντα, σκοπῶ (Madvig), not…εἶναι, τὰ τοιαῦτα πάντα σκοπῶ.

2.6.5   εὔνους, not εὔοικος.

2.6.17   οἶδα, ἔφη ὁ Σωκράτης, ὃ ταράττει σε. The OCT, following other MSS, omits οἶδα, ἔφη ὁ Σωκράτης.

2.6.28   ἐπιθυμῶν ξυνεῖναι [καὶ] ἀντεπιθυμεῖσθαι. The OCT retains the καὶ.

2.6.32   ὡς <οὖν> οὐ προσοίσοντος (Cobet).

          The OCT has οὐδὲ τὸ στόμα οὖν. Bandini omits the οὖν, not present in all MSS. I translate the OCT reading.

2.6.39   οἶμαι δεῖν ἡμᾶς <οὕτω ποιεῖν> (Bandini, after Bessarion). The OCT marks a lacuna after ἡμᾶς.

2.9.5   καὶ εὐθύς <του> τῶν συκοφαντούντων (Gilbert). The OCT marks a lacuna after εὐθύς.

2.10.3   παραμόνιμον [καὶ τὸ κελευόμενον ἱκανὸν ποιεῖν] ἔχειν (Schütz). The OCT retains the bracketed phrase.

3.3.12   χορὸς [εἷς] (Dobree). The OCT retains εἷς.

3.4.4   στρατιᾷ, not στρατηγίᾳ.

3.4.12   οἷσπερ <οἱ> τὰ ἴδια οἰκονομοῦντες (Zeune).

3.5.2   ἐξ Ἀθηναίων (Löwenklau), not ἐξ Ἀθηνῶν.

3.5.3   μεγαλοφρονέστατοι (Cobet), not φιλοφρονέστατοι.

3.5.8   ὧν οἱ πάλαι εἶχον (Orelli), not ὧν οἱ ἄλλοι εἶχον.

3.5.26   ἐκεῖνο <οὐκ> ἀκήκοας (Hindenburg).

3.6.8   ἡ τῶν ἐναντίων (Hirschig), not ἥττων τῶν ἐναντίων.

3.7.5   ὥρμημαι <ὅτι> οὔτε (Castalio).

3.8.1   <οἱ> πεπεισμένοι (Schneider).

3.9.4   τῷ τὰ μὲν καλά…..τῷ τὰ αἰσχρὰ (Heindorf). For the τῷ……τῷ in Bandini's text the MSS have either τὸ……τὸ or τὸν……τὸν. The OCT prints τὸν……τὸν, both obelized, but in his corrigenda Marchant changes his reading to τὸ……τὸ.

3.9.5   σοφίᾳ πράττεται (Reiske), not ἀρετῇ πράττεται.

3.9.8   τοὺς ἠλιθίους δὲ [ἀεὶ] πάσχειν αὐτό (Brodaeus).

3.10.8   εὐφραινομένη (Weiske), not εὐφραινομένων.

        τὰ ἔργα τῷ τῆς ψυχῆς εἴδει (Hartman), not τὰ τῆς ψυχῆς ἔργα τῷ εἴδει.

3.10.15   αὐτό......λέγω (Schneider), not αὐτός......λέγεις.

3.11.7   <οἱ> τὸ μικροῦ ἄξιον (Heindorf).

3.11.12   <μετα>μελήσει (Schaefer).

3.12.6   δοκεῖς ἐλαχίστην σώματος χρείαν, not δοκεῖ ἐλαχίστη σώματος χρεία.

3.14.1   ἠσχύνοντο τό τε [μὴ] κοινωνεῖν (Leisner).

4.2.8   <ἄκοντος> ἀκούοντος (Weiske).

4.2.14   θῶ, not θῶμεν (twice).

        κλέπτειν, not κακουργεῖν.

4.2.28   προΐστανταί τε (Richards), not προΐστασθαί γε.

4.2.38   οἶδα γοῦν (Bandini), not οἶδα [γὰρ].

4.3.8   Bandini has ὧν καιρός. I translate ὧν καιρὸς διελήλυθε, the OCT reading.

4.3.14   παμφαὴς, not πᾶσι φανερός.

4.4.24   νόμιμον <μέν>, ἔφη (Cobet).

        θείοις (Brodaeus, not θεοῖς) ταῦτα πάντα ἔοικε.

4.5.1   ἠσκηκὼς αὐτὴν (Richards), not ἠσκηκὼς αὐτὸν.

4.5.9   ὥσπερ ἡ μὲν ἀκρασία. The OCT omits ὥσπερ.

4.6.2   δεῖ τοῦτο ποιεῖν, not δεῖ τοὺς θεοὺς τιμᾶν.

4.6.7   ᾧ <οἱ σοφοὶ> σοφοί εἰσιν (Heindorf).

4.6.9   ἢ [εἰ] ἔστιν <ὃ> ὀνομάζεις (Ernesti). The OCT obelizes the MSS' †ἤ, εἰ ἔστιν, ὀνομάζεις†.

4.8.6   μάλιστα ἐπιμελομένους (Koraïs, from Bessarion), not ἄριστα ἐπιμελομένους.

4.8.10   οἶμαι γὰρ ἀεὶ, not οἶδα γὰρ ἀεὶ.

4.8.11   ἄλλους.....ἁμαρτάνοντας, not ἄλλως.....ἁμαρτάνοντα.

Apology

11   ἄλλοι (not οἱ ἄλλοι) οἱ παρατυγχάνοντες.

22   Perhaps read ἀσεβὴς for the MSS' ἀσεβῆσαι given in both the Budé and the OCT.

24   οὔτε ὀμνὺς οὔτε ὀνομάζων (not νομίζων).

28   μᾶλλον ἂν ἐβούλου, not μᾶλλον ἐβούλου.

INDEX

References to *Memorabilia* are to Book, chapter, and section (e.g. 4.2.10), and references to *Apology* are to sections, preceded by *Ap.* (e.g. *Ap.* 17). The headings of the more important entries are given in bold capitals, and references of particular relevance or importance are printed in bold.

2.6.24, 2.6.27, 2.9.8; position of citizen women, **2.7.2–13**; conditions caused by the war, 2.7.2–12, 2.8.1
— **resources**: revenue and expenditure, 3.6.5–7; silver mines, 2.5.2, 3.6.12; food supply, 3.6.13 (loss of crops, 2.7.2, 3.6.10–11); defence of the country, 3.5.25–7, 3.6.10–11; **military**: 3.6.9; army, 3.5.2 (disasters at Lebadea and Delium, 3.5.4); frontier guards, 3.5.25–7, 3.6.10–11; cavalry, **3.3.1–15**, 3.4.1; hoplites and cavalry supposedly 'the elite', 3.5.19, but lack of discipline in both, 3.5.19, 3.5.21; mounted archers, 3.3.1; navy, 3.5.5, 3.5.18 (disciplined); no military training at public expense, 3.12.5
— **past and present**: potential inspiration of previous history of achievement, 3.5.3, **3.5.7–14** (legendary past, 3.5.9–10, Persian Wars, 3.5.11, arbitrators and protectors, 3.5.12); Themistocles, 2.6.13, 3.6.2, 4.2.2; decline from earlier success and reputation, 3.5.1, 3.5.13; general moral infection, **3.5.15–18**; Athens under oligarchy, 1.2.12, 1.2.31–8 (the Thirty), 2.7.2 ('the civil war'); Athens harmed by Critias and Alcibiades, 1.2.12–25; Athens' reputation enhanced by Socrates, 1.2.61
— **the Athenian character**: collective sense of pride, 2.3.13, 3.5.3; lack of discipline and obedience, 3.5.5, 3.5.16–21 (exceptions, 3.5.18); quarrelsome, litigious, 3.5.16, 4.4.8; Athenian practice and attitudes contrasted unfavourably with Spartan, **3.5.14–21**
athletes, athletics: boxing, 3.10.6; pancratium, 3.5.21, 3.10.6; running, 3.8.4, 3.10.6; wrestling, 3.5.21–2, 3.8.4, 3.10.6; contestants in the Olympic Games, 3.12.1; athletic trainers, 3.5.21; successful athletes neglecting their training, 1.2.24, 3.5.13; the reluctant athlete, 3.7.1, 3.7.7; sculpted figures of athletes, 3.10.6–8
athletic games 1.2.24, 2.6.26, 3.5.13, 3.5.18, 3.7.1, 3.12.1; Olympic Games, 3.12.1

Attica 2.8.1; threatened Boeotian invasions, 3.5.4, 3.5.25–7; invasions by Peloponnesians, 2.7.2, 3.6.11; geography facilitating defence, 3.5.25–7; frontier-posts, 3.6.10–11

bad characters, lower sorts (*ponēroi*) 1.2.20, 2.3.16, 2.6.14–16, **2.6.19–20**, 2.6.24, 2.6.27, 2.9.8
barley 2.7.5–6
'BEAUTIFUL': relativity of the term, **3.8.4–7**, 4.6.9; the identity of 'good' and 'beautiful' in relation to the same things, 3.8.5–7; beauty of a thing inherent in its utility for purpose, 3.8.5–10, 4.6.9
— 'beautiful and good' (*kaloskagathos*) applied to people, 3.8.5 (*see further* **'MAN/MEN OF QUALITY'**); 'beautiful/fine and good' (*kala kai agatha*) applied to things or actions, 1.2.23, 1.3.11, 1.5.1, 2.1.20, 2.1.28, 3.8.7, 3.9.4–5, 3.10.5, 4.2.22, 4.3.13, 4.5.10
BEAUTY: Socrates' search for definition, 1.1.16, 3.8.4–10, 4.6.9 (relativity of the quality); an 'ambiguous good', 4.2.34–5
— male beauty: 1.2.29, 4.2.1 (Euthydemus); 1.2.24 (Alcibiades); 1.3.8–13 (Alcibiades' son: Socrates' warning of dangers of infatuation); 1.6.13 (good and bad use of youthful beauty); 2.6.22, 2.6.30–3, 4.1.2, 4.2.35; 'beauty wounds from afar', 1.3.13; **female beauty**, 1.1.8; 3.11.1–2 (Theodote); beauty of soul, 2.6.32, 3.10.3, 4.1.2; **beauty of the world**, 1.4.13, 2.2.3, 4.3.11, 4.3.13
betterment: of oneself, 1.6.9, 4.2.23, 4.8.6; Socrates making his associates better men, 1.2.61, 1.4.1, 2.6.37, 4.8.7, 4.8.10
birds: kept for pleasure, 1.6.14; hunted, 2.1.4, 2.6.9; in divination, 1.1.3–4, *Ap.* 12–13; quails and partridges, 2.1.4
BODY: the gods' providential design of the human body, 1.4.5–7, 1.4.11–12, 2.3.18–19; naturally strong or weak, 3.9.1; good/bad condition, 2.1.20, **3.12.1–8**, 3.13.1, 4.5.10, *Ap.* 19

— **body and soul:** 1.2.4, 1.2.19, 1.2.23,
1.2.53, 1.3.5–6, 1.3.14, 1.4.9, 1.4.14,
1.5.3, 2.1.19, 2.1.25, 2.1.31, 3.9.1,
3.11.10, 3.14.7, 4.1.2, *Ap.* 7; relation of
soul and body, 1.2.4, 1.2.23, 1.2.53,
1.3.5, 1.3.14, 1.4.9, 1.4.17 ('mind'),
2.1.20, 4.1.2
Boeotia, region NW of Attica: threat to
Athens, 3.5.2, 3.5.4, 3.5.25
books: Socrates and friends poring over
wise books of the past, 1.6.14;
Euthydemus' collection of books, 4.2.1,
4.2.8–10; medical treatises, 4.2.10;
complete poems of Homer, 4.2.10
bread, bakeries 2.7.5–6; the proper use
of bread at dining clubs, 3.14.2–5
breastplates, discussed by Socrates with
armourer Pistias 3.10.9–15
brothels 2.2.4
brothers **2.3.1–19** (Chaerecrates and
Chaerephon at odds)
burial 1.2.53, 2.1.33, 2.2.13 (obligation to
tend parents' graves)
BUSINESS: successful management of
a business, 3.4.4–12; successful
businesses in Athens during the war,
2.7.3, 2.7.6; a start-up business,
2.7.11–12; businessman, 2.6.3–4

call-girls 1.5.4
carpenters 1.1.7, 1.2.9, 1.2.37 (in
Socrates' talk), 3.7.6 (typical
assembly-goers), 4.2.12, 4.2.22, 4.4.5
carriage-driver 1.1.9
Carthaginians 2.1.10
cattle 1.2.32, 1.2.38, 1.4.14 (ox), 2.4.5
(oxen), 2.7.6, 3.11.5, 4.3.10, 4.4.5 (ox),
4.5.11
cavalry **3.3.1–15**, 3.4.1; lack of discipline,
3.5.19, 3.5.21; 'the elite', 3.5.19
Cebes, associate of Socrates from
Thebes 1.2.48, 3.11.17
Cecrops, legendary early king of
Athens 3.5.10
celestial phenomena: moon and stars,
4.3.4; sun, 3.8.9, 4.3.3–4, 4.3.8–9,
4.3.14, 4.7.7; planets, stars, and their
orbits, 4.7.5; Socrates' disapproval of
speculation, **1.1.11–16**, **4.7.5–7**
Ceramon, successful Athenian
businessman 2.7.3–4

Chaerecrates, brother of Chaerephon,
associate of Socrates 1.2.48, 2.3.1–19
(Socrates' advice on reconciliation with
his brother)
Chaerephon, brother of Chaerecrates,
associate of Socrates 1.2.48, 2.3.1–19
(at odds with his brother), *Ap.* 14 (his
question to the Delphic oracle about
Socrates)
Charicles, one of the Thirty Tyrants
1.2.31–6
Charmides, son of Glaucon [1], uncle of
Glaucon [2] and Plato 3.6.1, 3.6.14–15
(his household needing reform),
3.7.1–9 (reluctant to engage in politics)
chefs 2.1.30, 3.14.5–6
CHILDREN: procreation, 1.4.7,
2.2.3–4, 4.4.22–3 (consequences of
incest); pregnancy, birth, nurture,
2.2.5; education, 1.5.2, 2.2.6;
guardianship of children, 1.5.2,
4.4.17; parents' care for children's
future, 2.2.4–6, 3.12.4; parents' care
for children when sick, 2.2.8, 2.2.10,
4.2.17; children's duty to parents,
1.2.49, 2.2.3, 2.2.13–14, 4.4.17, 4.4.20
chorus: Athenian chorus sent to Delian
festival, 3.3.12–13, 4.8.2; sponsorship
of a chorus at Athens, 3.4.3–5;
discipline in a chorus, 3.5.5,
3.5.18; chorus-training, 3.4.3–4,
3.5.21; chorus competitions, 3.4.5,
4.4.16
Circe, goddess and witch 1.3.7
Clito, sculptor: conversation with
Socrates, 3.10.6–8
CITIZEN: ability to do good for one's
city, 1.2.48, 1.2.59, 1.6.9, 2.1.19,
2.1.28, 2.6.25, 3.3.2, 3.3.4, 3.5.28,
3.6.3, 3.7.2, 3.12.4, 4.1.4, 4.4.17,
4.5.10, *Ap.* 31; the function of a good
citizen, 1.6.13, 4.2.11, 4.6.13–14; duty
of a citizen to engage in politics, 3.7.2,
3.7.9, to keep himself fit, 3.12.1–8
clothing: Socrates' clothing, 1.2.5, 1.6.2,
1.6.6; Theodote's expensive clothes,
3.11.4; manufacture of clothing,
2.7.5–6, 2.7.12
cobblers 1.2.37 (in Socrates' talk), 3.7.6
(typical assembly-goers), 4.2.22, 4.4.5
comedians 3.9.9

Heracles: Prodicus' fable of the choice of Heracles, **2.1.21–34**

Heraclids, descendants of Heracles (Dorians) 3.5.10

herdsmen 1.2.32, 1.2.37–8; *see also* shepherds

Hermes, god 1.3.7

Hermogenes, son of Hipponicus, associate of Socrates 1.2.48, **2.10.3–6** (fallen on hard times); his account of Socrates before, during, and after his trial, **4.8.4–9**. *Ap.* **2–26**

Hesiod, epic and didactic poet: quoted, 1.2.56 (*Works and Days* 311), 1.3.3 (*Works and Days* 366), 2.1.20 (*Works and Days* 287–92)

Hippias of Elis, sophist: conversation with Socrates about justice and law, **4.4.5–25**

Hippocrates, Athenian general defeated and killed at Delium in 424 BCE 3.5.4

Homer, epic poet 1.4.3, 4.2.10, *Ap.* 30; **quoted:** 1.2.58 (*Iliad* 2.188–9, 198–202), 2.6.11 (*Odyssey* 12.184), 3.1.4 (*Iliad* 3.170), 3.2.1 (*Iliad* 2.243 etc.), 3.2.2 (*Iliad* 3.179), 4.6.15 (*Odyssey* 8.171); **referenced:** 1.3.7 (*Odyssey* 10.230–60, 281–300), *Ap.* 30 (*Iliad* 16.851–4 and 22.358–60)

hoplites 3.4.1, 3.5.2, 3.5.19, 3.5.21, 3.9.2

HORSES 1.6.14, 2.3.7, 2.4.5, 2.6.7, 4.3.10, 4.4.5; cavalry horses, 3.3.2–4, 3.3.8, 3.3.14; thoroughbred horses, 4.1.3; purchase of horses, 4.2.25; horsemanship, 3.3.9–10, 4.2.6, 4.4.5

HOUSEHOLD, management: 1.1.7–8, 1.2.48, 1.2.64, 1.5.2, 2.1.19, 3.6.14–15, 4.1.2, 4.4.16, 4.5.10; **household slaves:** 1.5.2, 2.1.9, 2.1.15–17, 2.3.3, 2.4.2–3, 2.4.5, 2.5.2, 2.10.1–3, 3.13.3–4, 4.4.5, 4.4.17; slaves in positions of responsibility, 1.5.2, 2.5.2; head of household as guardian, 2.7.12–13; duty to one's household, 1.2.48, 2.1.19, 4.4.17

houses: building of a house, 1.1.7, 3.1.7, 3.8.8–10; the ideal house, both beautiful and useful, 3.8.8–10; private quarters, 2.1.5; number of houses in Athens, 3.6.14

hunger: control and resistance, 1.3.5–6, 1.4.13, 2.1.2, 2.1.4, 2.1.17–18, 2.1.30, 2.6.22, 4.5.9; sexual hunger, 3.11.13–14

HUNTERS, HUNTING 2.1.4, 2.1.18, 2.6.9, 3.11.7–8; hunting dogs, 3.11.8, 4.1.3; hunting nets, 2.1.4, 3.11.8–10; night-hunters, 3.11.8, 4.7.4

— metaphorical: hunting for the right friends, 2.6.8–9, 2.6.28–9, 2.6.35, 3.11.5–11, 3.11.15; Socrates 'a hunter of men', 2.6.29, 3.11.15

idleness, laziness 1.2.57, 2.1.16, 2.1.20, 2.1.30, 2.1.33, 2.4.7 (lazy in caring for friends), 2.6.1, 2.7.7–8

ignorance 1.1.16, 1.2.49–50, 3.6.16–17, 3.9.4–6, 3.14.6, 4.1.4–5, 4.2.2–3, 4.2.27, 4.6.1; ignorance of self, 3.9.6, **4.2.25–30**

incest 4.4.20–23 (prohibition of incest a god-ordained 'unwritten law')

independence *see* self-sufficiency

INTELLIGENCE, MIND: in the universe, 1.4.8, 1.4.17; gods' gift to humans, 1.1.9, **1.4.13–14**, 4.3.11 (animals mindless, 2.1.5, 4.5.11); in the human soul, 1.2.4, 1.2.53, 1.4.13–14, 1.4.17, 2.1.31, 3.11.10, 4.3.11; limitations of the human mind, 1.1.7–9, 1.4.17, 4.7.6, 4.7.10; loss of mental capacity, 3.12.6, 4.8.1, 4.8.8, *Ap.* 6; mind affected by lack of physical health, 3.12.6–7; 'mindless is worthless', 1.2.55

see also **SOUL**

juries, Athenian 1.1.1, 1.1.17, 4.4.4, 4.4.8, 4.8.5, *Ap.* 4, 14–15 (uproar)

JUSTICE/INJUSTICE: Socrates' discussion and search for definitions, 1.1.16, 1.2.37, 3.9.5, **4.2.11–23**, **4.4.5–25** (dialogue with Hippias), 4.6.5–6, *Ap.* 16; justice equated with wisdom, 3.9.5, with lawfulness, 4.4.12–25, 4.6.5–6; justice teachable, 4.2.20 (but no ready teachers of justice, 4.4.5); ingratitude an injustice, 2.2.1–3; enslavement and deception of enemies justified, 2.2.2, 4.2.14–16; unjust condemnation to

Ap. 24–6; alienation of the jury, *Ap.* 9,
14–15, 32; **the verdict:** 1.2.62–4,
Ap. 23; refusal to propose alternative
penalty, *Ap.* 23; **after the trial:** 30
days between verdict and execution,
4.8.2; Socrates' bearing after the trial,
Ap. **27–30**; support of his friends,
Ap. 22–3, 27–8
— the memory of Socrates, 4.1.1, 4.8.10,
Ap. 34
SOPHISTS: Anaxagoras, 4.7.6–7;
Antiphon, 1.6.1–15; Dionysodorus,
3.1.1; Hippias, 4.4.5–25; sophists
charging fees, 1.2.6–7, 1.5.6, 1.6.13
(akin to prostitution), 3.1.11
Sophocles, tragic poet 1.4.3
SOUL: gods' gift to humans as their
dominant faculty, **1.4.13–14**; the soul
partakes of divinity, and reigns within
us, 4.3.14; the soul as faculty of
reason/intelligence, 1.2.4, 1.2.53,
1.3.14, **1.4.13–14**, 1.4.17, 2.1.20
(knowledge), 2.1.31, 3.11.10, 4.3.11;
the soul invisible, 1.4.9, 3.10.3, 4.3.14;
strength of soul/spirit, 4.1.4, 4.8.1, *Ap.*
30, 33; beauty of soul, 2.6.32, 3.10.3,
4.1.2; the condition of the soul
portrayed in art, 3.10.3–5, 3.10.8;
delightful food provided by the soul,
Ap. 18; care/training of the soul,
1.2.4, 1.2.19–20, 1.3.5; harm to one's
own soul, 1.5.3, 1.5.5
— relation of soul and body, 1.2.4,
1.2.23, 1.2.53, 1.3.5, 1.3.14, 1.4.9,
1.4.17 ('mind'), 2.1.20, 4.1.2
see also **INTELLIGENCE**
SPARTA: Spartan practice and attitudes
contrasted favourably with
Athenian, **3.5.14–21**; admiration of
Sparta, 3.5.14–16 (Socrates and
Pericles [2]), 4.4.15 (Socrates);
Spartan obedience to the laws, 3.5.16,
4.4.15; lawgiver Lycurgus, 4.4.15,
Ap. 15; Spartan support of Boeotia,
3.5.4; hoplite weapons, 3.9.2;
Gymnopaidiai festival, Lichas famous
for his hospitality, 1.2.61
speech: gods' providential gift to
humans, 1.4.12, 4.3.12; primacy of
the spoken word, 3.3.11; the time
when animals could speak, 2.7.13

sperm, quality dependent on the man's
age 4.4.23
spiders 3.11.6; widow-spiders, 1.3.12–13
study *see* **EDUCATION,
KNOWLEDGE, PRACTICE**
SUCCESS 1.6.8, 2.4.6, 3.4.12,
3.9.14–15, 4.2.26, 4.2.28; principle of
success in any management role,
3.4.3–12; 'successful action' the best
pursuit for a man, 3.9.14; admiration
of success, 4.2.28; pleasure at success
of one's friends, 2.4.6, 2.6.35, 3.10.4,
3.11.10; envy of friends' success, 3.9.8
sun 3.8.9, 4.3.3–4, 4.3.8–9, 4.3.14;
Anaxagoras' equation of sun with
fire, 4.7.7
sycophants, blackmailers bringing
vexatious lawsuits 2.9.1–8, 4.4.11
Syria 2.1.10

talents: natural or taught, 3.1.6, 3.9.1–3
(courage), 4.1.2, 4.2.2 (Themistocles);
natural talents most in need of
education, 4.1.3–4, and self-control,
4.3.1; the most talented capable of
both great good and great harm,
4.1.3–4, 4.3.1; wealth no substitute for
talent, 4.1.5
tanning: a 'servile occupation' arranged
by Anytus for his son, *Ap.* 29–30
TEACHERS: give personal
example, 1.2.17; turn out replicas of
themselves, 1.6.3; not responsible for
subsequent deterioration of their
pupils, 1.2.27; lessons forgotten,
1.2.21; primacy of spoken argument,
3.3.11
— teachers of young children, 2.2.6; of
arts and crafts, 4.2.2, 4.4.5; of
generalship, 3.1.1–11; of medicine,
4.2.5; of music, 1.2.27, 4.2.6; no
teachers of justice, 4.4.5
temples and altars: best location for their
purposes, 3.8.10; temple of Asclepius,
3.13.3; shrine of Amphiaraus,
3.13.3; temple at Delphi, 4.2.24
Thebes, city in Boeotia 3.5.2,
3.5.4; Cebes and Simmias associates of
Socrates from Thebes, 3.11.17
theft, justified in some circumstances
4.2.14–17

American Literature

British and Irish Literature

Children's Literature

Classics and Ancient Literature

Colonial Literature

Eastern Literature

European Literature

Gothic Literature

History

Medieval Literature

Oxford English Drama

Philosophy

Poetry

Politics

Religion

The Oxford Shakespeare

A complete list of Oxford World's Classics, including Authors in Context, Oxford English Drama, and the Oxford Shakespeare, is available in the UK from the Marketing Services Department, Oxford University Press, Great Clarendon Street, Oxford OX2 6DP, or visit the website at www.oup.com/uk/worldsclassics.

In the USA, visit www.oup.com/us/owc for a complete title list.

Oxford World's Classics are available from all good bookshops. In case of difficulty, customers in the UK should contact Oxford University Press Bookshop, 116 High Street, Oxford OX1 4BR.